Western Society
After the Holocaust

Westview Replica Editions

The concept of Westview Replica Editions is a response to the continuing crisis in academic and informational publishing. Library budgets for books have been severely curtailed. Ever larger portions of general library budgets are being diverted from the purchase of books and used for data banks, computers, micromedia, and other methods of information retrieval. Interlibrary loan structures further reduce the edition sizes required to satisfy the needs of the scholarly community. Economic pressures on the university presses and the few private scholarly publishing companies have severely limited the capacity of the industry to properly serve the academic and research communities. As a result, many manuscripts dealing with important subjects, often representing the highest level of scholarship, are no longer economically viable publishing projects--or, if accepted for publication, are typically subject to lead times ranging from one to three years.

Westview Replica Editions are our practical solution to the problem. We accept a manuscript in camera-ready form, typed according to our specifications, and move it immediately into the production process. As always, the selection criteria include the importance of the subject, the work's contribution to scholarship, and its insight, originality of thought, and excellence of exposition. The responsibility for editing and proofreading lies with the author or sponsoring institution. We prepare chapter headings and display pages, file for copyright, and obtain Library of Congress Cataloging in Publication Data. A detailed manual contains simple instructions for preparing the final typescript, and our editorial staff is always available to answer questions.

The end result is a book printed on acid-free paper and bound in sturdy library-quality soft covers. We manufacture these books ourselves using equipment that does not require a lengthy make-ready process and that allows us to publish first editions of 300 to 600 copies and to reprint even smaller quantities as needed. Thus, we can produce Replica Editions quickly and can keep even very specialized books in print as long as there is a demand for them.

About the Book and Editor

Western Society After the Holocaust
edited by Lyman H. Legters

Based on an International Scholars' Symposium convened to recall the infamous *Kristallnacht* in Hitler's Germany, this book represents an effort to distill from the ensuing Holocaust experience those lessons that seem most applicable to the contemporary world. The principal conference papers, focusing on such concepts as ideology, popular response, collaboration, resistance, and human rights, are gathered here with critical responses and authors' rejoinders not to recite the horrors of that time but rather to highlight continuing dangers and potential threats. The authors, all renowned for their contributions to the elucidation of the Holocaust experience in one or another of its dimensions, are united in the attempt to extract generalizable conclusions from that episode. At the same time, the volume preserves much of the controversy that emerged in the conference discussion.

Dr. Lyman H. Legters, senior fellow with the Institute for the Study of Contemporary Social Problems, is the editor of *The German Social Democratic Republic: A Developed Socialist Society.*

A Publication of the
Institute for the Study
of Contemporary Social Problems

Western Society
After the Holocaust

edited by
Lyman H. Legters

Westview Press / Boulder, Colorado

A Westview Replica Edition

Copyright © 1983 by Westview Press, Inc.

Published in 1983 in the United States of America by
    Westview Press, Inc.
    5500 Central Avenue
    Boulder, Colorado 80301
    Frederick A. Praeger, President and Publisher

Library of Congress Cataloging in Publication Data
Main entry under title:
Western society after the Holocaust
    (A Westview replica edition)
    Based on an international scholars' symposium convened to recall
the Kristallnacht.
    1. Holocaust, Jewish (1939-1945)--Congresses. 2. Crystal Night, 1938--
Congresses. 3. Arendt, Hannah, Eichmann in Jerusalem--Congresses.
4. Weber, Max, 1864-1920--Views on Judaism--Congresses. I. Legters,
Lyman H.
D810.J4W493   1983   940.53'15'03924   83-10322
ISBN 0-86531-985-5

Printed and bound in the United States of America.
10 9 8 7 6 5 4 3 2 1

To the Memory of
Harriet Lewis Littell
1914–1978

Contents

ix

x

Preface

Although individual scholars performed signal service earlier, coordinated work in America to research and interpret the lessons of the Nazi assault on Judaism and Christianity began little more than a decade ago. During the last ten years there has been a tremendous expansion of the number of courses offered on college and university campuses and of the number of professors and students engaged in the pursuit. Dissertations on the Holocaust and the Church Struggle abound.

From the beginning we have maintained that a fruitful result could only be obtained when the approach is interfaith, interdisciplinary, and international. Moreover, participants should include leaders in religious and civic agencies as well as academics.

There are compelling reasons for insisting upon an interfaith approach. In treating a traumatic event like the Holocaust, the gentiles must wrestle with the constant temptation to flee into abstractions and general formulae ("theodicy," "man's inhumanity to man," "genocide," etc.) without first confronting the Holocaust as a discrete event. The presence of Jewish colleagues guarantees that that escape route will be cut off. On the other hand, there is a marked tendency in some Jewish circles to slide into preciousness, to dwell morbidly upon the Holocaust as another illustration of Jewish misery and defeat. The presence of gentile scholars of Christian or humanistic persuasion helps to remind their colleagues of the universal lessons to be drawn from study of the event.

Interfaith study and publication on the record of the churches is also imperative. There has emerged in some churches' publications in recent years a neotriumphalism, signalized by the statement "...of course the Jews suffered... but the Christians

were persecuted too." The truth is that during the
fateful period of the destruction of Central European
Jewry, most of the baptized in Hitler's empire
apostatized, betrayed their calling. There were
perhaps 11-12,000 authentic Christian martyrs,
including some of the most worthy witnesses to the
truth ever to appear in Christian history, but the
total is in no sense symmetrical to the 6,000,000
Jewish martyrs. The presence of Jewish colleagues
helps to keep study of the Church Struggle honest.
On the other hand, it is important for Jewish
scholars and community leaders to be aware that there
were some Christians who, under pressure and
temptation, remained faithful.

The case that work on the Holocaust must be
interdisciplinary is equally strong. Every academic
department has the tendency to become locked into
specialized methodologies and esoteric vernaculars
which exclude or distort some truths as well as
illuminate others. The Holocaust is a credibility
crisis for traditional religion. It also puts the
modern university to the question. What kind of
medical schools produced a Mengele and his
associates? What kind of law schools turned out the
lawyers, judges, and civil servants who so skillfully
managed and systematized that monstrous crimes could
be committed "legally?" What kind of teachers'
colleges produced those who prostituted their
stewardship of young lives? Nobel Prize winners and
other professors of international reputation used
their talents in the laboratories and lecture halls
to strengthen Hitler's death machine. Not ignorant,
illiterate, superstitious savages but technically
competent barbarians mounted the genocide program.

Every academic discipline is affected by the
lessons of the Holocaust. Alumni of every skill and
professional association can learn from what
university men did during the Third Reich. The
function of the university itself, both as a social
and economic institution and as a partner in
designing and directing the modern engines of death,
must be rethought in the shadow of the Holocaust.

From the beginning it has been clear that the
work required international cooperation. Professors
from Israel, the German Federal Republic, and America
have usually taken the lead, but there has been
important input from other countries as well. The
pathological elements of the story--antisemitism,
totalitarian ideologies and governments, the
corruption of science, genocide--are worldwide, and
the lessons to be learned and transmitted concern all
peoples.

Writers and speakers often refer now to the personalia of the Holocaust as threefold: perpetrators, victims, and spectators. Certainly the third category, the special problem of Christian theologians, is the hardest to handle. And related to the problem of the spectators is a critical question: when did they first know that they were watching mass murder? The choice of <u>Kristallnacht</u> as a signal event in the history of the Third Reich was an appropriate one, for on that occasion the dictatorship made perfectly clear for any willing to see what was intended toward the Jews.

The first International Conference on the German Church Struggle and the Holocaust, held in 1970, announced a subtitle: "What Can America Learn?" Step by step, study of the destructive adventure which was the Third Reich has moved from presentation of the brute facts to discussion of the lessons to be learned and applied if the next generations are to have a chance at life.

The Institute for the Study of Contemporary Social Problems, which sponsored the <u>Kristallnacht</u> Memorial Symposium, combines the approaches which have proved so productive over the last decade: interfaith, interdisciplinary, and international in scope, its research programs, seminars and conferences are devoted to study of problems of the recent past and of the present for the sake of a better future. Moral commitment and scientific method are combined.

Since a chief mark of the misuse of knowledge which the Nazi adventure involved was precisely the severance of the link between moral commitment and scientific competence, the work of the Institute has something to say to <u>Academe</u> as a whole. Although certainly not romantically addicted to the notion that higher education should simply return to the early definition of <u>consensus fidelium</u>, this book shows some ways in which the "republic of learning" can be reintegrated to serve the common good.

The editor and I want especially to thank Hubert G. Locke for his vision and statesmanship in making the Symposium possible. Dr. Locke also served as manager and host of the first International Conference more than a decade ago.

Franklin H. Littell
Symposium Chairman

Acknowledgments

The International Scholars Symposium was made possible by the financial support of a number of foundations and organizations. The Board of Directors of the Institute and the Symposium Planning Committee takes this opportunity to acknowledge, with deep gratitude, gifts and grants from:

- The Catholic Archdiocese of Seattle
- The Dial Foundation
- The William Randolph Hearst Foundation
- The Jewish Federation of Seattle
- The Memorial Foundation for Jewish Culture
- The Harvey and Lenore Meyerhoff Philanthropic Fund
- Seattle-First National Bank
- The Samuel and Althea Stroum Foundation
- ZACHOR: The Holocaust Resource Center National Jewish Conference Center

During the week of the Symposium, more than twenty public lectures, addresses, and forums on Holocaust-related topics were presented to community groups and organizations throughout the State of Washington. These community appearances by scholars attending the Symposium were made possible by a grant from the Wshington Commission for the Humanities, to which the Institute expresses grateful appreciation.

Finally a special note of thanks is owing to Linda Christian for preparing the proceedings for publication.

Introduction

Lyman H. Legters

When the Institute for the Study of Contemporary Social Problems announced, for November 1978, the convening of an international scholars' symposium on "Western Society After the Holocaust," it was doing at least two distinct things. It was returning to its own roots and origins; and, simultaneously, it was proclaiming a commitment for its own future.

There is a direct connection, as Professor Littell emphasizes in his Preface, between the foundation of the Institute and several scholars' conferences held at Wayne State University in the early 1970s on Church Struggle and Holocaust under the Third Reich. Those early meetings, recognizing that scholarly attention needed to be focused on an episode of overriding moral implication in recent western history, gave enormous impetus to a continuing process of concerned inquiry and social criticism. The establishment of the Institute in 1972 intersected with the realization that the process demanded an organizational framework dedicated to a continuous critical inquiry into those events and tendencies in modern societies that signal their dissolution into caricatures and perversions of what we are wont to regard as civilizing achievements of humankind in history.

The Institute has proceeded to undertake a variety of investigations, most of them not explicitly related to the phenomenon of Nazism, but all of them united by two pertinent considerations. The Institute's topics—racism, law and justice, the quality of urban life, and critical theories of society—have had in common their life-and-death manner of challenge to contemporary civility and their general neglect, at least in their most threatening dimensions, within the fashion-governed research thrusts of the scholarly disciplines as those subsist within the academy.

1

It was thus doubly significant when the Institute seized upon the fortieth anniversary of <u>Kristallnacht</u>, the first thoroughly overt onslaught upon the Jews of Germany, as the occasion for further assessment of the Holocaust. It was a renewal of attention to a paradigmatic instance of social dissolution, the one that had set the Institute upon its course in the first instance; and it was a restatement of commitment to keep energies and resources applied to those tendencies (which some of us would group under the name "social pathology") that most severely threaten both justice and civility in modern western societies and that most consistently elude the capabilities of scholarship as it is sustained in the university.

The choice of title for the symposium followed directly and logically. This was not to be one more recital of the horrors of the Holocaust, still less an exercise in that form of self-righteousness that tends to surface when we are contemplating the wrongs committed by another set of people in another time. Rather, we were attempting to extract from the experience of the Holocaust some generalizable lessons for the present and the future, some concrete, i.e., historically rooted, analyses applicable to a world four decades removed from the largely unsuspecting one for which the Holocaust had been prefigured in the night of shattered windows.

The individuals participating in the November 1978 symposium had the most varied relationship to the Holocaust events that formed the background for deliberations. Some of those relationships are mentioned in the chapters that make up this volume. Many of those involved in planning and conducting the symposium had also been engaged, in various ways and with greater or lesser continuity, in the intellectual discourse that has sought, at least since 1945, to make sense of the practices, policies, and horrors of the Third Reich. We were fully aware that, in our attempt to treat the Holocaust as a real and terrible challenge to the contemporary world, we might run afoul of at least two disparate difficulties.

We knew that we might—and rather hoped that we would—unsettle those for whom the Holocaust is a completed chapter safely locked away in the past. I do not of course refer here to those who would deny the very reality of the Holocaust: they are beneath intellectual contempt, though—since they manifest some of the precise tendencies that animated National Socialism—one must be wary of pronouncing them unworthy of notice. I refer rather to those for whom the absorption of an event into the historical record represents a moral buffer, an excuse to ignore present moral implications in favor of measuring degrees of savagery or comparing numbers of victims, a perspective that effectively reduces an unexampled episode of resurgent barbarity, still contemporary to a significant fraction of those now living, to just one more recorded instance of the demonic capabilities of humankind. We hoped, I repeat, to issue a reminder that the Holocaust retains a moral cutting edge for our times even as it recedes into the past.

We realized too that we risked offending those for whom the Holocaust is such a unique set of events as to defy any attempt to generalize or to link its defining features with kindred phenomena. Our attitude toward this second, and much more problematical, difficulty was one of respectful diffidence. For it would be reprehensible to obscure the real suffering that still attaches to the Holocaust in the interest of cold-blooded intellectual analysis. But to that diffidence we sought to join a certain sort of stubbornness about the need, dictated not least out of respect for the victims of the Holocaust, to conceive the problem in a theorizing way, one that moves beyond sheer uniqueness without losing sight of that quality. Here the issue becomes acute of course, for any theoretical bent implies the identification of salient analytical features unclouded by horrific particularities. And that in turn risks affront to those for whom precisely the particularities distinguish the Holocaust from other instances of genocide.

The aforementioned notion of "social pathology" may afford some small help in this context. Although it does not enjoy currency in academic social science, the term has the virtue of denoting a category of social phenomena that signify a decisive breakdown of civilization and society in its proximately humane forms. As a metaphor drawing on the medical concepts of health and illness, but insisting at the same time on the social location of those attributes, social pathology may be taken as a concept looking beyond mere tension, conflict, and dislocation to a condition best described as dissolution. It has the further merit of fastening attention on the possibility of therapy, in the best case therapy of the preventive sort.

We lack any common understanding of the term in conventional intellectual discourse, so a definition is not readily available. But if resort is had to definition by enumeration, it might at least be possible to secure agreement that genocide, slavery, mass terrorism, and thought-control fall within the extreme condition suggested by the notion of social pathology, or, in other words, beyond the "ordinary" play of controversy over preferences and choices in the rational context of social decision-making.

Since the purpose of introducing the term here is merely suggestive, it will suffice to note that the Holocaust belongs within the concept on any definition however narrow. That being so, we have a basis for analyzing the Holocaust in somewhat detached terms in order to refine our powers of discernment as to what is unique about it and therefore improbable of recurrence and as to what attributes it shares with other pathological occurrences that might aid us in recognizing threatening developments in time for preventive response. Far from detracting from the uniqueness of the Holocaust in its particularity, this approach acknowledges that other such events are conceivable and, to the extent that they can be recognized in time as the Holocaust was not, perhaps preventable. These at any rate were the considerations we had in mind as we planned the Symposium and settled on the anniversary of <u>Kristallnacht</u> as a fitting occasion for our purposes.

The procedure adopted for the Symposium, replicated so far as possible in this book, was to confront each major speaker with two critical commentators whose remarks were then subject to rejoinder by the speaker. Beyond that point, the floor was open for discussion by the invited scholar-participants and observers, the main speakers remaining for the most part as participants throughout the conference. The symposium included some other elements as well: two major addresses, open to the public, by Joseph Borkin, the late author of <u>The Crime and Punishment of I.G. Farben</u>, and by Chaim Herzog, former Israeli ambassador to the United Nations and now President of Israel; a full day of scholarly panels devoted to aspects or lessons of the Holocaust; and a wide range of appearances by the scholar-participants, facilitated by a grant from the Washington Commission for the Humanities, at public meetings throughout the state. Many of those elements will find outlets outside the pages of this volume. But our first aim was to make available in print the principal scholarly papers that formed the heart of the symposium. The commentaries and author's rejoinders are designed to preserve for the reader something of the flavor of the Symposium discussions.

Lyman H. Legters
Editor

NOTES

1. Littell, F.H.,and Locke, H.G., (eds.), <u>The German Church Struggle and the Holocaust</u> (Detroit: Wayne State University Press, 1974), the proceedings of the first Wayne State conference; proceedings of later conferences await publication.
2. (New York: The Free Press, 1978).

1
Genocide and Ideology

Leszek Kolakowski

The Holocaust may be viewed from different perspectives: as the bloodiest chapter in the incredible history of the people of Israel or as an aspect of 20th century nationalism and totalitarianism. My remarks deal with the latter. I have nothing interesting to say about the history of Holocaust and I am not going to discuss the relevance of the massacre of Jews to the present state of the 'Jewish question,'in particular to the situation of the state of Israel. I do not deny the validity of such reflection, of course: on the contrary, it seems that it is almost the last moment when such questions can be discussed in the framework of living memory, and not as a matter of scholarly inquiry. In 10 or 15 years the world will be ruled by people to whom the Second World War will appear as a closed chapter of the past: the link between these events and the existence of the state of Israel will be forgotten and political decisions will not depend any longer on people who were witnesses to or victims of the atrocities of those years. But that is not my subject on this occasion.

A short self-introduction is not out of place in discussing a topic which can hardly be treated in a strictly scholarly and dispassionate manner. I am not a Jew or of Jewish origin myself. I spent the war in Nazi-occupied Poland as a boy for 12 to 17 years. I lived in various places, including Warsaw. I remember the destruction of the Warsaw ghetto, seen from outside, and I lived among Poles who were active in helping Jews and who every day risked their lives trying to save from the inferno those few who could be saved. Most of the time I lived with Jews hiding from hangmen. As you know, about 6 million Polish citizens perished in the genocide, about half of them Jews or Poles of Jewish descent. I and all people I knew in this period had and still have a clear feeling of the community of victims, and I admit that

7

our memory does impose a bias on all possible
analysis of these events.
                    ****
     We wonder sometimes what was horrifyingly new in
the massacre of European Jews in the Second World
War. Genocide is clearly not an invention of the
20th century, let alone of Nazis, apart from the more
efficient technique of killing people and of
transporting them to slaughter. Neither is
ideological genocide, by which I mean a mass
extermination that is justified not simply by the
exterminators' need to have more room for themselves
or to enrich themselves, but by an elaborate
'philosophy' implying that the victims <u>deserve</u>
annihilation for metaphysical, historical, or moral
reasons. As far as I know, the mass slaughter of
Anatolian Armenians during the First World War was
not supported by any ideological considerations;
neither were the massacres of Indians in North
America. In the history of European conquest in
South America in the 16th and 17th centuries we might
occasionally find a sort of 'philosophical' basis to
the effect that Indians were not properly human
beings endowed with souls; yet this theory (soon to
be denied by the Church) was referred to only
infrequently and even if adopted it did not provide a
reason for mass killing. It could only yield the
conclusion that in moral terms killing was
indifferent. As a whole it appears that these
massacres were not ideological and that the killers
did not bother much about working out a legitimation
of their performances. They were after wealth and
power, they knew that they were, and at best the
total 'otherness' of victims in terms of religion and
culture helped the conquerors to overcome any
inhibitions they may have had. The same may be said
about most of the atrocities committed throughout the
early stages of colonization, whether or not they
deserved the label of 'genocide' (a word which is
obviously impossible to define with perfect
precision). [1]
     Yet Nazis may not claim to have been the
inventors of ideological genocide either. Mass
extermination in religious wars of the past fall
under this category, no matter which other
reasons--more or less sophisticated than the victims'
wrong opinions about divine grace and the holy
Trinity--were invoked. The massacre of Cathars in
Southern France at the beginning of the 13th century
might deserve the name of ideological genocide. Yet
the heretics, at least theoretically, had a choice:
they could have converted to the orthodox doctrine,
renouncing their errors and repenting. The Jews had

no such option. Jewishness being hereditary in Nazi doctrine, one could not get rid of it; one was incurably corrupted and irrevocably condemned.

Of the two components of the Nazi ideology which are relevant to this discussion--the inborn superiority of the Germans and the intrinsic incurable evil of Jewishness--neither was new, to be sure. We know various attempts to trace back the origin of this ideology to German romanticism or further in the past; Thomas Mann and Lukács may be mentioned in this context or, in America, Peter Viereck. Even more effort has been devoted to the historical background of the phenomenon of Nazism in terms of economical, social, and emotional conditions of Germany after World War I. Some authors, mostly the former Marxists, went further in philosophico-historical explanations and tended to believe that Nazism, far from being a monstrous accident, was a typical symptom of a general totalitarian trend, of which the Soviet system was another striking example, and that both announced a new political formation which, cruel and inhuman as it might be, was a natural product of tremendous changes in technological development. This gloomy outlook may be found in writings of Brune Rizzi, Friedrich Pollock, James Burnham. Within the specific Nazi ideology seemed to be of little importance; the general economic and political features of the new order being, as it were, fatefully preordained in the very character of recent technical development, it is a matter of chance or of contingent local tradition which ideological shape the system would take in a given country--communist in Russia or Nazi in Germany. The ideology has no more than an instrumental function in mobilizing resources for the tasks which, however heavy, were imposed by history.

We may set aside this last question and state generally that, fortunately enough, there are no compelling reasons why we should accept the sinister prophecy and believe that irresistible historical forces lead the world unavoidably to a totalitarian order. We may admit that some aspects of technological change seem to favor such a development (the shift of more and more important decisions up to central power centers) but some counteract it (technological and economical inefficiency of totalitarianism) and it would be very pretentious to maintain that we know what the outcome of the clash between these opposite tendencies on the global scale might be.

However convincing the explanations of Nazism in terms of economic or cultural history might be, we cannot resist the impression that there was something devilishly innovative in this ideology and that its temporary success was to a large extent a personal contribution of Hitler himself (and of Rosenberg, of course.) His creativity is not to be underestimated or reduced to a simple expression of trends already in progress that merely produced the Führer as their necessary instrument. It might well have been the case that a militarization of the German economy was a possible solution for the country's problems and that an official pseudoreligion involving worship of the state and great power dreams were likely to emerge as an auxiliary device. Still, the specific Nazi ideology is not properly accounted for by such considerations. This is due perhaps to the natural disposition of the human mind that we are reluctant to admit that crucial historical events which changed the entire course of world affairs had been produced by a mere chance and by totally unpredictable coincidences instead of having occurred within an intelligible sequence of necessities. Even though it might be true that the upshot of the First World War made the second very likely or perhaps even inevitable, there was no preordained necessity in the rise and the victory of Nazism or, for that matter, in the fact that the Third Reich ultimately lost the war. Nazism was a creation of human mind, not of impersonal historical forces, and its doctrine was not a fortuitous and passive instrument to achieve goals which were otherwise ready-made independently of this doctrine. However miserable intellectually and however abominable morally, this ideology was real not only in the sense that people actually believed in it but in the sense that it effectively influenced the leaders' behavior as an independent variable.

This is particularly true in the case of antisemitism. It has been repeatedly pointed out by historians that the extermination of Jews in the last phase of war was actually harmful in terms of warfare, since the Endlösung required a huge mass of means of transportion badly needed for military purposes, and since the Jewish slave labour could have been usefully employed. The action went on, nonetheless, for ideological reasons. Nazi antisemitism was supported not only by specific accusations like those of traditional Christian antisemitism. Essentially, the Jews were guilty of being Jews and thereby doomed to destruction. They were the embodiment of evil and simultaneously an abstract symbol of evil: whatever was touched by Jewishness was evil and, conversely, whatever was evil seemed to be of Jewish origin. Plutocracy was

Jewish, and Communism was Jewish, and so were liberalism, pacifism, vanguard art, and the theory of relativity. The Holocaust was not only a cunning means to achieve objectives which were set up independently of it; it was a goal in itself, an act of great historical justice, a definitive victory over evil.

In this context I call attention to a book published this year in Poland under the title Conversations with a Hangman. The author, Kazimierz Moczarski, was an officer of the Polish underground army fighting against the Nazi occupation. He was involved, too, in organizing help for the Ghetto fighters before and during the 1943 uprising. Like many soldiers who had fought in the non-communist anti-German underground, he was imprisoned after the war by Polish communist authorities, savagely tortured, and eventually sentenced to death. He was not executed, however, but was released in the late 1950s. During his ordeal in prison he spent nine months in one cell with SS Gruppenführer Jürgen Stroop, the hangman of the Warsaw ghetto (Stroop himself was to be subsequently sentenced to death by a Polish court and executed in 1952). After his release Moczarski wrote this fascinating book relating his long conversations with the Nazi criminal in a Warsaw prison. This is perhaps a unique document, the best portrait of a genuine Nazi who persisted to the end in his macabre creed: he believed that the reason why the Nazis had lost the war was that they had been too good and not resolute enough in uprooting all the poisonous tendencies in Germany.

In this sense we have to do perhaps with an ideological genocide of a new kind, though it leads us nowhere to say that this ideology was a product of madness or of paranoia. There are no paranoiac states or mass movements, and the Nazi doctrine, though perhaps exceptional in its open barbarity, was not at all exceptional in the degree to which it was outrageous to common sense. In any case, we are brought to the proper question I am purporting to discuss: what is the legacy of Nazi ideology in today's world or what changes in the contemporary clash of ideas may be reasonably attributed to the record and outcome of National Socialism?

In discussing this I would dismiss the marginal phenomena of contemporary Nazism in the literal sense. Some small groups of fanatics who here and there are still using symbols and phraseology of Hitler's Germany seem to me unimportant; hideous as they are, they have no future and no role to play any more and they attract a disproportionate amount of attention in the press. The very fact that they stick to Nazi symbols proves their hopeless position. And indeed I believe that what remains from the Nazi heritage are not direct or even indirect continuations of this ideology but certain transformations occurring in the entire postwar ideological struggle as a result of the collapse of Hitlerism.

A remarkable aspect of Nazism was its overtness. It had very little of mendacious facade. It displayed its goals and uttered them aloud: to erect the German superstate, to destroy Jews, and to transform Poles and other Slavs into slaves after having exterminated their educated layers and thus annihilated their culture. This program was in progress and its executors in the army, SS, police, and party hardly needed what is called 'false consciousness': they were doing what the ideology explicitly expected them to do, no matter how ridiculous might have been the justifications of this ideology in a race theory.

Though physical exterminations of Jews was not explicitly required in <u>Mein Kampf</u> or in other representative ideological documents, the implications were perfectly clear, as we know. In <u>Mein Kampf</u> Hitler states "merely" that the Jews are devils, pernicious bacilli, plague, vampires, parasites, irreformable enemies of the human race, that they hate all culture and try to destroy everything sublime and beautiful, and that "the Jew's instinct towards world domination will die out only with himself." [2]

In a speech in the Reichstag a few months before the war (January 30, 1939), he announced that if the Jews succeeded in provoking a war the outcome would be the annihilation of their race. [3] There was nothing equivocal in such and many other pronouncements, and it was only after enormous delay that people started asking themselves why these promises had not been taken at face value then or later, when the massacre was already in progress and when the reports from the Polish underground were simply not believed in the West, so that in Western countries, in spite of the information available, hardly anbody had a clear notion before the end of the war what was in fact going on under the Nazi occupation.

The importance of this aspect of Nazism is brought into relief when we confront it, as has been frequently done, with another ideology of a totalitarian state, that is with Communism in its Stalinist period. Convincing though many analogies might be, one difference is not negligible or secondary: in contrast to Nazism, Stalinism was all facade. It used--and quite successfully--all the ideological instruments belonging to the socialist, humanist, internationalist, universalist tradition. It never preached conquest, only liberation from oppression; it never extolled the state as a value in itself, it only stressed the necessity of reinforcing the state as an indispensable lever to destroy the enemies of freedom, and it promised, in conformity with Marxist doctrine, the abolition of the state in the perfect world of Communism. It preached equality, democracy, self-determination for all nations, brotherhood, peace.

In both cases, the presence or the absence of a powerful ideological facade may have been responsible for some strengths and some weaknesses of the two orders. That Stalinism could have introduced itself as the legitimate heir of socialist dreams and values, as the embodiment of the old revolutionary humanism, was clearly its strength. Thanks to the skillful manipulation of words it was able--even when its oppressive and terroristic sides were at their peak--to attract a large number of intellectuals and thus to enhance its world-wide influence. That thousands of outstanding minds fell prey to Stalinist delusions and joined the cause of Communism in good faith, for a shorter or longer time, is a fact that cannot be dismissed with melancholic comments on human naivete; it deserves attention as the most striking example of the power of ideology in our century. Yet the same power generated dangers which were bound to appear in due course. Those who took the facade seriously--as very many did--and who assimilated the art of seeing all events and facts, however inconsistent with the verbal claims of the system, through the glass of ideology, and thus condoned the horrors of Stalinism, sooner or later were caught up by the independent force of their beliefs and began finally to confront the doctrine with the reality. Time and again, in human minds, the facade tore itself away from the reality, took on a sort of autonomous life, and was turned against the reality. Time and again communists used communist phraseology to attack the communist system, and therefore it might be said that the ideology, mendacious though it was, carried the germs of self-destruction, or that communism, thanks to its ideological contradictions, was capable of producing its own critics.

Not so with Nazism, though. The high degree of convergence between its real and its avowed aspirations made it stronger in one sense and weaker in another--at at least so it seems from today's

distance. Because of its self-confessed genocidal
ideology it had no chance to become an intellectual
movement of any size or to produce cultural
achievements of any value. Though it is true that
the intellectuals' resistance to Hitlerism was
astonishingly poor in Germany, their active
involvement in building the new culture was very poor
as well. In contrast to Communism which, for a
certain period, proved to be fruitful in various
domains of culture, Nazism was entirely sterile. It
turned out to be a pure cultural vandalism. In
literature, art, or philosophy it brought nothing but
devastation and left nothing which today would count
as anything but the decline of the human spirit.

It succeeded in attracting very few outstanding
intellectuals and the most famous of them, Martin
Heidegger, adhered to the ideology for barely one
year. Here was nothing remotely comparable to the
ideological prowess of Communism. And it naturally
selected people according to characterological
criteria much different from those typical of
communism when it was alive as a faith; the only
virtues it was capable of mastering and of attracting
were of military character: <u>Blut und Ehre</u>. On the
other hand this spiritual misery and the relative
lack of a false facade was not without advantages.
It prevented Nazism, except for a few episodes at the
beginning, from ideological splits: Nazism produced
few heretics and seldom nurtured the germs of its own
ideological dissolution.

It seems that the ruin of Nazism and its all but
unanimous condemnation all over the world greatly
contributed to an important shift in the ideological
aspect of postwar political struggles and that we
still witness the great impact of those events,
including the way 'the Jewish problem' is being
handled and antisemitism articulated. I believe this
observation to be commonsensically reasonable, though
I admit that it would be difficult to prove it--like
all cases where we try to grasp the meaning and the
causes of large scale social phenomena.

It is arguable that the racial and national
hatred in all parts of the world are more powerful
and more threatening than they used to be before the
Second World War, and that antisemitism is in quite
good health. So is the cult of, and the need for, a
'strong state.' This is probably not because of the
continuing impact of Nazi ideology. On the contrary,
this ideology or rather the fact that it has been
discredited, changed the way those hatreds and those
aspirations are being expressed. There are
apparently multiple reasons for the general growth of
nationalism and for the peculiar state form of

nationalism. Among them are the enormous growth of the economic role of the state under various political regimes and, at the same time, the emergence of a large number of new states without tradition and without any remotely homogeneous ethnic and cultural background. Next to nationalism of distinctive ethnic groups affirming their right to build states of their own, we see the phenomenon of nationalism without nation or a nationalism focused on a state which has no ethnic unity. Yet we notice that national movements and political bodies, including those admitting the label of 'nationalism,' almost never phrase their grievances and their claims in terms of a nation's right to dominate other peoples, of natural superiority, of _Lebensraum_, and the like. Not only are all the national aspirations expressed in terms of an indisputable right of self-determination or of right to regain possession of lost territories, but the very concept of fighting against a nation is very carefully avoided. Mussolini and Hitler were not afraid of revealing their imperial goals; they did not hesitate to admit that they pursued a policy of conquest, as they were entitled and called to do by virtues of the natural superiority of their peoples or by the laws of history. Hardly anybody does it today. Nationalist ideologies expressly condemning the idea of human rights, praising war as the seminarium of highest human values, preaching the inequality of men, appealing to instincts against reason, and laughing at the concept of justice, are marginal phenomena in political life (Mao Tsetung was an exception in explicitly dismissing the human rights concept). Racial and national hatred, imperial aspirations, totalitarian regimes and movements flourish under the cover of humanitarian, pacifist, and internationalist slogans. The concepts of national sovereignty, of progress, and justice turned out to be good enough to justify all manner of internal repression and expansionist policy, and this applies to cases of what may be properly called genocides in postwar history (like the massacre of Communists in Indonesia and the recent mass slaughter in Cambodia).

This applies to antisemitism as well. The patterns of antisemitism clearly changed after the horrors of Nazism. In fact explicitly anti-Jewish rightist movements and ideologies, albeit existing, are feeble and marginal; otherwise the concept of anti-Zionism is quite sufficient to absorb most of the traditional antisemitism. It would certainly be very unfair to say that all those who oppose Zionism are antisemites. After all, some Jews oppose it on political or religious grounds: old socialists who

in principle reject all political ideas and movements
based on national sentiments, and those pious people
who believe that Judaism is essentially a religious,
not a political, notion. Thus, if it is manifestly
untrue that all the anti-Zionists are antisemites, it
is true, on the other hand, that virtually all the
antisemites call themselves anti-Zionists and those
who define themselves as foes of the Jews as such or
who openly advocate the destruction of Jews appear
very infrequently. This has contributed to the
erosion of the inherited political patterns and
divisions.

Before the war Zionism in Europe was opposed
most strongly by segments of the Jewish socialist
movement and in various countries the antisemites
rather favored the emigration of Jews they wanted to
get rid of. Today antisemitism has found a
comfortable outlet in the form of anti-Zionism and
the latter has been adopted in the West both by
Communists and by various leftist sects. Thus, a
good deal of antisemitic tradition is on the side of
the political spectrum that calls itself left (again,
this may not suggest that all the leftists
anti-Zionists are in fact antisemites, yet it seems
that now to be antisemite and to call oneself an
anti-Zionist gives one a strong chance of being on
the side of progress, freedom, equality, and
universal human happiness). The government-sponsored
antisemitism--called anti-Zionism, of course, yet
very poorly disguised--reappeared endemically
throughout postwar history in European Comunist
countries, in the Soviet Union, Poland,
Czechoslovakia, and Romania. It has been
particularly virulent in the Soviet Union and it led
to a remarkable situation where to be a Jew is
compulsory and forbidden at the same time. It is
compulsory in that if you had Jewish ancestors you
have no right to define yourself as a Russian or a
Ukrainian and the Jewish nationality is written in
your internal passport by police authorities whether
you want it or not. And it is forbidden in that Jews
have no right to cultivate their separate cultural
tradition even in the miserably limited form allowed
to other nationalities. In Poland the official
Soviet antisemitism of the last years of Stalin's
rule (the campaign against so-called 'cosmopolites')
was not followed on any significant scale, but in the
turbulent years 1956-57 some factions in the ruling
party started exploiting antisemitic slogans for
their purposes. Yet the great antisemitic campaign
was launched by the party leadership in 1967, after
the Six-Day War, and again it had a background in the
conflict of party cliques vying for power. Given the

intensity and the omnipresence of antisemitic propaganda for quite a long period, the results must have appeared disappointing to its organizers, though the poison certainly was not harmless.

It may be said, as a whole, that the ideological effects of the Holocaust were not the same in East European Communist countries as they were in the West. In Poland, where a good deal of the massacre actually took place during the war, the Holocaust is mentioned in such a way as to efface or to disregard the special character of what happened to the Jews. It was not so in the first years after the war: then the Holocaust was discussed and depicted in many memoirs, novels, books, and films. In recent years, however, official propaganda, while devoting a lot of effort to keeping the memory of Nazi atrocities alive, stresses the universal character of genocide and--except for a few special and politically motivated occasions--avoids remembering the massacre of Jews as a separate and unique story. The same rule is much more consistently and thoroughly observed in the Soviet Union where the horrors of war have hardly even been mentioned with specific reference to Jews. The general tendency is to induce people to forget that there was anything special about Jews in Nazi genocidal policy. It is true, of course, that millions of Poles and Russians fell victims of the genocide, yet it is true at the same time that the case of Jews was special and the deliberate refusal to mention it is only one of many examples of how the history of the last war is being falsified in the official communist version.

Meanwhile the popular antisemitism in the Soviet Union, unceasingly encouraged and reinforced by state propaganda, displays features very similar to traditional antisemitic prejudices we can trace back to the destruction of the second temple. Party leaders are paid back for their antisemitism with the popular accusation that they are Jews themselves and that the communist rule is in fact the oppression of the Russian people by the Jews. This tendency can be noticed to a certain extent in some factions of the Soviet nationalist underground movement and it is expressed in the accusation that the Bolshevik revolution was in fact the work of foreigners--Poles, Georgians, Latvians, and Jews above all. Thus the same patterns we know from the history of socialist antisemitism (Jews identified as bankers, usurers, and capitalists; socialist ideas mixed with anti-Jewish stereotypes) come back in popular discontent against the communist system: this time the communist power is identified with Jewishness. This characteristically incoherent search for national innocence recurs time and again. In Poland, during the antisemitic campaign of 1968 the Jews were accused simultaneously of undermining Soviet-Polish friendship and of having been responsible for the atrocities of Stalinism.

We may ask how this deliberate verbal confusion, this impressive growth of Orwellian language and the noted changes in patterns of ideological struggle are to be assessed? Are the racist and chauvinist tendencies more, or rather less, threatening once they are wrapped in universalist, humanitarian, and pacifist phraseology? Do political slogans purposely designed to arouse national and racial hatred, antisemitism in particular, carry more or rather less danger when they are so transformed? This question may be put in a general way: is it as a whole better or worse if hatred is called love, slavery freedom, oppression equality?

The answer is not obvious. On the one hand racism and antisemitism seem to be more vulnerable when they appear in full light, as in the Nazi movement, and better protected if their expressive forms are elusive and embellished with humanist ornaments. One may look at the question from another angle, however. More hypocrisy in ideological expression reveals in general more respect for those universalist values and thus attests to their increasing recognition. If the movements more or less similar to Nazism may hardly employ the same ideology, this bears witness to the fact that the downfall of Nazism was more than military.

And therefore it is not at all clear what sort of practical and practicable morals we can draw from the frightening experience of Nazism 40 years after, and what is now the real meaning of the slogan 'never more' which resounded all over Europe after the fall of Hitler's Reich. Given the lavish use of political mimicry and given the trivial truth that history never repeats itself, it is bound to be quite a controversial question how we are to identify political and ideological phenomena which carry dangers similar to Nazism. The word 'fascism' has become an abuse devoid of content; who is not occasionally called 'fascist' by political enemies? Consequently the lessons we are expected to learn from the Holocaust are by no means easy to set forth, though at first glance the opposite seems to be the case. Should we be watchful of people wearing the swastika and worshipping Hitler? They are pathetic remnants of the past. Should we be alert to antisemitism? Yet antisemitism articulated as such is a marginal phenomenon, otherwise anti-Zionism gives it a respectable abode, and it would be exaggerated to say that the Ku Klux Klan poses an enormous menace to humanity. Or should we point out the perils of nationalism? But all of us, depending on our political allegiances, sympathize with some national movements and despise others. All over the world ideologies and parties which define themselves as 'left' support and label 'progressive' all the nationalist movements, including the most extreme, if on an international plane they happen to be damaging to the United States, any West European country, or Israel.

Thus there are regrettably not many clear and practical lessons we can learn from the history of Nazism except, of course, the general recognition of democratic values and of human rights. Yet for this purpose the negative material we can collect from the recent history is also only too abundant.

The Third Reich was an exquisite example of the ideological state, i.e. of a state supposed to be ruled by one <u>Weltanschauung</u> of which the truth was guaranteed by the higher wisdom of those having privileged cognitive position. Nazi philosophers were entirely right in terms of their doctrine when they concentrated their attacks on Descartes and the sceptical tradition.[4] What they wanted to destroy was the belief in universal standards of cognition and universal character of truth. Nazism had an 'epistemology' of its own, primitive though it might have been. It was based precisely on the abolition of universal criteria of truth and on the belief that some segments of mankind--the supreme race and its leaders--have a deeper insight which no arguments based on ordinary logical criteria could invalidate. That the claim to the absolute knowledge stored in a better part of mankind and immune to the scrutiny of universal criteria of rationality is a prescription for despotism and can justify anything is quite obvious, no matter how this privileged part is identified--in racial, political, religious, or class terms. And why Nazism caused such a shock in the Western world was not the fact that such claims had been made--they were not unusual, after all--but that they were applied with such a consistency in the very center of Europe, in a country which in terms of technical, scientific, and cultural achievements belonged to the most advanced segment of civilization.

For years people kept repeating the same question: how was it possible that Himmlers and Eichmanns were brought up in the same cultural setting as Thomas Mann and Einstein? In other words, the shock was produced not simply by Nazi atrocities but more specifically by the fact that they seemed to

have emerged from the same civilization we all
belonged to, as if there was something essentially
sick in the very foundation of this civilization.
Marxists tried to argue that Nazism was a natural and
inevitable product of capitalism--not a particularly
strong claim when confronted with the liberating
potential of Stalinism and with the fact that
democratic institutions have been so strongly and
clearly connected with the market economy.
Catholics, in their turn, devolved the main
responsibility on the atheism of National Socialist
philosophy and argued that an attempt to forget God
could not have failed to yield such results; again, a
doubtful argument, considering that a clear positive
correlation between a society's religious fervor and
its respect for democratic values is by no means a
well proven sociological fact, to say the least. If
it were so, some theocratic states of old or
contemporary traditional Islamic states should appear
as models of democracy. Catholic critics are right
however in pointing out that the cult of a nation, or
of a state, or of a nation-state as supreme and
absolute value carries a powerful totalitarian
potential and, if consistently upheld, provides the
justification for all the imaginble violations of
individuals' rights, including genocide if needed.

Many great Germans of the past were occasionally
singled out as spiritual ancestors of Nazism,
including Hegel, Fichte, and Luther; and Lukács
seemed to believe (in Die Zerstörung der Vernunft)
that all of German philosophy from Schelling onwards,
with the sole exception of Marxism, had been, as it
were, teleologically propelled by an urge to pave the
way for Hitler.

There is something artificial in reconstructing
such pedigrees, though. It seems that no ideology,
and certrainly no ideology with all-embracing claims,
is immune to the danger of being used as an
instrument of oppression and slavery, and this
includes all the religious systems, socialist and
anarchist ideals, national doctrines, and all sort of
high-minded utopias. To be sure, some are better
adapted to such use, and some less so, and Nazism was
obviously unusual in this respect; yet if we judge
various world views by their ostensible content alone
it appears that few could be less suitable than
Christianity to serve oppressive purposes, and still
it turned out to be quite serviceable when needed.
The evil can catch hold of any ideology, no matter
how well designed, and turn it into its tool. Except
for the virtue of tolerance there are hardly any
values which by force of their content,
intrinsically, could not be employed for evil

purposes, and the virtue of tolerance itself has been repeatedly attacked for protecting the evil and the lie from destruction and thus for being self-defeating. This is, as we know, a matter of persistent controversy: should tolerance be extended to people preaching and practicing intolerance, in particular to racist and totalitarian movements? This is the matter of the optimum strategy in defending democratic values, the absolute strategy--i.e., one that involves no cost--being impossible here or anywhere else. To suppress intolerant movements and ideas for the sake of tolerance is self-defeating and not to suppress them is self-defeating, which simply amounts to saying that as long as movements against tolerance exist their very existence makes the state of perfect tolerance impossible--an apparently tautological assertion. A democratic order enjoying strong support and working with a reasonable efficiency can survive when allowing intolerant movements however abominable, to express themselves and the idea that it has to stifle the freedom of speech in order to keep it intact can be easily expanded into a more general theory stating that we have to establish tyranny in order to prevent a tyranny from being established. After all, the saying 'we shall know freedom once more only when we have destroyed the foes of freedom"[5] is actually a quotation from Hitler.

Yet to tolerate totalitarian movements within a democratic society means nothing more than to tolerate them; it does not, or at least ought not to, imply that they should be given the same treatment by public institutions as the movements and ideas within the democratic spectrum. In other words, a constitution which is committed to defend democratic values cannot pretend at the same time, without self-contradiction, to be indifferent to these values, i.e. to treat ideologies and activities committed to their destruction on a par with all others. This is admittedly easier to state as a general rule than to convert into such practical measures which would be sheltered from abuses. Nevertheless the self-protection of democracy is simply abandoned if its enemies enjoy the same kind of respect as its defenders. And if, on the other hand, totalitarian or racist movements are powerful enough to tear apart the legal fabric of a democratic society, this does not prove that democratic principles have lost their validity or turned out to be inconsistent. It does prove either that democracy was incapable of mobilizing its resources to defend itself, or that in some circumstances many people are ready to give up these principles in favor of other expectations, however delusive these calculations might be.

How such circumstances can be defined, i.e. what sort of conditions produce or make likely totalitarian and highly oppressive systems, this is the crucial question in this context and indeed one of the main problems of our world. These conditions can be easily described on the basis of the existing experience, yet they probably cannot be expressed in a general theory with predictive power, given the amount of chance and the variety of utterly unquantifiable factors in such developments. Certainly no single economic, cultural, or political agent may be pointed out to explain why a democratic order, once set up, might collapse. It is not a matter of sheer propaganda technique, contrary to what Aldous Huxley seemed to believe; in his opinion the successes of Nazis proved that with a skillful indoctrination machinery anybody can be induced to believe in anything, however silly. This gloomy view is not credible and grossly overstated, I believe. With all his genius for propaganda Hitler could not have won had he not exploited a situation which large masses of Germans felt to be outrageous, had he not appealed to widely held feelings and grievances. To be sure, it is incomparably easier to mobilize hatred than tolerance, and the mastery of political indoctrination consists in properly singling out one easily identifiable target of hatred, which the Jews happened to become in Germany.

Totalitarianism is a possible solution for a society in deep crisis, plunged into despair. No theory with predictive power is capable of saying when exactly this solution will be chosen. It is the worst possible solution not only in terms of the horrors and suffering it brings about, but in that it drastically narrows down the range of further possible solutions and curtails to a minimum the adaptability of the society to any new conditions.

Jingoism is a 'natural,' as it were, though not absolutely necessary ideological form of totalitarianism, at least today. The easiest way of justifying a system which converts individuals into state property is to appeal to national values. One could once do the same by reference to God's glory, yet that is hardly practicable now. And to legitimate such a system by the progress of the whole of mankind proved to be much less successful: the continuous and inexorable transformation of communism into as many national communisms as there are communist countries shows the connections just mentioned. It goes both ways, though, which means that a consistent nationalism and jingoism have an enormous totalitarian potential. Once the national values are declared supreme, there are no rights of individual which could be defended if they happen to clash, or even just appear to clash, with the ideal of a strong nation, and there are no boundaries to mendacity and repression. Nazism was the most splendidly consistent example of national values raised to the source and the measure of all others.

This last moral might appear trivial, yet it is perhaps less so, if we take it seriously. It cannot teach us which side we should take in today's conflicts; still, it teaches us at least which ideas, however adorned with humanist phrases, have to be treated with utmost suspicion. The history of the Holocaust is equally important on both sides: the suffering of victims and the depravity of hangmen. The intensity of evil might not have been unique or unparalleled in history, or, for that matter, in our century, yet its ideological justification was apparently unique. Those who reject the content of this ideology--and only very few do not--must not avoid the question reaching beyond Nazi doctrine: to what extent are they ready to legitimate evil for the sake of ideological values of any sort? Those who believe that such limits cannot be defined or who simply refuse to define them are in the proper sense the spiritual heirs of Hitler.

NOTES

1. On the definition, see V.N. Dadrian, "A Typology of Genocide," International Review of Sociology, No. 2, 1975.

2. Mein Kampf, English translation (London, 1939), p. 539.

3. The Speeches of Adolf Hitler, edited by N.M. Baynes, Vol. 1 (London, 1942), p. 741.

4. St. Tyrowicz: Swiatlo wiedzy zdeprawowanej: Idee niemieckiej socjologii i filozosii 1933-1945 (The Light of Corrupted Knowledge: German Sociology and Philosophy 1933-1945) (Poznán, 1970).

5. The Speeches of Adolf Hitler, Vol. 1, p. 48.

Comment: Foreboding and Melancholy
John K. Roth

Leszek Kolakowski's paper leaves me with mixed reactions. I appreciate his effort to use understanding of the past to achieve a better grasp of where we are today and may be tomorrow. But as I contemplate his essay further, I find that appreciation slips into the background. Instead, foreboding and melancholy take the center of the stage.

These factors emerge not out of substantive disagreement with Professor Kolakowski, although I shall point out some areas where my views differ from his. On the contrary, foreboding and melancholy arise just because there is a tragic truth in the implications of his position.

Early on, Professor Kolakowski probes a question that has been asked many times: What was horrifyingly new in the massacre of European Jews during World War II? He doubts that the Nazis merit much distinction for originality in their efforts, at least insofar as ideologically-motivated genocide is concerned. However, Professor Kolakowski does not reject the conviction that there was something significantly unique about the Nazi program. As I follow him, he locates that uniqueness in two related phenomena. First, "the final solution" was not a means but an end in itself. It was to be a "definitive victory over evil." Second, Hitlerism was remarkably "overt" in its intentions vis-a-vis the Jews.

Putting together these unique factors from the past, Professor Kolakowski looks beyond them and perceives that they have significantly changed the conflict of ideas in our own day. This change has occurred not because Hitler was ultimately successful but precisely because he _failed_. In a word, Hitler's "overt" approach has been superseded. Shifts in ideological _content_ are much less important in this movement that are alterations in ideological _technique_. The latter are clearly reflected in political power that speaks of human rights, liberation, democracy, etc., but only to enslavé life, strip rights away, and entrench totalitarian authority.

Here it is well to pause for a more critical look at what Professor Kolakowski suggests. First, the configuration of forces that conspired to bring about the Holocaust--particularly in their bureaucratic, technological, and economic dimensions--leaves that event more unprecedented than he states. Even more central to his concerns, there

is also a question about the "overtness" of the Nazi
campaign against the Jews. It is well-known, for
example, that euphemistic language functioned in the
offices of the Third Reich where mass death was at
stake. "The final solution" itself provides one
crucial instance of a concept from that language. In
addition, the Nazis did not parade Auschwitz to the
world. Secrecy was a consideration. That reality is
revealed by the fact that we will always be wrestling
with the question of what people did--and did
not--know about the gas chambers and crematoria.

However, even if Professor Kolakowski does not
stress these points sufficiently, I remain convinced
that his basic proposition is of fundamental
importance. It _is_ fair to hold that the Nazis were
quite clear and explicit about much that they did on
"the Jewish question." Language and law, propaganda
and policy, belief and action--in the Nazi regime
these factors work rather openly and hand-in-glove.

Hypocrisy was not a major Nazi problem, nor was
inconsistency between theory and practice. In fact,
retrospective irony might conclude that the Nazis
were refreshingly straightforward. We might even add
that a lesson has been learned from them on this
score. But if so, it is a lesson learned more by
those who carry on non-democratic politics than by
those who oppose that outlook.

What is the lesson? According to Professor
Kolakowski, it is simply that the "overt" approach of
the Nazis failed, and therefore that the politics of
"facade" is dictated. True, the latter may produce
troublesome critics from within, owing to
disagreements that will emerge when language about
means and ends remains ambiguous. This system,
however, also has power to blunt all opposition just
because language can form a mask of idealism to cover
even the worst atrocities.

Here we have an instance of what Professor
Richard Rubenstein calls "the cunning of history."
Anti-human forces, surfacing openly in the thirties
and forties, now move into a verbal underground,
having learned that they can work there with greater
impunity and thus with greater effectiveness. As
debates in the United Nations testify, everyone is
"for" human rights and equally "against" racism and
imperialism. Torture, outright slaughter of life,
destructive forms of nationalism--all go forward
accompanied by humanistic rhetoric at every step.
Words assure us that "nothing is wrong," and thus
that no one can be held responsible for _doing_
wrong.

Again and again, the Holocaust illustrates how
difficult it was for "good" people to move from

knowledge of what the Nazis were doing, to comprehension of the significance of Nazi activities, and then to action aimed at thwarting Nazi success. Those difficulties--and they were substantial--existed in circumstances of relative openness as far as Nazi intent and technique were concerned. Professor Kolakowski thinks the advantage of that openness is ours no longer. Now, add to that possibility the cloud of nuclear threat that hovers about current struggles over race, rights, and power. Problems of getting from knowledge to comprehension to action compound themselves. My feelings of foreboding and melancholy start to sharpen. Perhaps, thanks to Professor Kolakowski, you share them, too.

Leszek Kolakowski permits one to take little comfort in the fall of the Third Reich. He implies that circumstances since 1945 have gotten more complicated, more difficult, more devastating in their destructive potential. Much of that outcome is due to Hitler's failure. Unfortunately, Professor Kolakowski's gloomy prognosis does not stop there. His concluding statements--perhaps unintentionally--push our plight one notch deeper: those who believe that ambiguity cannot be checked and controlled, those who believe that limits--moral limits, I take it--cannot be defined or who simply refuse to define them, are in a proper sense the spiritual heirs of Hitler.

None of us, I am sure, wishes to be Hitler's heir, spiritual or otherwise. And yet Professor Kolakowski's appraisal of our predicament indicates that we are going to need a lot of help to avoid such a fate. Professor Kolakowski gives us a boost with his various warnings: we should see that all ideologies or idealisms, especially those that are single-minded and absolutist, have perversive potential. Nationalism remains one of the most lethal examples in our day, and we must be vigilant against its destructive powers. Leszek Kolakowski's analysis of tolerance is also relevant here. Nevertheless, the force of his essay leaves me feeling a little empty.

How are we to cut beneath the mask of words, a death-mask that kills? Philosophical clarity about what people are actually saying when they speak and write, and how their actions square with words, seems to be one crucial remedy. But we can be clear about problems and still not be able to cure them. So where do we go from here? What is the next step? Specifically, how does it involve consideration of power--political and economic--as well as moral reflection?

Those questions are hard. I do not expect that
Professor Kolakowski has any quick answers up his
sleeve. In fact, I would not have posed these issues
overtly and starkly except for the fact that his
paper has left its mark on me. Could it be that the
Nazi version of ideology and genocide was in some
sense the _easy_ case to deal with, at least compared
to the subtleties of power that confront us today?
If so, where is Western Society after the Holocaust?
The overall theme of our symposium, Professor
Kolakowski has shown, really is the right one.

Comment: A Discrimination of Ideologies
Gavin I. Langmuir

When we were introduced last night, Mr.
Kolakowski responded, "Ah! You are my opponent,"
thereby demonstrating the sensitivity to a
dialectical context to be expected of an historian of
Marxist thought. My admiration for Mr. Kolakowski,
however, and my appreciation of his paper prevent me
from being a convincing opponent. He has asked
crucial questions and provided answers that provoke
reflection rather than negation.

Mr. Kolakowski's fundamental question is whether
the Holocaust ws unique, and if so how. Since the
Holocaust is subjectively unique for many people, the
question is guaranteed to set nerves on edge. Yet
Mr. Kolakowski seeks to view the Holocaust (if that
is the right term) as a phenomenon susceptible of
objective empirical and logical analysis, a procedure
I believe essential if we wish to recognize its
widest implications. And from that perspective he
concludes that it was unique only, or above all,
because Nazi ideology explicitly abandoned the
univeral humanitarian ideals of Christianity and
Marxist thought, rejected the universal
epistemological ideals of the Greeks and the
Enlightenment, and in their place made national
values or thinking with the blood supreme. The Nazis
affirmed that the elimination of Jews would be a
definitive victory over evil; and unchecked by any
recognition of common humanity, they were able to
give that goal top ideological priority and apply all
necessary means of modern technology to achieve it.
And because the Final Solution was an end, not a
means, the Nazis openly proclaimed their goal and
pursued it tenaciously, even when it conflicted with
other vital objectives, cloaking their actions only
for tactical reasons and not because they believed
them immoral or a contradiction of their ideals. In

this the Nazis were unique, clearly different from other persecutors such as the totalitarian communist regimes that have camouflaged their persecutions of Jews under lip service to universal humanitarian and epistemological ideals. This insight is highly illuminating even though we may feel that Mr. Kolakowski has not recognized fully either the novelty of the Holocaust or the number of people involved, however unwittingly, in the creation of Nazism.

Mr. Kolakowski asserts that the Nazis invented neither genocide nor intellectual genocide, but that limitation is possible only because he defines genocide with such generous biological objectivity as to deprive it of most of its distinctive moral implications. He apparently considers mass slaughter of any kind as genocide, while defining ideological genocide as mass extermination justified by the metaphysical, historical, or moral implications of some elaborate system of thought. Yet since all people have genes, any killings may be objectively described as involving genocide great or small unless the element of intention is included in the definition. To avoid reducing genocide to a synonym for killing, I would prefer to use the term only for those cases in which the killers consciously believe that the hated cultural characteristics they ascribe to their victims were predetermined by the biological nature of all members—past, present, and potentially future—of the group they are trying to eliminate.

The sophistication of the rationalization connecting biological characteristics with perceived cultural threats may vary greatly; the killers do not have to use the language of modern genetics so long as they belive that humanity is divided into groups whose social comportment is the inevitable result of sexual intercourse among their members. But there cannot be genocide according to this definition without some such rationalization. All genocide is, therefore, inherently ideological. But all ideologically justified mass killings are not genocide. However elaborate a system of thought, the slaughter it justifies is not genocide unless the ideology includes some form of the biological rationalization. Consequently, although justified by very elaborate systems of thought, neither the massacres of Cathars, Jews, or other victims of religious conflict nor the killing of the Kulaks can be considered genocide; and the same may be said of the Americans.

This definition compels us to see the Holocaust as more clearly unique and the Nazis less so than Mr. Kolakowski does. The Nazis were not only the first

to attribute top priority to genocide; they were also
the first to commit it on any significant scale. The
Holocaust is therefore unique as the first
indisputable instance of massive genocide. Yet the
Nazis did not invent the pseudo-scientific
rationalization that made the slaughter genocide.
Although Mr. Kolakowski attributes the creation of
Nazi ideology primarily to Hitler and Rosenberg in
order to free human creativity from the bondage of
historical determinism, the Aryan myth, like the term
"antisemitism" itself, was primarily a German product
of the later nineteenth century, one expression of
the desire to give a national society as absolute a
basis of identity as contact with God had provided
religious societies. Although Hitler made that
potentially genocidal rationalization the controlling
premise of Nazi ideology, he was rather its creation
than its creator.

Mr. Kolakowski acknowledges that belief in the
superiority of Germans and the evil inferiority of
Jews antedated Hitler, but he pays little attention
to the problem of why Hitler gave top priority to
antisemitism and genocide. We can agree that
Hitler's personality was not determined by
irresistable forces that controlled German history,
and that the ideological priority was in some sense
his choice, without disassociating that choice from
previous history. The charisma of a leader depends
upon his ability to redefine a crisis in ways that
appeal to the sensibilities and satisfy the needs of
his followers; and without that elective affinity
Hitler's creativity would have had little effect.
Both he and those who willingly followed him were
molded by a preexisting ideology, German
antisemitism.

I was struck by how little space Mr. Kolakowski
devoted to antisemitism in a paper on genocide.
Perhaps that was because we typically use that term
very loosely; and in conferences dealing with the
Holocaust, where the emotional level is high,
cold-blooded definition in neat terminology of a
phenomenon that embraces Auschwitz seems unnecessary
and out of place. But some precision is needed if
what made Hitler's extreme nationalism and
totalitarianism unique was the priority attributed to
genocide, and if the primary target was Jews.

Mr. Kolakowski asserts, and I fully agree, that
not all forms of hostility against Jews or against
types of collective Jewish conduct should be
considered antisemitism. There can be realistic
hostility provoked by real Jewish competition for
scarce goods, including the prestige of proclaiming
supreme truth, hostility that may seem undesirable to

Jews but is perfectly rational from the point of view of a competing group. Less rational is a second form of hostility, which I will call xenophobic, in which those who hate Jews overgeneralize radically from the real conduct of some Jews to the nature of all Jews. Thus Jews have been accused of being Christ killers, usurers, communists, and capitalists; and while it is true that some Jews hve been prominent in each of these kinds of conduct, all Jews have not. This kind of overgeneralization, however, although irrational, is typical between competing groups: we have only to look at the way many French people between 1870 and 1945 described Germans. All significant groups have had to face both realistic and xenophobic hostility. There is, therefore, nothing unusual about such hostility directed against Jews, nothing that warrants the use of a special term, antisemitism.

Some hostility against Jews is, however, different from such normal intergroup hostility in that characteristics are attributed to all Jews that no one has ever empirically verified. Thus no one has ever seen Jews commit ritual murder, drink human blood, profane the consecrated wafer of the Eucharist, cause the Black Death, or conspire against western civilization in a cemetery in Prague. This kind of hostility is far more irrational than realistic or xenophobic hostility, and I will call it chimeric because the monstrosities hated exist only in the imagination of the haters. Unlike realistic or xenophobic hostility, chimeric hostility is relatively rare: it has developed only in certain cultures against certain minorities such as Jews, Blacks, and some others. If the term "antisemitism" is intended to indicate an unusual kind of hostility against Jews, different from that directed against most other groups (a denotation consistent with the meaning of the term when it was coined in 1873), then it should refer to chimeric hostility directed against Jews.

The fundamental function of chimeric hostility is to make those already hated realistically or xenophobically the fearful symbol of what is feared as inhuman or subhuman. Chimeric hostility against Jews or antisemitism first appeared, not with the destruction of the second Temple, but in the late thirteenth century when large numbers of northern Europeans first came to believe that all Jews did such frightful things as eat defenseless children and were conspiring to destroy Christendom. The inhuman conduct ascribed to them was accompanied soon after by the ascription of distinctive subhuman biological characteristics: the belief spread rapidly that all Jews had a distinctive physiogonomy, strange ailments, a strange smell, and horns. By the fourteenth century, socially significant antisemitism was fully developed in northern Europe and became particularly rooted in Germany where the worst massacres initiated by chimeric charges occurred. A continuing tradition that Jews were subhuman was established.

The only major change introduced by the Aryan mythologists and seized upon by the Nazis, a change corresponding to the replacement of metaphysical or theological beliefs by empirical or scientific premises as social and cosmic foundations, was the inversion of the causal relation between conduct and physiology. Whereas chimeric Christians had explained Jewish physiology as a consequence of, or punishment for, their allegedly monstrous conduct, the Aryan mythologists and Hitler explained their allegedly monstrous conduct as a consequence of their biological inferiority. That reversal, however, bore the fatal implication that the only way to end the menace was to eliminate Jews physically either from German society or from the world. The former was the solution of the self-styled antisemites of the late nineteenth century, the latter that of Hitler, whose creativity lay less in the priority he attributed to the elimination of Jews than in the deadly means which his political skills enabled him to envisage and employ. One can conceive of genocidal massacres occurring in Germany in that period without Hitler, but one cannot conceive of the Holocaust without Hitler's achievement of totalitarian power.

Despite these qualifications of Mr. Kolakowski's assertions about genocide and antisemitism, I agree completely with his major thesis that the Holocaust was the result of an ideology that abandoned universal humanitarian and epistemological ideals. But I do not agree that all systems of thought that proclaim how humans ought to live their lives, including religious systems, are ideologies and are potentially totalitarian. Granted that, outside of Utopia, all governments that seek to direct a society according to any set of convictions about how society should be organized must enforce some rules, that does not mean that all such systems of thought themselves encourage the use of force. Although any socio-political theory can be given a different meaning by those in power so that it becomes a different theory, some socio-political ways of thought cannot themselves justify totalitarianism, while others inherently encourage repression and have the potential to become totalitarian while remaining true to their basic premises.

Ideology I take to be that denial of the discontinuity between valuation and empirical knowledge which Mr. Kolakowski has described in another context as the standard characteristic of all mythologies. To say this is not to deny that empirical knowledge is needed for ethical evaluations; it is only to assert that the process of making an evaluation or moral judgment is not the same as that of making an empirical judgment. Ideologues, however, whether adherents of natural law, providential history, communism, or Nazism, affirm both that the structure of reality as empirically discovered is normative and that their knowledge of true values enables them to distinguish valid empirical knowledge from error. That fusion or confusion of moral and empirical judgment depends upon a weakening of the capacity to make either kind of judgment and therefore involves at least a partial abandonment of universal humanitarian and universal epistemological standards. Ideological rulers claim an omniscience beyond their capacities, and a first priority of ideological government is, therefore, the repression of the human capacity to make independent empirical judgments that can be used in making moral judgments.

Using this definition, we can distinguish two types of ideology, which may be called idealistic and idealizing. The first or idealistic type asserts an abstract ideal of universal human conduct, proclaims that it should be realized, and affirms that the way reality is patterned demonstrates empirically that the realization of the ideal is inevitable. The ideal is confirmed by the direction of history; what "ought" to be already "is" empirically. Idealistic ideology thus moves from the ideal to its concretization. The second or idealizing type of ideology is precisely the opposite. It is based on assertions about how people have acted, affirms the value of their conduct, and proclaims that those values are ideal. Specific historical conduct is justified as ideal; what "is" always "ought" to be. Idealizing ideology thus moves from the concrete to its idealization.

Idealistic ideologies are initiated, I would argue, by people who are alienated from existing societies, have a moral vision of humanity that criticizes and transcends existing social barriers, are therefore attracted by cognitive procedures potentially applicable by all people, and try to found a new society based on that universalizing vision, be it a church or state. These founders, for example, Christ and Marx, may or may not themselves be ideologues, but their thought may be transformed into an ideology when rulers of a society so founded compete for power. Yet so long as such ideological societies continue to rely on the authority of the founders, the leaders of subsequent generations are forced to reexpress--at least verbally--the universalizing ideals of their founding charter and defend its universlity. As Mr. Kolakowski has so usefully insisted, the foundation remains as a molding facade despite heresies and contradictory conduct.

Both Christian and Marxist ideologies are of the idealistic type, which explains why neither developed a genocidal theory, although both have made life miserable for Jews. Each found the existence of Jews ideologically valuable so that each has both condemned them and ensured their continuity. Mr. Kolakowski has mentioned the Soviet double-bind: that Jews are not allowed to be anything but despised and disadvantaged Jews but also are not allowed to cultivate their Jewishness. Similarly, when the Church was powerful in the Middle Ages, it imposed its own double-bind: Jews were damned, degraded, and ordered to wear clothing that would set them physically apart, but nonetheless they were also prohibited from studying the Talmud and developing their own conception of Jewishness. Both Christian and Marxist ideologues have tried to control Jews so that, as Christians from St. Augustine on have said openly, their existence would serve as negative testimony to the ideological truth.

The second or idealizing type of ideology, however, has affinities with romanticism, because it does not purport to establish new ideals but idealizes certain patterns of life of an established society. Ideologies of this type are initiated by people who feel their identity threatened by social change and seek to reinforce their sense of belonging by providing intellectual support for what they assert to have been the empirical characteristics that have valuably distinguished their society and themselves from all others. Here again the initiators and many of their followers need not be ideologues; no more than reformers or radicals or conservatives are necessarily ideologues. But this kind of thought can easily be transformed into an ideology by proponents who feel seriously threatened and proclaim that preservation of these idealized characteristics of their own society is not only vital but will always be the primary obligation of those who belong to the society, and will ensure their superiority over all others. Allegedly empirical assertions about past conduct in a

particular society are thus transformed into moral
criteria to judge all people at all times.

Where the first type of ideology creates
societies with a universalizing mission, the second
seeks to protect and strengthen existing social
differences. Idealizing ideologies are fundamentally
ethnocentric and therefore fertile terrain for the
belief that cultural differences are--or should
be--accompanied by physical distinctions. And if
that belief develops, the genocidal rationalization
may not be far behind, particularly if the society is
in close contact with a weak group with a markedly
different culture, and if political leaders appear
who appeal above all to ethnocentrism to justify
their authority.

Both types of ideology require repressive
government. Leaders who justify their authority by
either have to stress indoctrination and the
suppression of deviance in order to maintain the
plausibility of their wishful distortion of ethical
and empirical judgment. Leaders with idealizing
ideologies, however, have to use more force because
they are more at the mercy of empirically observable
reality, and it is harder to control reality than to
reinterpret abstract ideals to fit changing
conditions. Because the moral claims of idealizing
ideologies depend on allegedly empirical assertions
about how real people have acted and are acting,
empirical discrepancies that anyone could observe can
immediately call the moral authority of such an
ideology into question. It is therefore imperative
that people be made to act in accordance with those
assertions and that followers be distracted from
using their capacity to make independent empirical
judgments by emphasizing other modes of reaction.
Hence the extreme Nazi emphasis on emotionally
impressive ritual, on thinking with the blood, on
propaganda and the big lie, and on blind obedience to
the person of the leader. Hence also the need, not
merely to segregate Jews, but to eliminate them and
make impossible any contact with a reality that
patently contradicted the fundamental assertion of
Nazi ideology.

Nazism was the convergence of three highly
compatible forms of ideological thought, already well
established in Germany, that implicitly abandoned
universal humanitarian and epistemological standards:
antisemitism, was the oldest of them, and Hitler
hardly added a new idea to it. The originality of
Nazi ideology lay neither in its goals not its
political techniques, not even in its abandonment of
universal humanitarian and epistemological ideals,
but rather in Hitler's acute perception of the full

implications of idealizing ideological government, in
his delight at the possibilities of power they
offered, and therefore, as Mr. Kolakowski has so
brilliantly insisted, in the explicitness with which
he rejected those universal standards in word and
deed.

I agree wholeheartedly with Mr. Kolakowski that
the Holocaust was one horrible consequence of a
government ideology that openly rejected universal
humanitarian and epistemological ideals, made (some)
national values supreme, and legitimated
totalitarianism. I agree also that totalitarianism
is most likely to emerge in a society plunged into
despair by a deep crisis--a sobering thought in the
present condition of the world. But I cannot agree
with his diagnostic conclusion as stated, perhaps
because he uses the term "ideology" ambivalently so
that it is both positive and pejorative. He
considers any wide-ranging body of ideas about how
life ought to be organized--Christian, Judaic,
democratic, nationalist, or Marxist--as an ideology,
but then he warns us to limit our readiness to
legitimate evil for the sake of ideological values of
any sort.

There is something disturbingly
self-contradictory about a precept that assumes that
we can legitimate something (i.e., recognize it as
a lesser good) by the same values by which we have
already recognized and defined it as evil. The
contradiction can be resolved, however, if we assume
that the people labelled as having the same values in
fact do not, or that people with the same values can
make evaluations in different ways so that they
arrive at different conclusions. I have tried to
resolve the dilemma by distinguishing between what we
might call realists and wishful thinkers (while fully
recognizing that the distinction is relative). On
the one hand, there are people who, whatever other
values they affirm, place an equally high value on
making empirical judgments as uninfluenced by their
other values as possible, and who are therefore
forced to recognize the limitations of their present
knowledge and of the evaluations that rely on it. On
the other hand, there are people who make some of
those other values supreme, who are unaware of, or
degrade, or consciously reject the value of empirical
objectivity, and whose conception of what is going on
is so much at the mercy of their convictions about
how life ought to be organized that the world appears
to be organized in sympathy with their values. Hence
they feel omnisciently qualified to disregard or
eliminate those who disagree with them. The passage
of time may reveal the fatal flaw of their

understanding, but it will be too late for the victims.

It is this second kind of thought that I have defined as ideology. That definition permits me to accept Mr. Kolakowski's concluding precept, understanding it to mean that we must beware of thinking about our values ideologically, for if we do we will no longer be able to recognize conduct as bad that seemed clearly evil when we were not thinking ideologically. I would therefore reformulate the precept more briefly: "Beware of any ideologically framed values!" But I would still agree with Mr. Kolakowski's major thesis: that what I have called idealistic ideologies have less potential for totalitarianism than idealizing ones, precisely because they pay lip service to the value of distinguishing between what is and what ought to be. The value is drastically degraded but still recognizable. Yet we should beware of them too. Not only are idealistic ideologies inherently totalitarian, but if an idealistic ideology becomes localized as the justification for the government of a particular society, it may idealize certain historical forms of conduct in that society, gradually acquire some of the characteristics of an idealizing ideology, and develop a greater propensity to totalitarianism. The Inquisition of Latin Christendom is a case in point, the Gulags of Leninism--Stalinism even more so. Beware of any ideologically framed values.

Rejoinder
Leszek Kolakowski

I may not really complain of having been viciously attacked by my critics. In fact I have little to say except thanking them for having noticed some sloppy or unclear points in my remarks. [I might have indeed somewhat overstated my points in my remarks.] I might have indeed somewhat overstated my point concerning the "overtness" of Nazi ideology, as Professor Roth has said, even though I see with satisfaction that he did not question the core of my argument. "Satisfaction" is perhaps not an apt word in this context. I wish I felt capable of saying more about how the dangers which, we both agree, hang over our civilization can be better diagnosed and beaten off. And yet perhaps these very changes we were talking about and which made the contemporary ideologies so elusive and so empty, have a brighter side, as it were. Precisely because so frequently "freedom" means slavery, "anti-racism" means racism, "equality" means privileges, "social justice" means tyranny, "liberation" means invasion, "majority rule" means minority rule, "peace" means war, etc. (I call your attention to the old Soviet joke from the "Radio Erevan" series; question: "Will there be war?", reply: "No, there will be no war, there will be just such a fight for peace that not a stone upon stone will remain!"), the need for another language and the feeling of being simply cheated and pushed in a cul-de-sac by most of the ideological commodities in circulation is more and more strongly experienced. It is not unreasonable to expect that many of seemingly healthy ideologies will soon crumble under the weight of their own emptiness.

And I can only express my perfect agreement with Professor Langmuir's remarks about how important for the aggressive efficiency of ideologies is the deliberate failure to distinguish facts from values. I tried to substantiate my view on this question elsewhere and I am not going to dwell on the topic except to note that I have no criticism of what he said. I have to admit, though, that I failed to provide a definition of antisemitism--although my topic might give me a partial excuse--and that Professor Langmuir's objection is justified in this point. Is there anything peculiar about antisemitism when confronted with other kinds of "xenophobic hostility"? The latter is almost evenly spread over the surface of the globe, in particular when the neighboring ethnic entities are involved, and the Jews have been by no means immune to it. So, how is antisemitism different from anti-Germanism,

anti-Polishness, etc.? (Proviso being made for the
fact that all those phenomena have a variety of
forms, some of them more and some less virulent, and
that one does not become antisemitic, anti-German or
anti-Polish by the mere fact of opposing a policy
which at a certain moment happens to enjoy the
support of most of the Jews, Germans, or Poles).
Perhaps the uniqueness of antisemitism resulted
simply from the contingent historical fact of
diaspora which made the fate of Jews unique. The
minoritarian omnipresence of Jews in Europe and
America contributed perhaps to transforming the
"normal" xenophobic hostility into a kind of
quasi-cosmopolitan ideology identifying the universal
source of Evil and into a kind of multinational
nationalism. The instrument proved convenient and
has operated quite successfully; we should not expect
it to be abandoned now for no better reason than that
it is intellectually absurd and morally abominable.

2

The *Kristallnacht* as Turning Point: Jewish Reactions to Nazi Policies

Yehuda Bauer

Why should a conference, whose overall theme appears to be what Professor Legters defines as 'social pathology,' be organized around a forty-year memorial to the pogrom against the Jews in Germany in November, 1938? Is there is a universal meaning to the Kristallnacht? If so, what is it?

When an event such as Kristallnacht becomes a symbol, there seems to be a danger--at least in my probably prejudiced mind--of it becoming an abstraction, of its meaning becoming flattened, universalized out of recognition. We may then engage in moralizing, wagging our fingers at the evil man can do to man, and end up by seeing the Kristallnacht as another 'bad thing,' comparable perhaps to ill-treatment of children, persecution of political opponents by any of the vast number of contemporary dictatorships, or inequality of women, all of them one-dimensional and undifferentiated. But all these evils are separate, unique, differentiated--and have to be fought on their particular bases and in different ways. Universal generalizations, to be meaningful, can only be distilled from concrete events in a concrete way. And so I see my task tonight as starting with the historicity of the event, emphasizing one particular angle of it, in order to see what general categories, if any, we can extract from it.

By the historicity of the event I mean not only the factual background, but also the general cultural framework, or in our case the place of the Jews in the Nazi scheme of things. The specific angle I choose to emphasize is the angle of the victim, simply because it is more or less neglected in historical literature.

In the years 1933 to 1937, 129,000 Jews, out of a half million, left Germany. In Nazi eyes this was a failure, especially when compared with their success in other major areas of Reich-building.

Nazi policy at the time was clearly defined as requiring the speedy emigration of all German Jews--less than one percent of the country's population. The SS, and more particularly a special department (II 112) of its security service, the SD, were increasingly assuming greater control over the Jewish policies of the Reich. They were competing with such authorities as the Party and its Gauleiters, especially Julius Streicher and his pornographic antisemitic sheet Der Stürmer, or Goebbels and his propaganda ministry, or the economic powers-that-be under the wizard Hjalmar Schacht. Exactly what part did the Jews play in the Nazi worldview? Were they that important?

It has often been pointed out that one can see the development of Nazi policies towards the Jews from a quasi-teleological angle. In other words, up to a point one can talk of the unfolding of a Nazi Jewish policy from a quasi-religious, ideological starting point towards an ill-defined ultimate goal. This is not quite true, but there is sufficient merit in this argument for us to seek the starting point, without which the unfolding, and the Kristallnacht within it, remains unintelligible.

In the Nazi worldview there existed a basic dichotomy of good and evil, whose racial expression were Aryans and Jews. Aryans were humans, and among them the Germanic nations were supreme. Other Aryans could be subhuman or just barely human, such as Slavs, who had been contaminated by Mongol racial influences. The Jews were at the other end of the scale--they were not human at all. They were a parasitic anti-race, they were comparable to parasitic germs, they were the embodiment of evil. They were scheming to control and devour the earth, though if they succeeded, they would perish themselves as any parasite would when the body on which it feeds wastes away.

In his speech of April 12, 1922, Hitler stated this very clearly" "There are only two possibilities in Germany: either the victory of the Aryan side or its extermination and the victory of the Jews. Out of this, I would say, bloodily serious insight resulted the founding of our movement." [1]

There is any number of such statements by Hitler and some of his chief lieutenants. In his directives to Göring in 1936, regarding the four-year plan, Hitler postulates that Germany must be ready for total war within four years. The reason for this is the imminent danger of the extermination of the Aryan race by the Jews. Any delay, even of months, he says, could not be made good in hundreds of years. International Jewry, "whose most radical expression

is bolshevism. . .will not now bring about new
Versailles treaties, but the final destruction of
European nations, such as humanity has not known
since the decline of the ancient world." [2]

The most fantastic pronouncement of all,
perhaps, is Hitler's statement in Mein Kampf: "by
defending myself against the Jew, I am fighting for
the work of the Lord." [3]

The historic basis for this dualistic,
eschatological, and apocalyptic identification of the
Jew with the devil (and the Aryan with the angels)
lies, it appears, in the Christian view of the Jew as
possessed of evil powers and intentions. Only a
people corrupted by the devil, indeed itself
possessed by him, could have committed deicide. But
whereas medieval Christianity saw the Jew as a human
being possessed by evil powers and in deep error, it
also saw him as a scion of God's first chosen people
who must be preserved for the Second Coming finally
to recognize the Christian Messiah. Nazism took a
different view altogether. Basing itself on
Christian traditions, it also rebelled against them.
It used the eschatological as well as the apocalyptic
verbiage of the New Testament and infused
sacrilegious, neo-pagan content into it. [4] Many
so-called Christians in the past had seen the Jew as
a symbol of evil or of corruption; Judaism was a
rotting remnant superseded by a true faith and had to
be destroyed. But, following in the footsteps of my
colleague Uriel Tal, I would argue that Nazism
performed a hypostatic change, substituting the
content for the symbol, the Jew for Judaism, evil for
the symbol of evil. [5] If the Jew was, as the Nazis
preached, no longer evil's symbol, but the evil
itself, corruption personified ("eine
Fäulniserscheinung"--a case of decay, as Walter
Buch put it),[6] or the Devil incarnate, in vermin form
on the one hand and a Satanic force out to rule and
destroy the world on the other hand, then Nazism,
rebelling against the Judaic content of Christianity,
could discard Christian teachings of love and the
equality of man and destroy the bearers of Judaism
themselves.

For the Hitlerite movement, the one-sided
struggle against the Jews was a necessity of life,
its internal raison d'etre, one of the poles of its
policies. Antisemitism was not a tool in the hands
of Nazi cynics, as the well-known NBC Holocaust
series tried to present it--quite the contrary. It
stood at the very core of Nazism's motive forces.
The German historian Andreas Hillgruber has shown [7]
that Hitler's attack on the Soviet Union was to have
been the crowning point of his anti-Jewish policy:

already in 1928 he wrote (in his Second Book, published in New York in 1962) that Germany's attack on Bolshevism is essential because Bolshevism is the form International Jewry takes to destroy the world. By fighting the Russians Hitler was exorcising the devil, and ensuring the survival of the German race. This was the content of the language used in his directives for the Russian campaign in 1941.

This, paradoxically perhaps, does not mean that from the very beginning the mass murder of the Jews was planned by Hitler or by others, as Lucy Dawidowicz seems to suggest in her The War Against the Jews.[8] Hitler was concerned with the purification of German soil and German blood. The word he used as early as 1919 for dealing with the Jews was 'removal' (Entfernung), which apparently indicated his desire to force the Jews out of Germany. We know with fair certainty that there was no murder plan in existence until the end of 1940 at the earliest. In a very important German Foreign Office memorandum of January 25, 1939, the hope is expressed that by expelling Jews Germany will spread antisemitism and thus, while weakening her enemies with the Jewish poison, arouse pro-German sympathies among the healthier elements in the world.[9]

But if the policy in 1933-1937 was emigration, it had, as I already said, failed. It was inconceivable that Germany should approach the critical phase of her conquests with a Jewish population in her midst, with the devil incarnate still sitting right within her.

The Hossbach protocol of November 5, 1937, which records Hitler's speech to his chief executives, presents a clear picture of Nazism's plans:[10] the conquest of Austria, the dismemberment of Czechoslovakia, and the conquest of Eastern Europe which would guarantee German supremacy in Europe and the world. This new stage of conquests was intimately connected with the Jewish policy of the regime. You could not successfully conquer without cleansing your own hinterland of your archenemy. The Jews had to be coerced into moving faster.

The SS journal Das Schwarze Korps stated on October 14, 1937, that Jewish businesses should disappear, that is be confiscated. When in the course of strengthening the Party's control over German society in February 1938 Walter Funk became Minister of Economic Affairs replacing Hjalmar Schacht, Goebbels immediately demanded that the new minister remove the Jews from the German economy. The SS in its internal report of January 1938, quoted by Otto Dov Kulka in an important Ph.D. thesis in Jerusalem, demanded the removal first of all of the

Jewish poor from Germany. A similar line was taken in February by Das Schwarze Korps.[11]

The removal of the Jews from the German economy would obviously facilitate their emigration. The so-called law against the hiding of the identity of Jewish businesses of April 22, 1938, was followed on April 26 by an order to register all Jewish businesses worth more than 5000 marks.[12] Official marking of such establishments came on June 14. Until 1938, Jews had been deprived of their governmental or municipal positions, but private businesses, private lawyers' and doctors' practices, could operate, though under increasingly discriminatory conditions up to and including boycotting. Artisans and workers could still work, if they found somebody to employ them or give them orders. The spring 1938 laws were therefore of a new character qualitatively. The Jews were now being removed from the German economy, their property confiscated so as to serve the needs of the preparations for war, and the Jews themselves forced out, if need be by the threat of violence.

Violence seemed to the Nazis to become necessary especially after the annexation of Austria in March, 1938, with its nearly 200,000 Jews, or in other words more than had emigrated from Germany until then. Violence started on June 9, 1938, half a year before Kristallnacht, with the destructin of the synagogues in Munich. On June 15, some 1500 Jews were put into concentration camps (these were people who had had any kind of a brush with the law, including traffic violations). No great risk was attached to these steps internationally: the Evian conference in July, 1938, resulted in no practical steps to advance Jewish emigration, and Hitler in a speech at Königsberg could with cynicism offer to ship the Jewish "criminals" in luxury ships to the shores of the democracies. He was quite safe. There were no takers.

There being no takers, the SS gave instructions to enlarge the Sachsenhausen and Buchenwald concentration camps to absorb large numbers of Jews. Streicher was given the green light to destroy the Nuremberg synagogue on August 10. In October, at the suggestion of the Swiss, Jewish passports were marked with the letter J. In Austria, anti-Jewish actions were much harsher than those against German Jews. Four thousand Austrian Jews were arrested and sent to Dachau and Buchenwald by September, 1938. Suicides multiplied. In certain communities such as Horn (Lower Austria), the Burgenland, and elsewhere, mass expulsions took place in September and early October, as Herbert Rosenkranz has shown in an important

monographic study. On October 5, which was that
year's Yom Kippur day, an attempt was made by the
Party and the SA to expel all the Jews from three
Viennese districts. An order from Berlin cancelled
this, but it may have been a kind of rehearsal for
the Kristallnacht.[13]

We all know what followed: the expulsion of some
18,000 Jews with Polish passports in the night of
October 27 to 28; the refusal of Poland to accept
them; the concentration of some 5,000 of them in the
no-man's-land area of Zbaszyn; letters of appeal for
help written by many of them, including the parents
of young Herschel Grynszpan living in Paris; the act
of desperation of the young man in shooting the
secretary of the German legation, Ernst vom Rath, on
November 7; and the Kristallnacht pogrom on
November 9 and 10, with the destruction of the
synagogues, the Jewish shops and apartments, the
murder of about a hundred Jews and the incarceration
of probably around 30,000 Jewish men in concentration
camps.

The details and the immediate antecedents have
been clarified sufficiently.[14] They include the fact
that Goebbels tried to snatch away the initiative in
the Jewish question from his SS rivals and obtained
Hitler's agreement to utilize vom Rath's death to let
the Party and the SA vent their destructive instincts
at Jewish expense. Goebbels hoped that he could whip
up mass enthusiasm for the pogrom among the German
people. The SS was at first taken unawares. Only
after the start of the pogrom, in the middle of the
night, did orders go out from SS headquarters to
prevent the spread of fires to Aryan property, to
protect foreign citizens, to secure Jewish archives
kept in synagogues, and, most importantly, to arrest
Jewish men in large numbers.

It seems that Goebbel's plans misfired. There
ws no great enthusiasm among the populace for the
pogroms, if we are to believe the report of the
Sicherheitshauptamt of the SS for 1938, as quoted
by O.D. Kulka: "The actions against Jewry in
November were received very badly," though there was
more enthusiasm in the less industrialized and
Protestant North than in the more Catholic areas of
the South and the West.[15] All in all, the SS
rejected the SA's pogrom-mongering methods
contemptuously. The Jewish problem had to be solved
coldly, scientifically, with the exercise of terror
and brutality hidden from the eyes of the German
public. This indeed was the method which was pursued
after Kristallnacht. At a--by now famous--meeting
in Göring's Air Ministry on November 12, 1938, the
leading role of the SS in the Jewish question was

made clear. The Jews had to pay an indemnity of a billion marks for the killing of vom Rath, had to pay the insurance money for the damage caused to them, but, more importantly, were now to be finally removed from the German economy, in order to force them into emigration. [16]

By January 1, 1939, all Jewish businesses and other livelihoods were shut down, closed, barred. On January 24, the Central Office for Jewish Emigration was established in Berlin, on the model of a similar office opened by Eichmann in Vienna in the previous August. If the West seriously wanted the Jews, it could have them. Hitler agreed to a plan worked out by Schacht and George Rublee, the American head of an Intergovernmental Committee for Refugees set up at the Evian Conference, to try and expel Jews by giving them a part of their property to take out of Germany and confiscate the rest. But the plan failed, basically because the West did not want the Jews. [17] Many managed to flee nevertheless. How? Well, there were tiny quotas, there were loopholes in immigration laws, there were South American consuls who could be bribed to give visas, there was illegal immigration into Palestine, into South America, even into Holland, England, and France. From December, 1938, Britain was the only country easing her immigration laws and absorbing over 40,000 Jews, including some 10,000 children, largely because of bad conscience for having been responsible for the Munich capitulation and for having closed the gates of Palestine to Jews. In 1939, 122,451 Jews emigrated from Germany and Austria (68,000 from Germany and 58,541 from Austria), almost the same number as had left Germany between 1933 and 1937. Concentration camp inmates--those that survived the treatment there, that is--were released if they could emigrate. [18] The second stage of Nazi policy, that of removing the Jews by force and pressure, was in full swing. Paradoxically, had there been somewhere for these people to go, they would have been saved by this policy of expulsion from the next stages of Nazi policy.

Rumblings of the next two stages, that of extrusion to a reservation and that of murder, can already be discerned about the Kristallnacht. In 1938 Eichmann was preparing material about Madagascar, because one might possibly gather the Jews there in a vast concentration camp. And the Schwarze Korps wrote on November 24, 1938, that if the impoverished Jews became, as they would if they did not leave, criminal elements, they would be dealt with by sword and fire. There were no concrete plans behind this, nor were there any behind Hitler's

famous speech of January 31, 1939, when he threatened
the Jews with annihilation in case of another war.
But the climate was defined, the possibilities
opened.
Kristallnacht, then, was not a sudden
revolution. It stemmed basically from the threat
perceived by Nazism in 1937 of a process of
normalization setting in and turning the Nazi regime
into a traditional, right-wing dictatorship. But
Nazism was anti-normative. It did not want the
supremacy of the state and its bureaucracy. It
wanted to establish a regime in which the
anti-normative will of the leader--and of his minions
to whom he delegated that prerogative--would
establish the rule of an anti-humanist elite. The
Nazi revolution was in danger of getting bogged down.
It was then that the next stage in the regime's
development came--the blueprint for military
aggression, the acceleration of the war preparations,
the removal of those parts of the civilian and
military bureaucracy that could serve as brakes to
the regime's plans, and the hastening of the removal
of the enemy within, the Jews. The steps towards
expropriation, terror, and expulsion became
progressively clearer as the 'fateful year'
developed. The barracks in the concentration camps
were prepared for the Jews. The offices and
institutions that would serve the terror were
established. Then came a perfect opportunity--the
death of Ernest vom Rath. The deadly enemy, the Jew,
had revealed his card; the new policy could be
justified. The qualitative change, prepared by the
steps just described, could take place.
Kristallnacht ensued.
Let me turn to the reaction of the victim. I
think it is important to realize the extent to which
the Jews of Germany thought of themselves as Germans.
Their forefathers had settled in West Germany before
there was such a thing as Germany. They were
Germans, though they thought of themselves as coming
from a different tribe. The majority of German's
Jews had tried to adapt their different culture to
their German environment. The liberal reform of
Jewish religion was intended to universalize Jewish
religion, make it into a new prophecy that would
carry a mission to all mankind of what was thought of
as the best in Jewish tradition: the brotherhood of
man, the hope for eternal peace. The orthodox
minority among German Jews were no less eager to
denationalize themselves: the fulfillment of Jewish
messianism was to be in the future, and now, though
the old traditions were to be strictly observed, Jews
were Germans of a particularly strict religious sect.

The German version of the Yiddish languge was forgotten, or suppressed, and the Jewish universalists became good German patriots, because it was only through the medium of the state, as in Hegel's teaching, that true universalism could be achieved.

It was precisely this kind of tension between a super-patriotism (12,000 Jewish soldiers fell for Germany in the First War, out of the half million German Jews, or two-and-a-half percent compared, say, to the one percent of the Jews of Palestine who fell in the Israeli War of Independence, or the tenth of one percent that fell in the Yom Kippur War in 1973) and a universalism that was repugnant to German nationalism. But Jews simply were not Germans; even German liberals in the late nineteenth century thought that Jewish emancipation, if it was to be succesful, must lead to the abandonment by the Jews of their separatist customs, that is of their disappearance as a separate group. German Jews refused to acknowledge these facts. Antisemitism was a remnant from the distant past, and it would go away with progressing civilization. But German Jews were no cowards, they stood their ground on the basis they thought they had established for themselves. In 1893 they created the CV (Central-Verein deutscher Staatsbürger jüdischen Glaubens--Central Alliance of German Citizens of the Jewish Religion), an organization that fought bravely, if unsuccessfully, against German antisemitism from the standpoint of patriotic German liberalism.

It was only the small German Zionist movement that defined German Jews as members of a non-German minority. Since 1912 there was a very theoretical obligation for German Zionists to consider acting upon this conviction and participate in the building of a Jewish homeland in Palestine. German Zionists were no less deeply affected by the ancient German-Jewish symbiosis than were their opponents among the Jews. They quite consciously tried to educate the whole Jewish people in the light of the German cultural heritage, which would supplement and enrich the Jewish traditions.

In the twenties the tendency of the factionalized Jewish community towards greater centralization and organization became more evident. The basic split in the community between the liberals and the Zionist minority did not allow this to take place. Only in 1932 were there first moves towards such a centralization. Paradoxically, it was the anti-Zionist, assimilationist leadership of American Jewry, itself of German-Jewish origin, which for very practical reasons clamored for such centralization.

When it became clear that German Jewry would need American Jewish help, the demand that there should be one organization only to which aid would be sent proved to be a very effective catalyst for the centralizing tendency. After Hitler came to power, Rabbi Jonah B. Wise was sent by the Joint Distribution Committee and the American Jewish Committee to Germany to work for unification. Local initiatives, strengthened by this intervention, led to a first attempt to establish a Reichsvertretung, a National Representation, of German Jews in April, 1933. But the divisive elements were still too strong, and instead of a political representation of German Jews, only a Central Committee for Aid and Reconstruction (Zentralausschuss für Hilfe und Aufbau) was established. However, in September, 1933, the attempts at establishing a Reichsvertretung finally succeeded, and Rabbi Leo Baeck, Dr. Otto Hirsch, and others created, paradoxically, the only independent political organization in the Nazi Reich which had just abolished all other political groupings.

Only the Jews coud have a political organization in the Third Reich. They were foreigners, enemies, strangers, so they could; Germans had to be members of the only political organization for members of the super-race that was permitted: the Nazi Party. Jews were not really humans. Therefore, what they did amongst themselves, and especially their cultural activities, was of little interest to the Nazis, as long as the Jews did not defile Aryans authors and composers by playing their works or discussing them. A flowering of Jewish culture started among German Jews, who were thrown back onto their own heritage. This regeneration of Jewish cultural traditions is associated with the name of Martin Buber, who was for a number of years the guiding spirit of the Jewish Kulturverband, whose activities were permitted by the Nazis. It is hard to describe the intensity with which lectures, concerts, readings, performances by Jews for Jews were engaged in. In the midst of cultural barbarism, of eradication of individual creativity, the Jews were an island of feverish activity. On the political side, the Reichsvertretung was, during the first years, active in trying to protect Jews. Public protests against Nazi antisemitism were made as late as 1935, an unheard of and almost suicidal thing under the Nazi dictatorship.

What I want to emphasize is the independence of the Reichsvertretung. Of course, it was under constant Nazi pressure. It was under Gestapo control, in the sense that reports had to be submitted, Nazi agents were present at Jewish gatherings, and orders were given that had to be obeyed, albeit under protest. But there was no attempt, or at least no successful attempt, to influence the personal composition of the Reichsvertretung, or even to prevent contacts with Jewish organizations abroad. The Reichsvertretung had been established by Jewish initiative, and the Nazis did not try to substitute something of their own creation for it. Of course, The Nazis supported everything that favored emigration; for this reason, they tended to lend support to the Zionists--after all, the Zionists both worked for emigration and denied that the Jews were Germans. But the Nazis refrained from interfering in the elective democratic processes of the internal Jewish self-government, not despite the fact that these stood in contradiction to the Nazi principles, but precisely because they stood in this contradiction. In its report of late 1937, the SD explained its policy of non-intervention by saying that if they did intervene, in order to assure the ascendancy of the pro-emigration Zionists, the Liberals would leave the community organization--surely a very peculiar argument in a totalitarian regime.[19]

With the change of Nazi policy in late 1937, the bottom fell out of the Jewish hope that the worst had been experienced with the Nuremberg laws and that the Jews could either survive in Germany until the Nazis fell from power or they could effect an orderly emigration over a period of years. As early as March 28, 1938, Nazi tendencies were made clear to the Jews when a law suddenly denied Jewish communities their status of legal personalities. That meant that from now on no taxation could be imposed by the communities on their membership. The Reichsvertretung, until then a voluntary alliance of communal organizations, was now outmoded. The Jews saw that they had to establish a new political basis for themselves. Again, there is no evidence of Nazi pressure: the idea of Jewish centralization developed among the Jews themselves. Discussions were held in April and May. They were thorough, and took place within the democratic framework of Jewish life. The SD commented that this was "incisive proof as to the inefficiency of the principle of democratic government and to the total failure of the Jews in the administrative field, even at a time when their very existence is at stake."[20]

Historiography up till now has largely presented German Jewish leadership after the Kristallnacht as cowed and yielding, completely responsive to Nazi pressure.[21] What I am trying to show is that, just

as similar judgments about the Jewish Councils
established by the Nazis all over conquered Europe
are in many cases inaccurate, so the view expressed
about this first Judenrat, the Jewish
self-government in Nazi Germany itself, is simply
wrong. The changeover from the Reichsvertretung to
a more centralized organization was the result of
Jewish initiative, though it was prodded or, perhaps,
forced by Nazi action. In June, 1938, the
Reichsvertretung, in a communication to the Nazis,
still protested what they called moderne
Sklaverei (modern slavery), [22] but they saw they had
to adapt themselves to these new conditions, whose
revolutionary quality was swiftly becoming clear to
them. The deliberations culminated in a decision by
the Reichsvertretung executive of July 27, 1938, to
set up a new centralized organ. This, called at
first Reichsverband, and then Reichsvereinigung,
or National Alliance, was not officially recognized
by the Nazis until July 4, 1939, but existed in
effect from just after the Kristallnacht, having
been carefully prepared and organized for months
before that event. [23]

What was the difference between
Reichsvereinigung and the Reichsvertretung? The
RVE (Reichsvereinigung) was a centralized organ of
self-government which tried to get hold of the
property of the communities in order to be able to
support German Jews in the new conditions of
expropriation and approaching pennilessness. Yet,
true to Jewish tradition, in the new RVE the old
communities were represented, the big ones directly
and the smaller ones through 18 local representative
organs of the RVE. The Führerprinzip was
decisively rejected even under these conditions. The
Jews did not win--they ultimately lost; but yield
they did not. The RVE had to look after the
education of the children, deal with social problems,
and look after families whose men were in
concentration camps. But the main problem was how to
get out quickly. Again, if I may refer to the
Holocaust TV series, the picture presented there,
with Mrs. Weiss after Kristallnacht admitting her
mistake of not wanting to move out of Germany, is not
quite accurate. While it is true that a section of
Germany Jewry persisted in their illusions until
after the Kristallnacht, or even later than that,
this is not so for the large majority of German Jews.
The process of trying to flee started before the
Kristallnacht: after that, it turned into a panic,
an unsuccessful run on the consulates to get visas
somewhere, anywhere. The RVE, together with the
American JDC, then perfected the system of getting

Jewish funds from America without paying dollars to the Nazis despite Nazi pressure. Jews who emigrated, left their German marks to the RVE or the Viennese Jewish community, and in return received their tickets and landing money in dollars after they left German soil. Through that system about a third of the funds necessary for the maintenance of the Jews in Germany were obtained.

What interests us most in this connection is the behavior and attitude of the persons who stood at the helm of German Jewry. I say German, in order to differentiate between them and Viennese Jews. In Vienna, a cowed, obedient and submissive Jewish community under the leadership of Dr. Josef Löwenherz fell pray to demoralization and despair. Not so in Germany. Hirsch, Julius Seligsohn, Cora Berliner, and, to a lesser extent perhaps, Paul Eppstein, continued the tradition of moral steadfastness inherited from the Reichsvertretung. This carried on into the war. Hirsch, Seligsohn, and Eppstein were all arrested in 1940 and 1941 because of protests against Nazi policies. They knew perfectly well that they would be punished for protesting, but they did so nevertheless. Nor were their protests public. Their martyrdom was private; it might never be acknowledged by future generations. They did it out of a deep feeling of moral responsibility. Eppstein was arrested in June, 1940, for protesting against the desecration of cemeteries. Hirsch was arrested in October, 1940, for declaring a closing of the RVE offices in protest against the deportation of West German Jews to the French concentration camp of Gurs; and Seligsohn was arrested for protesting against the deportations to Poland. Seligsohn was outside of Germany when the Kristallnacht broke out; in January 1941, he was in Lisbon. Both times he returned, because he thought he owed it to German Jewry. I think he deserves to be mentioned in the same breath with Anilewicz, the commander of the Warsaw Ghetto rebellion.

The same applies, I think, to the behavior of most rabbis in Germany. German orthodoxy would not yield on questions of Jewish law, and both liberal and orthodox rabbis found their strength not in what they had considered to be their German qualities, but in their Jewish traditions.

The picture painted by some historians, and widely accepted by the public, of a Jewish victim mesmerized by the dictatorship in which he lived, appears to be factually wrong. Just as the Nazi policy did not undergo a sudden change with Kristallnacht, so the Jewish response was based on a continuation of the historical development, from the Reichsvertretung on. One might say with some justification, that the collapse of the democratic parties in Germany was fairly complete--though with some honorable exceptions. Jewish leadership may have been living for too long a time under illusions; they may have misinterpreted some of the Nazis' measures. But they did not collapse into demoralized submission, in contrast perhaps to their Viennese brethren.

Let us sum up. The Jews are a disturbing element in the Christian-Moslem world. In Franklin Littell's terminology, they are a counter-culture, bearers of a culture different from that of their surroundings. Not better, not worse, but different. They are the bearers of the religion and the culture which the Western world inherited and rebelled against. They adapted or created (or both) concepts which formed, together with the Greek and Roman heritage, the basis for the more advanced societies of the contemporary world. They stuck to their religious and cultural guns, they refused to be superseded, a constant ancient prophetic reminder. Trained through long centuries to live by their wits, they emerged into the modern world with traditional skills that were useful and productive, and that created jealousy. Modern societies in crisis, societies whose pathology if you will, is considerably more pronounced than that of others, will be tempted, on the basis of their Christian or Moslem stereotype of the Jew, to identify the Jews with whatever they are fighting against, and turn him into the archenemy who has to be superseded, or evicted, or, finally, murdered. Jew-hatred then can become a central issue in the ideology of that society; in the Nazi ideology, Jew-hatred became the central negative pole. Jews, unfortunately for them, inescapably and sometimes tragically, are important to the modern world, though they are such a small group of people. In the Nazi world, they were one of the poles--the negative one--around which that ideologically-motivated regime operated.

The eschatological-apocalyptic tendencies inherent in Nazism were partially suppressed, or remained partially latent, in the years up to 1938. The change of the Nazi regime into the open threat that it became to world civilization began in late 1937 and can be documented throughout 1938. At least within the German leaders' circle, Nazi expansionism becomes explicit. So do the motivations behind that drive. The 'fateful year' witnesses the manifestations of that transformation which make it possible for us to define Nazism as the nearest to absolute evil that man has produced to date. It can

serve as the prototype for all that civilzation does
not stand for, and its attitude to the Jews is then
a central issue. The Kristallnacht was not a
sudden transition. But it was both a culmination and
a dividing line. The Jewish reaction to it was to
keep one's moral standards; to try and find refuge in
a world that did not understand and did not want to
understand; to appeal to the nations of the world to
help. The results of that appeal are well known.
But it would be a vast exaggeration to say that the
Jews really understood the full import and
implications of Kristallnacht. They were still
fighting old battles, protecting their lives against
what they thought was a retreat into the Middle Ages,
whereas what was happening to them was something
quite different, something frighteningly modern.
Assimilation, the attempt of Jews to submerge their
uniqueness and blend with some undefined world at
large, had proved to lead to disaster--but there were
Jews in Germany and elsewhere who failed to recognize
this. There still are. Chaim Weizmann was one of
the few who did see clearly. He wrote on April 29,
1938, that Jews do not understand "the apocalyptic
nature of the times." He described how despondent he
was not to have his associates realize that the Jews
were threatened with real physical danger. On April
19 he wrote how that was an oppressive nightmare.
His advocacy at that time of a Jewish State in a
partitioned Palestine stemmed from this realization.
"Notwithstanding the great numbers of Jews (about six
million) who are threatened with extinction, I
believe that a Jewish State . . . Could substantially
relieve the situation." But the Jews then were
powerless. Their reaction, even had it been united,
could not have brought about the removal of the
threat.
     The threat to the Jews was a symbol and a
content. The content was specific--it concerned the
future of the Jewish people. For the world at large,
Kristallnacht was a symbol of things to come, a
portent, an omen. For any study of the contemporary
world and its pathology, it is vital to understand
the extreme of Nazism and its works, in order to be
able to judge what the sociologists would probably
term the threat to the accepted norms of developed
societies, and what some theologians I know would
probably call the works of the devil. In
Kristallnacht, the hypostasis was complete. The
Jews were accused of wanting to control the world,
imbue it with the evils of liberalism, socialism, and
humanism; therefore, their houses of worship were
committed to flames and their physical existence
threatened. Through Kristallnacht, Nazism sent a

54

warning that it wanted to control the world, and imbue it with the opposite of what the Jews were accused of. That is the universalist meaning of Kristallnacht, a meaning that becomes evident only when we stick to its concrete content. It happened to a well-defined group of humans, with a tradition, a culture, and certain characteristics. Jews, as we all know, are just like all the others, only more so. It follows, therefore, that Kristallnacht has meaning for all of humanity.

NOTES

1. "Es gibt nur zwei Möglichkeiten in Deutschland: Entweder Sieg der arischen Seite oder ihre Vernichtung und Sieg der Juden. Aus dieser, ich möchte sagen, blutig ernsten Erkenntnis heraus ist die Gründung unserer Bewegung erfolgt." My translation. The quotation, unfortunately not translated accurately, also appears in Lucy S. Dawidowicz: A Holocaust Reader, (New York: Behrman House, 1976), p. 31.

2. Wilhelm Treue, "Hitler's Denkschrift zum Vierjahresplan," Vierteljahreshefte für Zeitgeschichte (VJHZ), 3 (1955), pp. 184-210. My translation.

3. Adolf Hitler, Mein Kampf (Boston: Houghton Mifflin, 1943), p. 65.

4. Cf. for instance Uriel Tal: Religious and Anti-Religious Roots of Modern Antisemitism, The Leo Baeck Memorial Lecture No. 14 (New York: Leo Baeck Institute, 1971); and the very large bibliography contained in the notes there.

5. Idem, "Forms of Pseudo-Religion in the German Kulturbereich Prior to the Holocaust," Immanuel, No. 3, Jersualem 1974, pp. 68-73 (esp. p. 72).

6. Helmut Krausnick, "Judenverfolgungen," in: Krausnick et al: Anatomy of the SS-State (London: Paladin, 1970), p. 309.

7. Andreas Hillgruber, "Die Endlösung und das deutsche Ostimperium," VJHZ, 2 (1972), pp. 133-153.

8. (London: Weidenfeld and Nicholson, 1975), p. 17.

9. Documents on German Foreign Policy, (Washington: Department of State, 1949), Series C, Vol. 5, pp. 853-857, 859-862.

10. Documents. . ., Series D, Vol. 1, pp. 29-31, 34-39.

11. Otto Dov Kulka, "The Jewish Question" in The Third Reich, unpublished Ph.D. thesis (Hebrew), Hebrew University, Jerusalem, 1975, Vol. 1, p. 227; Das Schwarze Korps, 14 February 1938.

12. See the text of this law in Dawidowicz: A Holocaust Reader, p. 50-51.

13. Herbert Rosenkranz: Reichskristallnacht, (Vienna: Europa Verlag, 1968).

14. Cf. Lionel Kochan: Pogrom. 10 November 1938, London, 1957; Hermann Graml: Der 9. November, Reichskristallnacht, Schriftenreihe der Bundeszentrale fur Heimatdienst, Heft 2, Bonn, 1955.

15. Kulka: The Jewish Question. . ., p. 226.

16. Nuremberg Doc. PS-1816.

17. Yehuda Bauer: My Brother's Keeper (Philadelphia: Jewish Publication Society, 1974), pp. 273-285.

18. Idem, pp. 260, 270-271.

19. Kulka: The Jewish Question. . ., Vol. 2, pp. 61-62, Note 212.

20. Idem, Vol. 1, pp. 54-55.

21. Cf. Shaul Esh: Studies in the Holocaust and Contemporary Jewry (Hebrew) (Jerusalem: Institute of Contemporary Jewry, 1973), pp. 257, 275-291. Esh's view is not quite clear. He was the first to establish the development leading to the establishment of the Reichsvereinigung. The text follows closely his presentation of the facts. On the whole, Esh seems to tend more towards the view that the RVE was imposed on the Jewish leadership. Raul Hilberg: The Destruction of the European Jews (Chicago: Quadrangle Books, 1961), p. 122, has no hesitations: to him, the RVE was imposed by the Gestapo. See also Lucy S. Dawidowicz: The War Against the Jews, (London: Weidenfeld and Nicholson, 1974), pp. 105, 196.

22. Quoted in Kulka: The Jewish Question. . ., Vol. 2, pp. 234-235, note 111.

23. Idem, and Esh, as in note 21, above.

Comment: Holocaust and Genocide
Marie Syrkin

As I am essentially in accord with the views expressed by Dr. Bauer I shall limit myself to one comment on the issues he has raised in regard to Jewish rections to the Holocaust. Dr. Bauer's reference to Chaim Weizmann's complaint in 1938 that even the latter's sophisticated associates did not realize that Jews were threatened with physical danger raises one of the most troubling questions about the Nazi extermination program; namely, the inability of Jews as well as of the rest of the world to believe that Hitler meant precisely what he had promised in his well-publicized utterances in Mein Kampf and in later speeches. Few took literally the sanguinary declarations of the Führer before and after he took power. This scepticism proved to be the fatal ally of the Nazis at every stage in the development of their program from the enactment of the Nuremberg Laws to the finale of Auschwitz. Dogmatic Nazi ideology in regard to the Jews was dismissed as rhetoric. This progressive litany of self-delusion is all too harrowing to recall: first Jews believed that the Nazis would not enact the antisemitic legislation they had threatened; then, that they would surely balk at establishing ghettos in the heart of twentieth century Europe; and finally, despite the deliberate starvation and killings in the ghettos and despite reported acts of mass carnage by the Einsatz commandos, Jews almost to the end stubbornly refused to accept the meaning of deportation and "resettlement." We are all familiar with the devices by which the Nazis deceived their victims to ensure their compliance and the smoother functioning of the German scheme.

The psychology of the doomed who sought desperately to discover some rationale according to which their sufferings could be interpreted as an accident due to a given locality--it could happen in Warsaw but not in Vilna or vice-versa--or that it was caused by the savagery of a particular Nazi henchman, is understandable. Because of its diabolic senselessness, Jews could not give credence to the existence of a rigid total plan of extermination from which there would be no exemptions and which would remain unaffected even by the requirements of the Nazi war machine. Surely the Nazis had better employment for their trains in the final stage of the way than the shipping of Jews to the gas chamber when soldiers were needed at the front. Such were the hopes on which the steadily diminishing ghetto inhabitants fed. Nothing in the long history of

Jewish martyrdom, in which sporadic massacre and persecution were constants, had prepared Jews for an absolute and all-encompassing decree of destruction.

Equally understandable was the inability of Jews outside the Nazi charnel house, particularly American Jews, immediately to credit the reports of extermination they began to recieve. When American Jewry learned of Nazi outrages, each act however extreme its nature, still seemed to be a dreadful episode rather than a part of a systematic, inexorable program. Let me give you an example of this state of mind--an example which though slight is tragically illuminating.

In August 1942, shortly before Dr. Stephen Wise, despite a reluctant State Department, was informed via Great Britain of the reality of the extermination program, I was summoned to a small private meeting of Jewish publicists and spokesmen in New York City at which Dr. Leon Kubowitsky gave us information that he had received about the existence of death camps and gas chambers. All those present were in the forefront of the campaign steadily waged by American Jews at the time to arouse American sentiment against the Nazi persecutions. Hence the auditors at that meeting were neither uninformed nor indifferent but they had no inkling of where these persecutions would lead. Though from the vantage point of later knowledge it has become fashionable to excoriate American Jewry for passivity during the Nazi era, every person who listened to Kubowitsky's report was passionately involved in seeking to arouse the American public and the "conscience of the world," and to discover havens for Jewish refugees. Nevertheless we left the meeting in a kind of haze in which shock was muted by disbelief. I can think of no more accurate way of describing our state of mind.

I had come as a representative of the Labor Zionist monthly, the <u>Jewish Frontier</u>. Its editor-in-chief, Hayim Greenberg, a leading figure in Labor Zionism and American Jewry, was also present. Since the mid-thirties hardly an issue of the <u>Jewish Frontier</u> had failed to react as vigorously as possible to the unfolding drama of Nazi antisemitism. In editorials and articles we offered whatever information we could garner, we demanded a revision of American immigrantion quotas, in short to the fullest extent of our limited resources and abilities, we dealt with one over-riding concern--the fate of European Jewry. It must be remembered that in that period the general press gave minimal attention to the subject. Unlike the situation today when some aspect of "the Jewish problem" is likely to be daily front-page fare, the Anglo-Jewish press was almost the only instrument for publicizing whatever could be learned about events in Nazi Europe insofar as these affected European Jewry. Therefore, as Greenberg and I left the meeting we had an immediate editorial problem: if we unreservedly believed what we had just heard our obvious function was to sound the alarm. At approximately the same time, in August, 1942, we had received from the Polish Bund a circumstantial account of the extermination of the Jews of Lodz by means of gas-filled trucks driven to the neighboring woods. Every monstrous detail from the initial deceptive "bath" to the looting of corpses was given. I must confess to you that we read the document without the emotional capacity to accept its truth. Yet we hesitated to dismiss the report outright as an incredible horror story. So we hit on an editorial compromise for which I can give no reasonable post-facto explanation and which today I recall with shame. To assuage our misgivings, in our September, 1942, issue we printed the dread account--which now reads so matter-of-factly--in fine print, in the back of the magazine, as a story that had reached us and for which we could not vouch. The title of the article, "Murder in Poland," was not even featured on the cover.

Kubowitsky's report at the meeting heightened our fear without effecting conviction. Within a few weeks, however, information from Stephen Wise and other sources no longer left room for doubt. So we skipped the October issue and devoted all our energy to amassing whatever documentation could be gotten at the time. Our November, 1942, issue, printed with heavy black borders and devoted exclusively to the Nazi program, revealed in its editorial that a systematic extermination of European Jewry was under way. This issue represented, as far as I know, the first attempt in English to alert the American public as to what was happening. A few radio stations commented briefly on our tidings. The general press could be reached primarily through advertisements paid for by Jewish organizations. The information was definitely not front-page news. Except for the Jewish press, the silence was almost complete.

The evolution in consciousness--the ability to think the unthinkable--illustrated so graphically by the September and November issues of the Jewish Frontier indicates how difficult it was as late as 1942 for even the most alert and nationally sensitive sector of American Jewry to make the psychic leap from an awareness of bloody persecution to acknowledgement of the reality of the Final Solution. Part of this disbelief stemmed from the failure to realize--to quote Dr. Bauer's significant distinction--that antisemitism was not a tool of Nazi policy but constituted its very core.

Forty years after <u>Kristallnacht</u>, we were no longer afflicted by disbelief either in regard to the past, or what is worse, the future. One abiding legacy of the Nazi regime is not only a new word for the dictionary, "genocide," coined by a Jew, Raphael Lemkin, in response to the Nazi experience. More fundamental is the fact that a generation has come of age for whom genocide is a familiar concept whose possible realization in any part of the globe few would question. The gas chamber and the death factory have invaded the imagination of mankind. These Nazi achievements of modern technology are no longer accorded the moral tribute of disbelief. What has once happened can happen again. On more than one trivial occasion in recent years popular displeasure has found expression in an imprecation never heard before: "throw them in the gas chamber." This represents not merely a triumph of technology. The crossing of a threshold in the human mind so that acts which a few decades ago appeared incredible are now viewed as a mater-of-fact possibility indicates how thoroughly we have assimilated the Nazi bequest. We taste its poison when we read with comparative tranquility of mass extermination in Cambodia or some other country, not because we do not credit the reports but because we have been conditioned to tolerate the atrocious. In this respect I believe that <u>Kristallnacht</u> represents a turning point in modern history, not only because it was a portent as to where the treading of a given path might lead but because amid its broken glass a barrier fell whose shattering increased rather than diminished the area of possible evil in the contemporary world. For this reason it seems to me important to reestablish distinctions among various forms of evil which afflict us, rather then to blur them with analogies whose ultimate result tends to justification. The attack on the Jews was <u>sui generis</u>. Unless this is perceived, it cannot be countered. "Genocide," a term that came into being as the result of Jewish experience to mean <u>willed</u>, <u>total physical annihilation of a people</u>, is today applied almost flippantly to a host of social injustices of various degrees ranging from defective school systems and inadequate housing to local conflicts in which the adversaries charge each other with genocide however few the actual numbers involved on either side. Such a corruption of the term is not a semantic or political question but a moral one. If we continue to dilute the specific meaning of genocide we run the risk of weakening our capacity to recognize its actual recrudescence and to summon the spiritual energy to fight this unique evil.

Comment: Prevention of Genocide
Eric H. Boehm

Yehuda Bauer relates clearly the historical nexus of the Kristallnacht of November 9, 1938. Kristallnacht was not an isolated event in Jewish persecution, although the extent of organized Nazi hooliganism and the ferocity of destruction was unprecedented and came as a surprise to Jews and non-Jews alike. As Bauer makes clear,that night can be seen as an antecedent of the "ultimate solution," namely evacuation and annihilation. Bauer points out that Hitler's Satanic drive to destroy Judaism was at the core of Nazi doctrine, and I agree with his assessment.

I also agree with Bauer's review of the history of Jewish responses in Germany and Austria, and the positive image of the Reichsvertretung and Reichsvereinigung. They were effective organs, and--a strange phenomenon in an authoritarian state--they were democratically organized. They were in no way a passive tool of the Nazi government. As Bauer said, "The Jews did not win, they ultimately lost; but yield they did not." In particular he singles out the heroism of Julius Seligsohn, one of the German Jewish leaders, as deserving of mention along with Anilewicz, the commander of the Warsaw ghetto rebellion. On the other hand Bauer's assertion that all but Zionists were going to succumb to assimilation or absorption is not substantiated in this paper.

Certainly one must agree with Bauer's statement that "universal generalizations, to be meaningful, can only be distilled from concrete events in a concrete way." He articulates what I perceive to be the theme of this conference: "For any study of the contemporary world and its pathology, it is vital to understand the extreme of Nazism and its works, in order to be able to judge what the sociologists would probably term the threat to the accepted norms of developed societies." I wish to address myself to the search for the meaning of the Holocaust.

First, we must acknowledge that it is exceedingly difficult to deal dispassionately and diagnostically with an event in history that is bound to arouse our deepest emotions, and that it is for us

a matter of contemporary history, a history of the
times we have lived through. Yet it is mandatory, if
we are to avoid a Holocaust in the future, that we
identify the multiplicity of causes. The sad words
spoken in 1948 by Lagi Countess Solf-Ballestrem, a
person who opposed the Nazis with great courage, are
a warning to us today: [1]

> I do not want to think of the past because it
> has lost its meaning. The world has learned
> nothing from it--neither slaughterers nor
> victims nor onlookers. Our time is like a dance
> of death whose uncanny rhythm is understood by
> few. Everyone whirls confusedly without seeing
> the abyss.

We must avoid surrendering to the comforting
rationalization that only a particular people is
capable of committing genocide. This was the
prevailing view shortly after the shocking exposure
of the death camps and the mass murders perpetrated
by the Nazi government. Such naivete is no longer
excusable.
     Humans by their nature are extrordinarily
adaptable to being either killers or victims. It
would be comforting to believe only perverse sadistic
devils could be killers. To be sure, Nazi policies
led to a natural selection of persons whose moral
restraints were minimal or non-existent and whose
pathological behavior was maximal. But genocide is
the result of deliberately organized behavior. The
executioners marshalled the instruments of violence
of the state, and planned in great detail the
logistics of death. Obedience, considered to be a
supreme virtue in a society with an authoritarian
orientation, or in a given situation such as war, can
greatly exacerbate the hazard of genocide. Hoess,
the head of the Auschwitz death camp, perceived
himself as a law-abiding citizen who did his duty.
When obedience is coupled with an expediential ethic,
in which all means are justified by a goal, we reach
a point of maximum hazard. In any deliberation on
the role of values we must also ask ourselves to what
degree the secularization of man and the denial of
positive values can facilitate the rationalizations
involved in genocidal behavior.
     Two human experiments of recent years have shed
some frightening light on dangerous patterns in human
behavior.
     There have been several references during our
discussion to the experiments by Stanley Milgram, a
professor at Yale. These experiments, carried out in
1960, were precipitated by the questions Milgram

posed concerning Germans: were they different, especially in their willingness to obey authority? Did Germans have a basic character flaw that brutalized them? To get an answer to his questions Milgram designed an experiment in which readiness to obey was tested. A volunteer "teacher" was to administer on a "learner" what he was led to believe were electric shocks. The pain from the shocks was simulated by the learner who had been instructed by Professor Milgram. The teacher had no way of determining if these shocks, which allegedly went up to 450 volts (for wrong answers!), might not in fact electrocute the learner, and the experiment was so set up that there was genuine reason to believe, when the learner no longer gave evidence of pain as the voltage was escalated, that he might be in a coma or dead. Some teachers resisted, but not to the extent that they defended the victim against the perpetrator of the "experiment" (or crime?), Professor Milgram. These are Milgram's conclusions: [2]

> The results, as seen and felt in the laboratory ...are disturbing. They raise the possibility that human nature or more specifically the kind of character produced in American democratic society, cannot be counted on to insulate its citizens from brutality and inhumane treatment at the direction of malevolent authority. A substantial portion of people do what they are told to do, irrespective of the content of the act and without limitations of conscience, so long as they perceive that the command comes from a legitimate authority. If, in this study, an anonymous experimenter can successfully command adults to subdue a fifty-year-old man and force on him painful electric shocks against his protests, one can only wonder what government, with its vastly greater authority and prestige, can command of its subjects.

Another well known experiment pertains. Philip G. Zimbardo, Professor of Social Psychology at Stanford University, hired students to simulate a prison situation. He concluded: [3]

> At the end of only six days we had to close down our mock prison because what we saw was frightening. It was no longer apparent to most of the subjects (or to us) where reality ended and their roles began. The majority had indeed become prisoners or guards, no longer able to clearly differentiate between role playing and self. There were dramatic changes in virtually

every aspect of their behavior, thinking and feeling.

The extraordinary vulnerability of human beings thus illustrated does not suggest a totally undifferentiated conclusion, that all human beings are always capable of mass slaughter under any circumstance. Such a jump in logic is not only wrong, but is also dangerous, as it could support criminal rationalizations. Instead we need to examine the factors which heighten or minimize the hazard. In what context does a particular historical circumstance reach the critical mass that leads to genocidal behavior? By contrast, what are the conditions of safety?[4]

Clearly we must recognize that the nature of the government is critical. A highly authoritarian and totalitarian state, without restraints on its leaders, creates a much more dangerous context. If in addition some leaders at the top of the hierarchy are deeply flawed personalities and they are able to co-opt similar personalities to act out the pathological fantasies of their more paranoid followers, then we have an explosive situation of the type experienced with Hitler in Nazi Germany. Albrecht Haushofer expressed it well in one of his Moabit Sonnets when he wrote shortly before his execution that in times ruled by madmen the best men are put to death.

A critical factor is the tolerance level of a people, and a gross disparity between expectation and fulfillment. A people that has been severely traumatized and brutalized as the Germans were in World War I, with their whole society destroyed and further affected by successive traumas (the defeat itself, post-war revolutionary activities, inflation, depression, and polarization of the people) the situation is maximally hazardous. In Germany, events contributed to a widespread surrender to pat ideologies, simplistic solutions, and rationalizations. The result was the exacerbation of pathological tendencies toward scapegoatism. There appears to be a direct relationship between a person's or a society's pathology and the readiness to escape self-blame through the search for a scapegoat. Then sadism may become enshrined in government policy.

In the modern era governments enjoy the technological capability to render mass killing both easier and more remote. Modern warfare engenders horrible genocidal potential, and remoteness makes rationalization easier.

The society that legitimizes brutality, and
codifies the search for scapegoats, also creates
victims. What of the victim? The victim is
defenseless in a society that does not observe the
rule of law. In the twentieth century we have had
numerous demonstrations of the relative inefficacy of
the people resisting the state, with its ability to
marshall the instruments of power and its monopoly on
the tools of violence. What, then, are the means of
survival? The potential victim has the option of
escaping to another country if he can. If he cannot,
he must try to create a situation in which he is
never subjected to the arbitrariness of the agents of
death. His home becomes his last tolerable
environment. If he is not organized for defense,
then learning how to engage in passive resistance can
be another resort, although one of very limited
effectiveness. (This option was difficult to
conceive of in the case of Central European Jews
whose orientation to law and order represented part
of their national character.) And finally,
marshalling public opinon, both within the state and
outside, is a tool in the victim's arsenal of
defense. But we should be under no illusion that
outsiders remote from the scene, with concerns of
their own, will rise to the occasion as need demands.
The ineffectiveness or callousness of response can
be extrapolated from the examples provided by the
authorities in Washington and the Vatican during the
Holocaust, as documented in the literature of the
period.

In conclusion, what is the paradigm of the
nation that has maximum potential for engaging in
genocidal behavior? It has a government of an
authoritarian nature that has persuaded its people,
through circumstances promoting consensus and through
propaganda, that its particular ideology justifies an
expediential ethic. Psychologically, it is likely to
be a culture that is inclined towards severe
childrearing habits, physical punishment, and
instruction in absolute obedience. Its people have
been severely traumatized by recent historical
events, and brutalized by a war or wars. Timing
itself is critical: a war or violent event in itself
enhances the expediential ethic and leads to
callousness. The emerging situation can be of such
severity that a scapegoat is ultimately identified,
and is perceived as subhuman. Sadism gone rampant
results in slaughter, the elimination of the
scapegoat.

What, by contrast, is the paradigm of a nation
that is safe for those who could be identified as
potential victims? It is a society committed to the

rule of law, a culture in which childrearing habits are supportive of loving and caring relationships. It is a society with high moral principles that are not disturbed by those deep traumas or instances of brutalization that lead to an expediential ethic. It is a society in which heterogeneous views are openly expressed, and where impedances against arbitrariness are well developed. It is a nation in which the government is federal rather than centarlized, in which there are effective checks and balances, and a pluralistic rather than monistic environment, in which a large number of minorities display well-developed and positive self-identities, with strong organizations, and awareness of the possible need for self-defense. Such a society offers safety against genocide.

I conclude with an exhortation: the study of the Holocaust is not merely an esoteric or antiquarian subject. It is a matter of deep concern to us all. It is a matter that demands constant alertness and analysis. Else, as Santayana said, those who do not learn from their history are condemned to relive it.

NOTES

1. E.H. Boehm, We Survived, (New Haven: Yale University Press, 1949 and Santa Barbara: Clio Press, 1966), p. 149.
2. Philip Meyer, "If Hitler Asked You to Electrocute a Stranger, Would You? Probably," reprinted in Readings in Psychology, (Guilford, CT: The Dushkin Publishing Group, 1978), pp. 78-79, p. 288.
3. Op. Cit., p. 289.
4. I refer readers to an excellent review article: George M. Kren "The Literature of the Holocaust," Choice, January, 1979, pp. 1479-1490, and to Kren's "Psychohistorical Interpretations of National Socialism," German Studies Review, Vol. 1, No. 2 (May 1978), pp. 150-172.

Rejoinder
Yehuda Bauer

Neither Marie Syrkin nor Eric Boehm take issue with what I have had to say in my paper on Kristallnacht and the Jewish reaction to it. My good friend Marie Syrkin's harrowing account of the way the news on the Holocaust was received in the U.S. in 1942 surely speaks for itself. I do, however, with all due respect, believe that she does not quite do justice to the way in which Nazi plans regarding Jews evolved in time. It is a fact that the Nazis did not know that they were going to murder Jews, should we be so very strict in accusing the future victims of not having been clearsighted enough to see the danger?

Hitler did not threaten the Jews with murder, either in Mein Kampf or his Second Book (published in New York in 1962). He did say, in Mein Kampf, that had a number of Jews been gassed instead of German soldiers, during World War I, the war would have been worth its while. Frankly, there are worse passages in antisemitic literature than this. The first time Hitler uttered a threat was in his Reichstag speech in January, 1939--after Kristallnacht--when he threatened European Jewry with extermination in case of another world war. We know now that this was not backed up by any planning or any concrete preparation. Until late in 1940, ghettoization, starvation, humiliation, and persecution were aimed at expelling Jews from the Reich. In 1940 the idea was to establish a vast ghetto in Madagascar for three to four million Jews with possibilities for ransom by American Jews.

Despite its lack of real knowledge of what the Nazis were about to do, over half of Central European Jewry--450,000 out of over 700,000 German and Austrian Jews--fled from the Reich before emigration was forbidden in 1941.

All this is not to deny that there were many German Jews who deluded themselves as to the nature of Nazism, or that Western Jewry did not succumb to its liberal traditions that ruled out the possibility of government-planned murder. But I do wish to make the point that the epistemological problem of information versus knowledge, or the problem of how much the Jews (and others) could have known, did know, how they reacted to this information, or how they internalized this into knowledge leading to action, is very complicated indeed and needs separate treatment.

Eric Boehm's points are also in the main well taken--again, he discusses a problem I did not really touch upon. His analysis approaches the problem from one angle only--the psychological-political one. The idea that the top Nazis were "deeply flawed personalities," coopting similar individuals to act out pathological fantasies is debatable, and in any case begs the questions of where the paranoid followers come from whose fancies needed to be satisfied. Top Nazis were ethically flawed, no doubt, but I am not sure that psychological analysis would not place them squarely among so-called normal people. Ethically flawed normal people, so to speak. I find no abnormality with Göring, Himmler, Frick, Bormann, Kaltenbrunner or even Hoess that would distinguish them from bureaucrats or managers anywhere. I think that some of the stars of the Watergate affair, some of the leaders of the PLO, not to speak of some of the Soviet leaders would qualify for the epithet of flawed personality much more easily--yet the Holocaust was committed by Nazis.

Boehm's prescriptions seems to me rather simple--though basically very appealing. Federal democracy is good, decentralization is good, dictatorship is bad. If you want to avoid repetition of Holocausts, support one and oppose the other. That is undoubtedly true, but again--how does one do it? Where exactly are the signs of beginning rot? How do we square demands for a free society with the exigencies of a modern technology in which the value of humans is reduced by technical advances induced by those very same humans? I did not try to solve these problems in my paper on Kristallnacht. I just tried to put up a warning sign. I would be very wary of general prescriptions, though I am in complete sympathy with Boehm's direction of thought.

Boehm queries my statement that only Zionists opposed assimilation. He is right in a sense--I had no occasion to expand on this in any detail. But it should be clear that if by assimilation we mean the gradual shedding of religio-ethnic traditions and identities, then the mainstream of German Jewry, represented by the Centralverein, was clearly assimilationist. Zionists, arguing for a separate national Jewish identity, were not, or were less so.

3

The German Popular Response to *Kristallnacht:* Value Hierarchies vs. Propaganda

Willliam Sheridan Allen

In the historiography of the Holocaust, the year 1938 is generally seen as the beginning of the final phase of open, violent, Nazi antisemitic actions that was to lead to systematic genocide.[1] A key event symbolizing this turning point was Kristallnacht: the infamous Nazi pogrom of November 10, 1938, in which over 200 synagogues were burned, 7,500 shops and offices owned by Jews were sacked, 91 Jews were murdered, and 26,000 Jews were imprisoned, all for the "crime" of having been born. Prior to this staggering iniquity the Nazis had persistently excoriated Jews through propaganda, periodically subjected them to random individual violence, intermittently boycotted or dispossessed them, progressively excluded them from legal equality, and persistently harrassed them bureaucratically. But Kristallnacht broke the prior approach of "cold pogrom" and inaugurated a new pattern of systematic and total persecution that eventuated in mass murder.

Yet accurate as this overall analysis may be, it still simplifies and thus distorts reality, for there was no straight line from Kristallnacht to the crematoria: instead, as we know from that superb study of the evolution of Nazi policy by Karl Schleunes,[2] the road to Auschwitz was a twisted one, replete with hesitant explorations, backtracking, policy shifts. And nothing seems more paradoxical in this story than the German public's reaction to Kristallnacht plus the implications this has for our understanding of the origins and nature of the Holocaust.

How is this paradoxical? A basic supposition of prior Holocaust studies has been the natural assumption that the pressure of popular antisemitism in Germany made the Holocaust occur, or at least facilitated it. This supposition has logical tenability as a causal factor, but the actual German response to Kristallnacht challenges it. On the one hand, it seems that the German public was opposed to antisemitic violence; on the other hand, this opposition may actually have contributed to making the Holocaust worse than it might otherwise have been.

Certainly there can no longer be doubt, from the evidence unearthed by historians, that Germans did not rejoice in <u>Kristallnacht</u>. On the contrary, they were stunned, dismayed, and disgusted by the actions of the storm troopers on the night of November 9-10, 1938.[3] Nazi surveillance agencies, such as the <u>Gestapo</u>, the Security Service, and the various governmental offices, were virtually unanimous in their description of a widespread public revulsion over <u>Kristallnacht</u>. Even otherwise fanatical Nazis shared this attitude. Such a prominent Nazi as Baldur von Schirach, head of the Hitler Youth, protested so vehemently against the employment of his young Nazis in the pogrom that he was removed from his office and drafted into the German army as a common soldier in punishment for his heresy. Ordinary Nazis also protested; so did many ordinary Germans. The regime's records show that public disapproval was almost universal.

Nor do we need to depend upon Nazi sources for evidence as to how the German public reacted to <u>Kristallnacht</u>, for we have extensive corroborating data from non-Nazi observers. For example Brooks Peters, the <u>New York Times</u> correspondent who scooped the world with his eyewitness reports of the pillaging of Jewish stores in Berlin, has reported that the only looting he observed was done by prostitutes, while the only Germans who commented to him on the arson of the <u>Fasanenstrasse</u> synagogue were two workmen who wanted him to stress that the crime was not done by German workers.[4] The <u>chargé d'affaires</u> in Britain's Berlin embassy reported to his home government that he had not met a "...single German from any walk of life who does not disapprove to some degree of what has occurred." The American Consul in Leipzig reported that in that city the crowds were "benumbed and aghast." The strongest statement of all came from the British Consul General in Frankfurt a/M, who informed his government as follows:

> I am persuaded that, if the government of Germany depended on the suffrage of the people, those in power and responsible for these outrages would be swept away by a storm of indignation, if not put up against a wall and shot.

A further non-Nazi source on public opinion in Germany, and one that has not been sufficiently exploited by historians, consists of the eyewitness reports of the German Social Democratic underground inside Nazi Germany, collected and circulated to foreign opinion leaders by their Executive Committee-in-Exile. [5] These have shown themselves to be accurate in virtually every instance where they can be checked against other sources; even the Gestapo admitted that they gave an excellent picture of German public opinion. [6]

As the initial series of assessment came to the Social Democratic leadership in November, 1938, the general reaction to Kristallnacht was summarized with these words: [7]

> All reports agree in stating that the riots have been sharply condemned by the vast majority of the German people. In the first days of the pogrom hundreds of aryans all over Germany were arrested for openly expressing their opposition. The question was frequently asked: "After the Jews, who will be next?" But one must also clearly understand that, no matter how great the general disgust may be, the brutalities perpetrated by the pogrom-hordes have increased the level of intimidation among the population and reaffirmed the conviction that any resistance would be pointless in the face of the Nazis' unlimited power.

A month later, when virtually all reports were in, this conclusion was reached: "...Since the establishment of the Third Reich, there has never been such a unanimous and public rejection of Nazi methods." [8]

Descriptions of individual reaction showed the population to be disgusted by the plundering and violence of the storm troopers and stressed that there was no popular participation in the pogrom. [9] There were numerous reports that even Nazis protested, [10] that many policemen said they were ashamed of their own uniforms, [11] that some storm troopers and SS men refused to participate, [12] and that actual fistfights broke out between German workers and Nazis over the events of Kristallnacht. [13] The Gestapo dealt with this by an unprecedented wave of arrests, seizing anyone heard protesting. [14]

One member of the Social Democratic underground summarized his conclusions in the following way: [15]

> Goebbels has tried to persuade the world that the German people are fundamentally anti-Jewish

in order to defend and excuse the atrocities for which the state is responsible. Those who had an opportunity of watching the Berlin population during the days of the pogroms know that the people have nothing in common with this brown barbarism. ... The German people as a whole have not been greatly infected by the poison of antisemitism. If the antisemitic propaganda had produced the desired effect, this whole action would not have been necessary.

To which one should add that the German people's reaction raises fundamental questions beyond those concerning the effectiveness of Nazi propaganda, though that is an issue we shall be returning to. One must also question the general level of antisemitism in Germany (including not just that derived from the Nazis, but also the residue from their predecessors) and ultimately the relationship between the German public's attitudes and the origins of the Holocaust.

Of course we can never know precisely how much of the antisemitic propaganda that the Germans had been bombarded with (in the decade or so prior to <u>Kristallnacht</u>) was actually internalized by them. But we do know that Nazi antisemitic <u>actions</u> ran counter to a number of long-established historic German attitudes. Thus when the Nazis moved from abstractions to actions, their deeds were condemned, despite the intensive propaganda and even despite residual bigotry. Other concerns obviously became paramount.

It may be helpful if we conceive of German attitudes as ranged in hierarchies of values.[16] These would vary from individual to individual, each having his own hierarchy; thus it is not possible to create a common rank-system for the whole of Germany. But neither is that necessary since the key question is: "Where did antisemitism as a value rank in any one of them?" The answer, based on reactions to <u>Kristallnacht</u>, is that while the value hierarchies of Germans may have also included antisemitism, for one reason or another it was apparently well down the line of priorities and therefore was subordinated when it conflicted with other, higher-ranked values. To specify this we need to identify some individual value commitments.

For example: private property was sacrosanct to many Germans, a prime value. Thus when the Nazis looted Jewish stores the point that was noted by those who valued property rights highly was that <u>private</u> stores were being plundered, not that they were privately owned <u>Jewish</u> stores (which was evidently of secondary significance). What speaks to this is the frequency with which words like "plundering," "looting," or simply the legalistic term "larceny" (Diebstahl) are mentioned in the eyewitness reports.[17]

Frugality was another long-standing value inculcated by German culture. When Jewish merchandise, office equipment, and household goods were thrown into the streets, burned, or--as was most often the case--simply smashed to bits in systematic wantonness, the common response was simply: "What a waste!" The eyewitness reports of the Social Democratic underground indicate clearly that there was widespread knowledge of and revulsion toward the senseless destruction of Kristallnacht, though it is difficult to ascertain whether this or the moral corruption involved in Nazi looting (or even the pitiful experience of the victims) was resented more in the cited popular reaction.

Another traditional concern in Germany was the defense of religion against state encroachments. As far back as the nineteenth century Kulturkampf, conservative Lutherans had grown so uneasy about Bismarck's attacks on the Roman Catholic Church that their restiveness was a major factor in Bismarck's abandonment of his campaign.[18] And of course the history of the Catholic Center Party in Germany showed continuous opposition to any state actions against minorities, especially religious ones. When those of either Christian faith who held such views (no matter how intolerant otherwise) watched synagogues going up in flames, their response was that houses of worship were being desecrated, regardless of the denomination. And let us not forget that these were the years of the German Church Struggle, so the republic was sensitized to the issue of state persecution of organized religion. In Bavaria, for example, there was openly expressed fear that the Catholics would be "next in line." [19]

Respect for "law and order" is another long-standing German tradition (albeit with its own special ambiguities), so much so that Hitler was careful to observe the rules of pseudolegality in his takeover in 1933, as Karl-Dietrich Bracher has so heavily stressed.[20] But Kristallnacht was a blatantly illegal and disorderly event, repugnant therefore to those who prized the tradition of the Rechtsstaat--the state ruled by laws rather than arbitrariness. Therefore antisemitic beliefs took a back seat to this value. The issue is obscured, however, by the relative safety of protests couched in terms of "law and order." It could even be stretched to include that marvelously delusive

74

formula: "If only the Führer knew about this...."[21]
But perhaps the more important point is that
pseudolegality has its limits, and there is no way it
could be stretched to cover arson, robbery, and
murder.
Another traditional German value was decency
towards one's neighbor, not in the generalized sense
(despite the prime Christian injunction to "Love thy
neighbor as thyself" which almost all Germans had
been exposed to), but in the specific sense of the
family-next-door. Even those Germans who accepted
abstract antisemitism were apparently appalled by
what was done to actual Jewish neighbors that night.
The Social Democratic underground reporters give
extensive examples of Germans who warned Jews in
advance, sheltered them, stored their property, all
at risk to themselves. Even Nazi party members did
this.[22] Himmler himself later recognized this in his
notorious statement that "Every German has his 'good
Jew,'" which, translated into other terms, means that
to some Germans the value of antisemitism was
subordinate to that of personal neighborliness. A
similar phenomenon was later noted in wartime Poland,
where formerly rabid antisemitic politicians helped
Jews during the Holocaust because personal responses
overrode ideology. [23]
Even middle class concern with external
appearances was a value that could rank higher than
antisemitism. Richard S. Levy, in his book on The
Downfall of the Anti-Semitic Political Parties in
Imperial Germany,[24] has pointed out that in the
Kaiser's time once an antisemite could be tagged with
the characterization "rowdy," he was henceforth
politically hors de combat. Of course the
intervening insidious preachments of the racial
theorists had gone a long way toward lending
intellectual respectability to bigotry, and the
destabilizing year of street fighting in the death
agony of the Weimar Republic had inured Germans to
overt violence, but Kristallnacht came after five
years of surface calm in Germany and so seemed a
shocking reversion to earlier excesses. During those
first years of the Third Reich the violence done to
German Jews was sporadic, covert (or hushed up),
localized, and contrary to Hitler's wishes--however
tactically expedient these were. [25] One could
successfully rationalize them as aberrant
excrescences. Kristallnacht dropped the mask by
being universal, patently official (despite Goebbels'
cover story about "popular rage"--which was so thin
as to insult everyone's intelligence), and overt.
Neither rationalization nor denial was possible.
Everyone knew about it, despite Goebbels' quickly

applied press censorship designed to minimize its extent. And virtually everyone was ashamed. It was so crude: a Kulturschände.

Admittedly such attitudes imply a sinister corollary: violence against Jews would be laudable if conducted in an "orderly" and secretive manner (the conclusion drawn by the SS and later applied in the Holocaust); but that evades the issue. Dictatorships like Hitler's encourage agnosticism and denial as general tools of control, but only because there are preexisting values they are afraid to violate lest they delegitimize themselves. If there had been sufficiently widespread, violent antisemitic sentiments in Germany prior to Kristallnacht, then even its "rowdiness" would have been condoned as a necessary evil. Since it was not, it seems that the value of "decent" appearances ranked higher than that of antisemitism.

Finally, one can note that even traditional nationalistic antipathies played a role in German public opposition to Kristallnacht. For years, especially before World War I, the German people had been told that the Slavs of tsarist Russia were German's national enemy and that Germanic Kultur was superior to barbaric Russia's. The Russians were repeatedly excoriated by the German press for their pogroms, which were cited as examples of Russian cultural backwardness. But Kristallnacht was enough like this "Russian" tradition to upset many Germans. The spontaneous descriptive term for it that was employed by virtually all the Social Democratic reporters was precisely the word "pogrom," There was a similarly ironic experience with the France of the "Dreyfus Affair," so that both of Germany's presumed hereditary foes were associated in the minds of patriots with antisemitic excesses.[26] Were such German patriots to forget these traditional arguments when confronted with the experience of Kristallnacht?

And there were other values that worked against Nazi antisemitism, even when it was not connected to the visible events of Kristallnacht. For example, in the world of Field Marshall von Hindenburg the most important attribute of an individual was whether he had served as a soldier; all Germans were divided into loyal veterans and others. According to such a value hierarchy, religion was of secondary relevance, an attitude Hindenburg hesitatingly verified when Hitler tried to purge all Jews (regardless of their military service records) from the civil service in 1933. Hindenburg's value hierarchy prevailed over Hitler's in this instance, though few people would think of Hindenburg as a champion of tolerance.[27]

Many German Jews had fought bravely in World War I
(on a relative basis, two-and-a-half times as many as
non-Jewish Germans had served). What were
superpatriots to think when these war heroes were
persecuted? Even Hitler had to take this sentiment
into account despite his personal conviction that
all Jews were evil and that Jewish veterans had not
been "front-fighters."

Or: consider such an apparently irrelevant
value as Victorian prudery. Certainly one reason
that many Germans opposed the chief antisemitic organ
of Nazi Germany, Julius Streicher's vicious Der
Stürmer, was not that its ideas were obscene (which
they were, profoundly), but that it was
semi-pornographic. Here too, antisemitic attitudes
played second fiddle in individual hierarchies.

Finally, it would be a distortion of the
historical record to ignore those Germans who opposed
Nazi antisemitism because they believed in human
equality, were philosophically opposed to racism, or
were ethically committed to protecting the rights of
their fellow humans. The reports of the Social
Democratic underground suggest that thousands of
Germans were simply appalled by what was being done
to innocent people. There were some willing to be
their "brother's keeper."

As for the others, it is undoubtedly a sad
comment on the human race that many Germans opposed
Hitler's antisemitic actions not out of simple
decency or a real abhorrence of evil, but because of
such varied motives as patriotism, prudery, a
commitment to property rights, dismay over waste,
institutional religious self-interest, respect for
legal appearances, shame over impropriety, or
inherited national antipathies. But even these
attitudes must be taken into consideration in an
assessment, especially when they keep us from
assuming artificial uniformities. However varied the
motivation, the central fact is that, at least with
respect to Kristallnacht, German value hierarchies
won out over Nazi propaganda. In this concrete
test--the only occasion they had to respond to
visible Nazi violence--most Germans opposed Nazi
actions. That was three years before Hitler
activated his "final solution" with the stipulation
that it be kept hidden from the German people.

Here we must distinguish clearly between
"opposition" as an attitude and as an activity,
for the record is equally clear that, whatever their
feelings, most Germans remained passive in the wake
of Kristallnacht. Collectively their stance was
very like what one Berlin taxi driver told an
observer for the Social Democratic underground: "God

knows this is the biggest <u>Schweinerei</u> I've ever experienced, but you have to keep your trap shut."[28] Acknowledging this passivity, one must also conclude that German disapproval of Nazi antisemitic violence means that they were not encouraging Hitler in his policy.

Now we must return to the issue of Nazi antisemitic propaganda. Of course, in the years since Leni Riefenstahl's notorious film "Triumph of the Will," with its explicit and nonverbal messages that the German people were one hundred percent behind Hitler and the Nazis, we have become more skeptical about the efficacy of Nazi propaganda in general. Where once it was simply accepted that Goebbels was a magician of mass manipulation who could make the Germans believe that night was day and down was up, we have now come to recognize that propaganda cannot make people accept ideas that run counter to their preexistent convictions. It can confuse people; it can suppress information and thus blind people; it can reinforce extant beliefs; it can isolate people by convincing them that everyone else agrees with the propaganda, so dissidents feel alone in their disagreement; but it cannot twist popular convictions 180 degrees.

There is ample evidence that Goebbels' other propaganda campaigns were unsuccessful. What were the main themes of Nazi propaganda, apart from antisemitism and the apotheosis of Hitler? War is desirable. The good Nazi must sacrifice his personal interests for the fatherland. All Germans must cooperate. Religion must give way to Nazi ideology. Germany must never surrender.

But the reality of the Third Reich belied every one of these propaganda goals. The people were afraid of war and hated it.[29] Hitler was so unsure of his people's willingness to accept economic sacrifice (and with good reason) that he never demanded it, but geared his plans to lightning victories and built his war machine primarily on plunder.[30] The individual Nazi leaders never cooperated in their common cause but cut each other's throats at every opportunity, for selfish reasons.[31] The campaigns for a new Nazi religion to replace Christianity won over fewer than five percent of the population.[32] At the end of the war, despite the most brutal repressive measures including on-the-spot executions of "defeatists," the German people could not surrender fast enough and even SS leaders sold out Hitler to make a separate peace, as in Italy.[33]

In short, since we know that Nazi propaganda was so ineffectual in these other areas, why should we believe it worked when applied to antisemitism? I doubt that it did, though we do not yet have decisive evidence either to substantiate or refute this thesis, since hardly anyone has even bothered to ask the question seriously. But even if Goebbels was successful in increasing the level of bigotry among the Germans, the evidence of Kristallnacht suggests that he never developed it to the point where the public condoned violence against the Jews.

This statement has extensive implications for the study of the Holocaust. If correct, it means that Hitler and his henchmen murdered the Jews of Germany and the rest of Europe against the will of the German people (though their oppositional attitude did not produce effective resistance--the other aspects of the Nazi dictatorship saw to that). How was it possible for Hitler to do this?

One return to the conclusion that he had a killing machine in the SS that could accomplish mass murder with only relatively few people directly involved, though tentative knowledge and passive complicity were widespread.[34] The opinion of the others did not matter, because every effort was made to keep them from knowing about it,[35] and terror was used to prevent people from interfering if they did find out about it. Let us not forget that of the three million people put into concentration camps during the Third Reich, about one million were Germans. Not that many were imprisoned for opposing the "Final Solution," though some were for aiding Jews or expressing disapproval, especially in the wake of Kristallnacht, but there was a general atmosphere of terror that inhibited overt resistance to any of the regime's policies. Furthermore, it is one of the characteristics of terroristic dictatorships that they foster personal withdrawal, privatisation, and a debilitating apathy in their subjects. People compartmentalize themselves, turn inward, and do their best not to know about matters that they are powerless to affect anyway. In any case, terror and censorship proved sufficient to let the Nazis get away with genocide, regardless of the German people's attitudes.

One of the bitterest consequences of those attitudes was that some German Jews took heart from the support given them by their "Aryan" neighbors during and after Kristallnacht and came to the wholly incorrect conclusion that the worst was past and the future could not possibly be so bleak, given the German people's attitude of opposition against antisemitic outrages. They thought opinion counted. In fact, it would have been better had all Germany's Jews despaired completely and dedicated themselves to fleeing the country at any cost (which was still fully possible at that time, as far as the Nazis were concerned, had there only been other places to receive them).

A second dreadful irony was that precisely the German public outcry after Kristallnacht led to Hitler's decision to turn control of antisemitic policy over to the SS.[36] With that organization in command, he expected more efficient and less disruptive action. And thus the fate of Germany's Jews (and, as it turned out, the fate of the 5,723,000 other European Jews who were to be killed) was sealed. For the SS not only had the skill and discipline to organize mass murder quietly, efficiently, and "tidily," it also had the cold brutality to carry it through to completion.

Thus on two crucial counts it would have been better if the German people had been coolly indifferent rather than supportive toward the Jews in their response to Kristallnacht.

As for the actual killing machine, the SS, we now know that it was a near perfect instrument for genocide: morally blind, devoted only to its own institutional self-interest, scornful toward the general claims of humanity, and fully bureaucratic in its treatment of human beings as though they were things. It killed dispassionately--not just the six million Jews, but as Simon Wiesenthal reminds us, a total of eleven million Europeans: anyone it was asked to murder. Lest we think of it as a uniquely German institution, and therefore comfortably discountable, the recent American experiences with the Manson and Reverend Jim Jones cults show that people like the SS can be found in other times and places too.

For future potentialities one of the most significant statistics of the Holocaust concerns the Einsatzgruppen, those roving execution squads that operated behind the lines in Russia, murdering Jews before the death camps were opened. In about fourteen months they killed some two million Jews, yet at any one point there were never more than three thousand people in the Einsatzgruppen.[37] With proper organization and modern techniques, three thousand kill two million.

All the above factors make one lesson clear. What is crucial is to prevent a movement like Hitler's from ever coming to power again. Once entrenched and equipped with modern techniques, it will have little difficulty in finding human beings like the SS and in conducting another genocide. It will be able to ignore the will of the people; opinion will be bypassed. The only time that public opinion does matter is before a regime like

Hitler's comes to power, because then it can prevent it from attaining power.

Our duty is thus to identify the characteristics of movements like the Nazis (or whatever they might call themselves in the future) so that we can be forewarned in time to take preventive action. Without this, public opinion can become irrelevant, as it largely was in Nazi Germany.

NOTES

1. Nora Levin: The Holocaust: The Destruction of European Jewry, 1933-1945 (New York: Crowell, 1968), pp. 74-94.

2. Karl A. Schleunes: The Twisted Road to Auschwitz: Nazi Policy Toward German Jews, 1933-1939 (Urbana, Illinois: University of Illinois Press, 1971).

3. The data and sources for the quotations that follow, unless otherwise noted, may be found in Sarah A. Gordon, "German Opposition to Nazi Anti-Semitic Measures between 1933 and 1945, with Particular Reference to the Rhine-Ruhr Area" (Ph.D. Dissertation, State University of New York at Buffalo, February, 1979), pp. 184ff and passim.

4. C. Brooks Peters, "Remembrances of a Berlin Correspondent: Kristallnacht, Berlin 1938" (Paper delivered at the International Scholars Conference, Seattle, Washington, November 10, 1978). Others, however, did see popular participation in the Berlin plundering: See Deutschland-Berichte der Sozialdemokratischen Partei Deutschlands, Vol. 5 (1938), No. 12, p. A-34.

5. The formal title of these reports is given in the previous note, though there were also English, French, and Danish translations issued (the English language edition being entitled "Germany Reports," etc.). They were issued monthly from March, 1934, to January, 1938, out of Prague and thenceforth through May, 1940, from Paris. The raw data from which they were compiled may be found in the Archiv der sozialen Demokratie, Bad Godesberg. Full runs are available in America at the Hoover Institution, Stanford University, and the New York Public Library. Their editor made every effort to have his agents report "objectively," which he defined as follows: "You must report fully and must cover items that show the regime in a favorable light as well as those that do not." (Author's interview with Erich Rinner, New York, September 5, 1966). Henceforth cited as DB.

6. Sicherheitsdienst, "Monatsbericht über Linksbewegung im Februar 1937," (Bundesarchiv Koblenz, R58/266, fol. 1-46. See also Lewis J. Edinger: German Exile Politics: The Social Democratic Executive Committee in the Nazi Era (Berkeley: University of California Press, 1956).

7. DB, Vol. 5, No. 11, p. A-44.

8. Ibid., No. 12, p. A-47.

9. Among the specific areas reporting were Baden (No. 11, p. A-30), the Palatinate (No. 11, p. A-32), The Sudetenland (No. 11, p. A-36), Saxony (ibid.), Silesia (No. 11, p. A-39), and Danzig (No. 11, p. A-40/41). In the following month (No. 12) signs of opposition were noted in Berlin (p. A-32 and A-46/47), Hamburg (p. A-35/36 and A-49/50), Silesia (p. A-36/37, A-45, and A-51), Southwest Germany (p. A-45/46 and A-48/49), Northwest Germany (p. A-50/51), and the Rhineland (ibid.).

10. Ibid., No. 11, p. A-44/45.

11. Ibid, pp. A-44 to 50. This entire section is on public responses, broken down city by city.

12. Ibid., p. A-29 (but the storm troopers finally agreed to join the pogrom if they could do it in another town, where they would not recognized) and No. 12, p. A-49 to 51.

13. Ibid., No. 12, p. A-48.

14. Ibid., No. 11, p. A-46 and A-49/50.

15. Germany Reports, Vol. 5, No. 11 (December 1938), p. A-29/30, citied in Gordon, p. 187.

16. A parallel analysis (undertaken at my suggestion) is available in Gordon, p. 203ff.

17. See any of the DB citations above; virtually all of them use these terms, nor was the congruence a matter of editorial policy since Rinner stuck closely to the language of the raw reports, except to limit redundancies, and the original reports consistently employ these terms.

18. Most recently and succinctly summarized in Gordon A. Craig: Germany: 1866-1945 (Oxford: Clarendon Press, 1978), pp. 75-78.

19. DB, Vol. 5, No. 11, p. A-34.

20. Karl-Dietrich Bracher: The German Dictatorship: The Origins, Structure, and Effects of National Socialism (New York: Praeger, 1970), pp. 191ff.

21. See DB, Vol. 5, Nos. 11 & 12, passim.

22. Ibid.

23. Wladyslaw Bartozewski and Zofia Lewin: The Samaritans: Heroes of the Holocaust (New York, 1966), p. 58.

24. (New Haven: Yale University Press, 1975), p. 26f and passim.

25. Schleunes: The Twisted Road to Auschwitz: Nazi Policy Toward German Jews, 1933-1939.

26. Peter Gay has posited the followng pre-Nazi conversation between two Germans: "In the future there may be outrages against the Jews." "Yes, you can never tell what the French may do."

27. Schleunes, p.95f, 105,109.

28. DB, Vol. 5, No. 12, p. A-46.

29. Marlis G. Steinert: Hitler's War and the Germans (Athens, Ohio: Onio University Press, 1977).

30. Timothy W. Mason: Sozialpolitik im Dritten Reich: Arbeiterklasse und Volksgemeinschaft (Opladen: Westdeutscher Verlag, 1977), especially pp. 208-321.

31. Though there have been innumerable studies of this, the classic formulation remains that of Sir Hugh R. Trevor-Roper: The Last Days of Hitler (London: Macmillan, 4th ed., 1971).

32. William Sheridan Allen, "Objective and Subjective Inhibitants in the German Resistance to Hitler," in Franklin H. Littell and Hubert G. Locke (eds.): The German Church Struggle and the Holocaust (Detroit: Wayne State University Press, 1974), p. 122.

33. Of course there are still authors who believe that Goebbels' propaganda must have worked, because it was so skillfully orchestrated. See Jay W. Baird: The Mythical World of Nazi War Propaganda, 1939-1945 (Minneapolis: University of Minnesota Press, 1974) or Robert Edwin Herzstein: The War that Hitler Won: The Most Infamous Propaganda Campaign in History (New York: Putnam, 1978). But for a review describing how the latter's own data contradicts his thesis, see The American Historical Review, Vol. 84, No. 1 (February 1979), pp. 198f.

34. Lawrence D. Stokes, "The German People and the Destruction of the European Jews," Central European History, Vol. VI, No. 2 (June, 1973), pp. 167-191.

35. Gordon, pp. 149-164 and 190ff.

36. Schleunes, pp. 251-254.

37. Lucy S. Dawidowicz: The War Against the Jews, 1933-1934 (New York: Holt, Rinehart and Winston, 1975).

Comment: Public Reaction and Paradox
John P. Burke

If it is one part of the historian's task to reconstruct the historical record of events and facts, it is surely another to offer analysis and interpretation of such evidence. If it is a virtue in the historian to attempt to remain open to new or neglected evidence, there is surely also a responsibility to consider some reasons why such evidence may have been previously neglected. For while we must be indebted to the historian who reveals an aspect of the historical record which has been undeservedly neglected, it is by no means true that all such neglect is undeserved. Professor Allen attempts to acquaint us with a relatively neglected area of Holocaust studies by an examination of some features of the German popular response to Kristallnacht.

Allen identifies an impressive array of factual incidents to show that the German people's reaction to Kristallnacht was far from that of unanimous or even widespread support. Indeed, the incidents cited are striking not only in their numbers but also for the quality of the disapproval of the Nazi destruction suggested by the popular response. Allen's explanation of this opposition is that the German public held to a hierarchy of values which all but immunized it against the antisemitic propaganda. It may be best to leave to other historians and Holocaust scholars the job of appraising the historical examples used. As a philosopher I propose to examine the structure of Professor Allen's argument and evaluate the conclusions drawn. But one need not be a philosopher to regard Allen's conclusions with serious scepticism.

Before examining the Allen thesis in detail, two general observations can be offered, both of which are less controversial than the Allen thesis. The first concerns the force of value commitments; the second concerns Kristallnacht as a focus of Holocaust study.

Although it is often more difficult than people ordinarily suppose to determine with reasonable clarity and certainty what values, if any, a group of people subscribes to, it can undoubtedly be useful to know of these values. Knowledge of the nature and meaning of people's value-conceptions and knowledge of the fact that they do subscribe to those values can often provide us with plausible explanations of some, though of course not all, of their behavior. Our knowledge of human nature is too imperfect to allow us to predict invariably how people committed

to some set of value will behave. For it is evident
that value commitments are not always the sufficient
or determining grounds of our actions. Our value
commitments can be overwhelmed, numbed, muted,
eroded, corrupted. To adopt a remark of the
contemporary American philosopher, Michael Scriven,
for the present context, "We are still an exceedingly
primitive tribe."

Second, Kristallnacht is without doubt an
arresting, haunting, pivotal incident in the whole of
what is termed the Holocaust. Such an event can be
studied legitimately in its own right. But one
Kristallnacht does not necessarily constitute a
sustained national policy of genocide. For some
purposes it is conceivable that a focus on
Kristallnacht would prove too narrow. For example,
one might be misled about the general effectiveness
of Nazi antisemitic propaganda during the period of
the Third Reich if one concentrated solely on
Kristallnacht.

With these observations in mind, it will be
useful briefly to reconstruct the general argument
Allen seems to make in order to see why I think both
scepticism and criticism are appropriate. Allen
challenges what he calls "a basic supposition of
prior Holocaust studies, . . . the natural assumption
that the pressure of popular antisemitism in Germany
made the Holocaust occur, or at least facilitated
it." I agree that this belief is eminently in need
of challenge for several reasons.

First one hopes this is not a "basic supposition
of Holocaust studies" since, as formulated by Allen,
it is unclear. Whatever sense may be made out of the
notion that antisemitism "made the Holocaust occur"
is muddled by saying that such antisemitism
"facilitated" the Holocaust. For there are, of
course, all sorts of degrees of facilitation.
Second, quite apart from its ambiguity as a thesis of
historical causality, it is an exceedingly crude and
simplistic claim. Third, however "natural" the
assumption is, if it is "a basic supposition of prior
Holocaust studies," that would be an unfortunate
irony since the proposition would be congenial to any
Nazi propagandist.

But Allen's challenge takes the form of citing
German popular revulsion to Kristallnacht, and he
thinks he can identify "hierarchies of values" held
by the German people to explain such revulsion. He
lists a number of values which were supposed to
constitute part of the attitudes of Germans. These
include a respect for the rights of private property,
frugality, defense of religion against state
encroachments, respect for law and order,

neighborliness, middle class concern with appearances, German nationalism, the honor due one who has served as a loyal soldier, and even Victorian prudery. Allen notes that we must not overlook those who opposed Nazi antisemitism on the basis of beliefs in human equality, human rights, and an opposition to racism.

These values are supposed to explain German popular reaction to Kristallnacht in the following ways. Because the Germans respected private property rights, they condemned the looting of Jewish stores. Valuing frugality, German people abhorred the "waste" in the destruction of Jewish merchandise, equipment, and goods. Since the Germans were uneasy generally about state actions against religion, they were a fortiori opposed to Nazi destruction of synagogues during Kristallnacht. The popular sense of law and order was violated by the arson, robbery, and murder of that night. Decency toward one's neighbor was outraged when Jewish neighbors were victimized. Middle class appearances and Victorian prudery were assaulted by the excesses and the obscenities of the Nazis. Germanic Kultur was deemed superior to Russian "barbarism," and Kristallnacht seemed like a domestic eruption of the latter. And since many German Jews had distinguished themselves in military service, indiscriminate assaults on Jews violated the honor due to veteran soldiers.

This is Professor Allen's case concerning German value hierarchies. It must be judged an embarrassingly fragile case, both in itself and with respect to further conclusions he attempts to draw. I have already remarked on the difficulty of determining with any accuracy what value commitment a people might hold. I must add that even if one can construct a rough summary of such value commitments, the concepts of value must be subjected to careful analysis and interpretation if they are to serve as valid explanations of people's behavior. We should be cautious in scholarly work about the uses we make of familiar value commitments, for what might suffice to render a recognizable portrait or stereotype of a people's character can prove to be insufficient as elements of an explanatory hypothesis about their behavior.

But if one agrees to engage in the enterprise of identifying certain value commitments as characteristic of a people, one should be prepared to acknowledge some values which also have been attributed to the German people and examine the relevance of these to one's explanatory hypothesis. Loyalty to the causes of one's country, concern with fidelity to duty, absorption with the appearance of

respectability, and deference and obedience to
authority have been frequently thought to
characterize some of the value commitments of the
German people (although they could characterize other
peoples as well). If these were actually values
subscribed to by Germans in the period discussed,
their possible connection with Allen's explanatory
hypothesis is left wholly unexplored.

To speak of "value hierarchies," as Allen does,
seems inappropriate and misleading. It is
inappropriate, for he simply lists some values
alleged to be characteristic of the German people,
and a list is not a hierarchy. It is misleading
because "hierarchy" is used apparently to suggest,
rather than demonstrate, that antisemitism typically
"ranked" lower than other values in a scale which
formed part of the German people's attitudes. Allen
concedes "it is not possible to create a common
rank-system for the whole of Germany." But he thinks
he is entitled to conclude that antisemitism ranked
"well down the line of priorities" and that it "was
subordinated when it conflicted with other, higher
ranked values." He defends that thesis by appealing
to the German popular response to Kristallnacht.
Unfortunately, this is an exercise in circular
reasoning for he also tries to explain that popular
response by appealing to the notion of a value
hierarchy in which antisemitism is taken to occupy a
low rank. Thus the "paradox" of the German public's
reaction to Kristallnacht is meant to be dissolved
by referring to value hierarchies, yet the limited
sense of a value hierarchy is derived by examining
cases of the public reaction to Kristallnacht.
Allen's thesis is slender to the point of fragility.

Despite its weaknesses, Allen is encouraged to
draw still further conclusions from it. There are
four which must be identified and commented upon
briefly. First he claims that "at least with respect
to Kristallnacht, German value hierarchies won out
over Nazi propaganda." For reasons I hope to have
brought out, this conclusion is not justified by his
present argument. Encouraging as are the examples of
public reaction to the atrocities during
Kristallnacht, one simply cannot say from the
evidence gathered and analyzed what force a set of
values manifested in the fact of a "prior decade" of
Nazi propaganda. Even if we could be certain of
their potency during Kristallnacht, it seems clear
enough that they were relatively unavailing to stem
the tide of the subsequent inhumanity practiced
during the Third Reich.

A second conclusion drawn by Allen seems to me
to be false, but at least it is not justified by his

present study of <u>Kristallnacht</u>. He asserts ". . . we have now come to recognize that propaganda cannot make people accept ideas that run counter to their preexistent convictions." If this is not false, it can be salvaged, I believe, only by giving it a crude interpretation which threatens to trivialize it as a proposition. Allen concedes that propaganda can confuse people, blind them, suppress information, isolate people, and persuade them that others agree with the propaganda. Perhaps the truth Allen is seeking is that very poor or very vulgar propaganda cannot have much expectation of success.

Allen seems to undermine, inadvertently perhaps, a third thesis he is willing to advance. He contends that Nazi propaganda was ineffectual generally and also specifically with respect to antisemitism. The general effectiveness of Nazi propaganda and its special effectiveness in promoting antisemitism are questions which call for research projects beyond the scope of Allen's present study. Nothing he presents in his paper suffices to establish decisive answers to the questions. He himself suggests that other scholarship is presently inadequate as well when he says "we do not yet have decisive evidence either to substantiate or refute this thesis."

His fourth conclusion betrays well the perils of "slippery arguments." The argument which produces this fourth conclusion may be reconstructed as follows: 1) Goebbels' propaganda succeeded in increasing bigotry among the Germans. 2) <u>Kristallnacht</u> evidence suggests the propaganda failed to secure public approval of violence against the Jews. 3) The latter supports the conclusion that "Hitler and his henchmen murdered the Jews of Germany and the rest of Europe <u>against</u> the will of the German people." Allen cushions this conclusion with a qualification: "(though their oppositional attitude did not produce effective resistance--the other aspects of the Nazi dictatorship saw to that)."

Assuming that the bigotry Goebbels increased included some degree of antisemitism, there are two obvious problems with this argument. First there is the "slide" from saying the public did <u>not condone</u> anti-Jewish violence to saying that violence against and murder of the Jews was undertaken <u>against the will</u> of the German public. But from the fact that I do not condone a practice, it does not follow that the practice is undertaken against my will. I may tolerate it or passively acquiesce in it. It is not implausible to attribute a significant degree of acquiescence to the German public. However that may be, there is a logical distinction between not condoning and being opposed to which Allen's argument slides over.

Second there is the "slide" from speaking of the evidence of <u>Kristallnacht</u> to speaking of the Holocaust in general. But it is entirely unclear how one can validly move from propositions concerning the German public response to <u>Kristallnacht</u> to a generalization about the German people's opposition to the Nazi extermination of both German and other European Jews throughout the Holocaust.

Allen begins and ends with two different paradoxes. The first paradox concerns the German public reaction to <u>Kristallnacht</u>. He offers to dispel that paradox by attributing a value hierarchy to the German people in which antisemitism had a low priority due to ineffectual Nazi propaganda. This then forms part of his case for claiming a <u>general opposition to the Holocaust</u> on the part of the German people, which in turn engenders the second paradox. Why did the Holocaust occur? To dispel this paradox Allen resorts to some remarks about the "killing machine" wielded by the SS and the <u>Einsatzgruppen</u>, widespread "passive complicity" and "tentative knowledge," and "terror and censorship proved sufficient to let the Nazis get away with genocide, regardless of the German people's attitude."

Even if those are genuine paradoxes, we may remain sceptical that they have been dispelled. Moreover, Allen's discussion leaves us with further paradoxes. It is paradoxical that he should focus his paper on the thesis that German popular value hierarchies won out over Nazi propaganda when he believes both that Nazi propaganda was generally ineffectual and that the Nazi machinery of oppression rendered German public opinion irrelevant. It is paradoxical to lament ("it is a sad comment on the human race") that many Germans opposed Nazi antisemitism for a variety of motives which are not conspicuously moral reasons, and yet to announce that "it would have been better if the German people had been coolly indifferent rather than supportive toward the Jews in their response to <u>Kristallnacht</u>." Professor Allen thinks that what "support" was given Jews falsely encouraged them and also inclined Hitler to resort to the SS for more efficient mass murder of Jews. Given the immense horror of the Nazi regime, it may always be uncertain to speculate about what "it would have been better" to do, but Allen's position leaves him with a most disturbing moral paradox.

Comment: The Double Edge of Public Reaction
Ernest A. Menze

Professor Allen contrasts what he takes to be long established German value hierarchies with the principles espoused by antisemitic propaganda and finds that, in November 1938, traditional German values conflicting with the brutality of the Kristallnacht pogrom were more important to the majority than the satisfaction of antisemitic urges. The Judenaktion of November 9-10, 1938, resulting in the destruction of synagogues all over Germany, mounds of broken window glass from vandalized Jewish establishments everywhere, violence, plunder, mass arrests, and even death for almost a hundred Jews thus, in Professor Allen's judgment, took place contrary to the inclination of the German people.

Professor Allen is not the first to suggest that this particular outburst of antisemitic violence was offensive to most Germans. Karl Dietrich Bracher long ago observed that "the barbaric acts were anything but spontaneous and most likely were disapproved of by the majority of Germans, as the British chargé d' affaires reported at the time."[1] Moreover, the action, principally engineered by Goebbels, at the time was an inconvenient and perilous interference with Göring's economic policies and Himmler's conception of bureaucratically efficient antisemitic practices.[2]

Many observers agree that the events of Kristallnacht mark a turning point in the Nazis' Jewish policies. Hitler was convinced by this "last fling" granted the radicals of his movement that it was time for him to assume a central role in the direction of anti-Jewish policy, from which he had been "strangely aloof" during the preceding five years.[3] Professor Allen's exposition of German popular reaction to Kristallnacht, supported by the researchg of Dr. Sarah Gordon,[4] must be examined especially in terms of this evident "turning of the tide."[5] The historian must not only note the existence of value hierarchies offended by these particular acts of violence, but the structures creating the values and, in turn, the pernicious role played by them in making possible precisely the flawless functioning of the policies taking the place of random violence after the fateful November night and leading, ultimately, to Auschwitz. Hitler's strength up to this point had rested on the broad support his policies received from the German people. The real significance of German popular reaction to--yes, revulsion against--the events of Kristallnacht lies in its effect on Hitler. A prominent biographer of the Führer, characterizing the German popular reaction to Kristallnacht in an address to representatives of the German press.[6] Was he apprised already at this point of the public's reaction and thus prompted to muse about the possible reaction of the masses to other failures?

It is well established by now that, whenever the German people showed reluctance to cheer one of Hitler's major initiatives, he was greatly disturbed and reacted bitterly.[7] His anger turned on those who, even as victims, denied him quick success and the "deserved" acclaim of his people, such as the Poles who dared to resist in 1939. The spectacle of the German people not merely passively watching a major step undertaken by their leader, as at the time of the invasion of Poland, but actually displaying an attitude bordering on disapproval--or widespread revulsion, if Mr. Allen is right--as in the reaction to Kristallnacht, undoubtedly disturbed Hitler profoundly. Whereas, in the case of opponents out of his reach, he could only rant and rave, in the case of the negative German reaction to Kristallnacht he could turn the cold fury of his frustration against the victims, the cause of this temporary alienation of his movement from his people. There is no quarrel here, then, with Mr. Allen's suggestion that German opposition to antisemitic violence, whatever its exact extent and intensity, "...may actually have contributed to making the Holocaust worse than it otherwise might have been." In effect, given the evidence at hand, a stronger statement appears to be called for. Hypersensitive to even indirect criticism and craving unity, Hitler could not allow any possible source of dissent to get in his way. Since the Jews didn't simply fade away in the face of violence, but now actually seemed to evoke the sympathy of Germans otherwise apt to look at them with indifference, if not passive dislike, a way had to be found to make them disappear as inconspicuously as possible. Indeed, the German reaction to Kristallnacht worsened the fate of the Jews.

If there is no argument with Professor Allen's contention that there was more disapproval of antisemitic violence in November 1938 than commonly assumed, one may still disagree with him over the extent and manner of this disapproval and its meaning. Professor Allen is right in pointing out that the German public reaction to Kristallnacht appears paradoxical only if one shares the view of prior Holocaust studies and considers the pressures of German popular antisemitism as the source of the "final solution." However, if one follows Professor Allen's argument and accepts the German hierarchy of values as he sees it, the German reaction to Kristallnacht, indeed, no longer seems paradoxical, but in keeping with these values.

Though I have no quarrel with the assumption that the average German's values were offended by such vulgar violence, the question still remains how widely such distaste turned into revulsion and was publicly expressed. For the historian the problem of substantiating tangibly a sense gained--due to profound familiarity with the subject matter in general, as in the case of Professor Allen--turns out to be a considerable one. Given the preponderance of non-Nazi sources cited by Mr. Allen, a few examples of what he calls the "virtually unanimous...descriptions of a widespread public revulsion over Kristallnacht" by Nazi surveillance agencies would have been helpful. This is especially so since most of Professor Allen's citations come from the Deutschland Berichte of the exiled Executive Committee of the German Social Democratic Party. A perusal of the pertinent numbers of these reports does indeed confirm Professor Allen's reading and Dr. Gordon's more elaborate exposition. Still, one does not question the accuracy of these reports by doubting the accuracy of the impression created by them when cited without collaboration from other sources, viewing the disaffection from different vantage points. Moreover, one does not question the integrity of the authors and editors by assuming that there was an element of wishful thinking in their hearts. Writing in pain over the sad state of the land they loved or, in the case of the editors, exiled and hoping to return one day to rebuild, does it seem unreasonable to suppose that they wanted to see the German people set apart from their oppressors? Even at that, one of the reports could not help noting that some people "evidently enjoyed this sad spectacle and grinned happily," though the majority was visibly disgusted, even if passively so.[8] A review of the Deutschland Berichte of the years preceding Kristallnacht serves well to balance the impression created of a people at odds with its leader's policies in November of 1938. A report on the "terror" of the year 1936,[9] perhaps summarizes more accurately the general mood by stressing that, though Streicher's methods generally were rejected, antisemitic propaganda was not without influence on the attitude of the people. As it was reported from Saxony,

Antisemitism, unquestionably, has taken root in broad circles of the population. If people, nevertheless, buy from Jews, they do so not in

order to help the Jews, but to anger the Nazis.
The general antisemitic psychosis affects also
the thinking people, our comrades too. All are
decidely opposed to excesses, but one is in
favor of breaking, once and for all, the Jewish
position of predominance, and of assigning to
the Jews a fixed field of activity. Streicher
is rejected everywhere but, basically, one
agrees in the main with Hitler in that he pushes
the Jews out of the most important positions.
The workers say: The Jews became big within the
Republic, but also within the party." [10]

And a report from Hessen added "people in general are
so brutalized that they do not perceive the low human
level of antisemitism."[11]
  If these reports reflect accurately the overall
attitude of Germans to antisemitism in 1936, there is
little reason to assume that the attitude had changed
in 1938. The negative reaction displayed by
Germans--whatever the extent--in face of the unusual
violence of _Kristallnacht_, accentuated by the
authors and editors of the _Deutschland Berichte_,
was fully in keeping with their values. But this
does not necessarily lead to the conclusion suggested
by Professor Allen. Pointing out correctly that
"...even if Goebbels was successful in increasing the
level of bigotry among the Germans, the evidence of
Kristallnacht suggests that he never developed it
to the point where the public condoned violence
against the Jews..." he concludes that "this
statement has extensive implications for the study of
the Holocaust. If correct, it means that Hitler and
his henchmen murdered the Jews of Germany and the
rest of Europe against the will of the German people
(though their oppositional attitudes did not produce
effective resistance--the other aspects of the Nazi
dictatorship saw to that)." Though the historian may
well speculate as to how people might have acted had
they been given a clear choice in the matter, he must
in the end confine his judgment to their actions
within the range of choices available to them. Here
we know that, confronted with certain acts of
violence in November of 1938, a considerable, but
undetermined, number of Germans reacted negatively,
but remained passive and, apparently, quickly forgot
about the incident. Moreover, as Professor Allen
argued, the negative reaction on the whole, was due
to the "un-German" Nazi offenses to "German" values
and only incidentally to the violence done by Jews.
  The Nazis' task of making up for their
"un-German" conduct at the time of _Kristallnacht_
was eased by Hitler's instinctive understanding of

the real German values and his skill in paying lip service to them. Though, as Professor Trevor-Roper recently pointed out, "Hitler hated bureaucracy, just as he hated law" and the <u>Führerprinzip</u>, to him, meant "to enforce his will through obedient agents, using or ignoring institutions as he pleased,"[12] he also knew that such obedience was sustained by the illusion of adherence to traditional "German" values. Perhaps the most deeply ingrained German value is a sense of order which, under conditions of properly legitimized authority, is at the root of a feeling of personal security and encourages willing obedience. This sense is part of all of the values listed by Professor Allen as offended by <u>Kristallnacht</u>. After <u>Kristallnacht</u> serious efforts were made by the Nazis to take care of the problems created by the "Jewish question" without offending this sense of order. Bureaucratic assembly line extermination was their answer.

Professor Allen, of course, perceived that the German reaction to <u>Kristallnacht</u> "may actually have contributed to making the Holocaust worse than it might have been." But, further on in his paper, in buttressing his argument that, to Germans, "decent" appearances rank higher than antisemitism, he concluded that the "admittedly...sinister corollary" of "violence against Jews..." as "...laudable if conducted in an orderly nd secretive manner...evades the issue." To this writer the "sinister corollary" <u>is</u> the issue. The fact that <u>violent</u> antisemitic sentiments were not prevalent before, during, and after <u>Kristallnacht</u> does not come as a surprise to one who lived there. The shock lies in what Hermann Glaser called the "ghastly idyll" as the ultimate source and locus (extended to the occupied territories) of the unimaginable terror following <u>Kristallnacht</u>.[13] The shock lies in the fact that virtually total obedience was possible even though, as Professor Allen pointed out, Nazi propaganda was not effective to the point generally assumed. Excesses of Nazi propaganda violating basic values or common sense as, for example, Goebbels' orchestrated call for "total war" in February 1943, were widely ridiculed. Such expressions of ridicule brought relief and eased the agony of unremitting fulfillment of duty. It does not seem unreasonable to suggest that the expression of revulsion at the sight of violated values during <u>Kristallnacht</u> also had a tonic effect and made continued loyalty to German law and order--as practiced by the Nazi state--less burdensome. In the end it was much easier to believe that the excesses were exceptions to the rule and not the true face of the fatherland. Once the violence of Kristallnacht had passed few asked the logical question as to what policies had taken its place. The return to normality meant a return to the comfort of obedience to legitimized authority, a state of being to which all men are to some degree conditioned.[14]

Embedded in structures systematically distorting those communications capable of facilitating individual autonomy, German society was unable to generate a popular will running counter to properly legitimized authority.[15] Whatever "will" there was of the German people, was directed to doing things within the framework of and in a manner corresponding to the hierarchy of values so aptly described by Professor Allen. From this point of view, then, Hitler and his henchmen did not act against the "will" of the German people in murdering cold bloodedly and bureaucratically those Jews still in their grasp after Kristallnacht. Rather, Hitler and his henchmen adjusted fully to what the reaction to Kristallnacht had persuaded them to be the overriding "will" of the German people and made sure to preserve outward appearances in conformity with it even in their most ghastly undertakings. Germans, on the whole, made this easy: "'Accustomed to governments acting correctly, not slave-like, but inclined to go along with authority (obrigkeitlich fühlend), we listened only half-way, did not see some things, and some things we could have seen.'"[16]

Professor Allen is right, it is our duty "to identify the characteristics of movements like the Nazis (or whatever they might call themselves in the future) so that we can be forewarned in time to take preventive action." More importantly, however, we must identify the structures leading to hierarchies of values that allow such movements to harness the masses obediently to their cause. Professor Allen's laudible effort to set apart German values from the conduct of Nazi rowdies during Kristallnacht notwithstanding, it was this system of values that allowed the rowdies to assume power and then, during their "last fling" in November of 1938, reminded Hitler where his power really was rooted, forcing him to act accordingly.

NOTES

1. Karl Dietrich Bracher: <u>The German Dictatorship: The Origins, Structure and Effects of National Socialism</u>, (New York: Praeger, 1970), p. 367.

2. Karl A. Schleunes: <u>The Twisted Road to Auschwitz: Nazi Policy Toward German Jews</u>, 1933-1939, (Urbana, Ill.: University of Illinois Press, 1970), p. 251, 244.

3. <u>Ibid.</u>, pp. 244-45, 251-52.

4. Sarah Ann Gordon, <u>German Opposition to Nazi Anti-Semitic Measures Between 1933 and 1945, With Particular Reference to the Rhine-Ruhr Area</u>, Ph.D. Dissertation, State University of New York at Buffalo, February, 1979. The author appreciates Dr. Gordon's making available to him a copy of her dissertation while he was preparing this comment. See also footnote 3 of Professor Allen's contribution to this volume.

5. In the words of Raul Hilberg, "every bureaucrat, in and out of the party, was henceforth convinced that measures against Jews had to be taken <u>systematically</u> and that the amateurish handling of the situation by Goebbels and other agitators was to be avoided under all circumstances. From now on, the Jews were going to be dealt with in a "legal" fashion--that is to say, in an orderly way that would allow for proper and thorough planning..." Raul Hilberg: <u>The Destruction of the European Jews</u>, (Chicago: Quadrangle, 1967), p. 29.

6. Robert G. L. Waite: <u>The Psychopathic God: Adolf Hitler</u>, (New York: Basic Books, 1977), p. 47. Waite cites the text of Hitler's speech from Wilhelm Treue, "Dokumentation: Rede Hitlers vor der deutschen Presse, 10. November 1938," <u>Vierteljahreshefte für Zeitgeschichte</u>, Vol. 6, (1958), pp. 175 ff. Joachim Fest, quoting the same passage, reads Hitler's misgivings as primarily addressed to his critics and "seditious intellectuals," though he considers the speech, on the whole, as "practically an order for psychological mobilization" [Joachim Fest: <u>Hitler</u>, (New York: Harcourt Brace Jovanovich, 1974), p. 569]. The text of the speech, in the main, was concerned with the aftermath of the Sudeten crisis and the need to shift propaganda from themes of peace to a more aggressive stance, lest the German people become "'..filled with a spirit of defeatism which in the long run would inevitably undermine the success of the current regime.'" The speech reflects Hitler's "concern about the lack of enthusiasm shown by the German people for war." In how far that concern had been

amplified by the reaction of the German public to Kristallnacht on the day after the event must remain up to speculation. But his emphasis on the fact that "...all of us can only survive if we do not let the world see our mistakes but only the positive things" may well have been prompted by reports of the morning after [Jeremy Noakes and Geoffrey Pridham, eds., Documents on Nazism, 1919-1945, "Hitler's secret speech to the German press, 10 November, 1938," (New York: 1974), pp. 549-50.]

7. See, for example, Alan Bullock: Hitler, a Study of Tyranny, (New York: Harper and Row, rev. ed., 1962), pp. 547-59.

8. D e u t s c h l a n d   B e r i c h t e   d e r Sozialdemokratischen Partei Deutschlands, 5. Jahrgang, Nr. 11 (Paris, 1938), p. 32, Reports from Homburg and Saarlautern.

9. D e u t s c h l a n d   B e r i c h t e   d e r Sozialdemokratischen Partei Deutschlands, Jahrgang 3, Nr. 1, (Prague, 1936), pp. A 13 - A 76.

10. Ibid., p. A 18.

11. Ibid., pp. A 19-20.

12. H . R .   T r e v o r - R o p e r ,   "Toady, Bully, Vulgarian," Review of Jochen von Lang: The Secretary: Martin Borman, The Man Who Manipulated Hitler, (New York: Random House, 1979), in The New York Times Book Review, July 1, 1979, p. 6.

13. Hermann Glaser: The Cultural Roots of National Socialism, (London: Croom Helm, 1978), pp. 231-44.

14. As Stanley Milgram has observed, in another context, in reference to man's inclination to obey properly legitimized authority: "...Something far more dangerous (than anger and rage against others) is revealed: the capacity for man to abandon his humanity, indeed the inevitability that he does so, as he merges his unique personality into larger institutional structures.

This is a fatal flaw nature has designed into us, and which in the long run gives our species only a modest chance of survival.

It is ironic that the virtues of loyalty, discipline, and self-sacrifice that we value so highly in the individual are the very properties that create destructive organizational engines of war and blind men to malevolent systems of authority." [Stanley Milgram: Obedience to Authority: An Experimental View, (New York: Harper and Row, 1974), p. 188. See also Milgram: The Individual in a Social World, Essays and Experiments, (Reading, Mass., 1977)].

15.   For a discussion of such "structural violence" see Jürgen Habermas, "Hannah Arendt's Communications Concepts of Power," in <u>Social Research</u>, Vol. 44, Nr. 1, (Spring 1977), pp. 3-24 and, by the same author, "Umgangssprache, Wissenschaftssprache, Bildungssprache," <u>Sonderdruck</u>, from <u>Max-Planck-Gesellschaft Jahrbuch 1977</u>, (Göttingen, 1977), pp. 36-51.

16. Hermann Heimpel: <u>Kapitulation vor der Geschichte</u>, (1956), p. 7, cited in Hans-Joachim Schoeps: <u>Bereit für Deutschland: Der Patriotismus deutscher Juden und der National Sozialismus</u>, (Berlin: Haude & Spenersche Verlagsbuchhandlung, 1970), p. 20.

Rejoinder
William Sheridan Allen

Do historians take particular glee in presenting revisionist challenges? On the contrary; they usually do so with foreboding. Any argument that questions accepted beliefs will inevitably upset people--especially when what is being undermined is an understanding acquired through considerable effort. So the revisionist must brace himself for angry attacks, often based on factors separate from the actual data. As John Kenneth Galbraith put it (in another context): "A vested interest in understanding is more preciously guarded than any other treasure. It is why men react, not infrequently with something akin to religious passion, to the defense of what they have so laboriously learned."[1]

On the other hand it is a historian's professinal duty to correct prior errors of analysis, because then the path is opened for a new way of looking at data that may bring us closer to the truth. Destruction of unsound foundations is a prerequisite for new and sounder construction. Further, a reexamination of issues, stimulated by revionist theses, may also suggest new topics for research so that the net result may be a general advance of human knowledge--at least in one area.[2] That seems worth the upset caused by challenging "vested interest in understanding."

The two responses to my revisionist essay neatly reflect both the major effects just discussed. Professor Burke is clearly very bothered by my analysis; his critique is noteworthy mostly for its emotional aura. Professor Menze, however, while by no means conceding my conclusions completely, still points the way toward new research and new interpretive options on the issues raised.

A few of Professor Burke's points will help clarify the matter under discussion, but most will not. For example, a rereading of the relevant passages in my essay will show that Professor Burke is distorting my point when he writes that I contend "that the German public held to a hierarcy of values which all but immunized it against the antisemitic propaganda." Since this involves a central issue in my analysis, I think it important to be precise. My concept of value hierarchies (not "a hierarchy") includes the existence of antisemitic values among the Germans of November, 1938 (whether from tradition or from recent propaganda), but--and this is the nub--I am contending that the evidence suggests a subordination of antisemitism to other values (where conflicts can be shown to have existed). In short, the issue is not "immunization," which would be <u>reductio ad absurdum</u> through exaggeration, but the <u>relative</u> significance of values. A comparative example: during the McCarthy era many Americans valued both anticommunism and the principle of fair play. The issue then became one of which value was more important to individuals. While McCarthy was riding high, anticommunism seemed more important or it was argued that his tactics were not unfair. Once it was shown that he was not fair, the value of fair play asserted dominance and McCarthy's tide of credibility and influence began to ebb. Naturally, there were other factors, too.

What I suggested was that no matter how much Germans expressed concurrence with Nazi antisemitic propaganda, they clearly did not accept its implications of violent <u>actions</u> against the Jews (on various grounds), at least in November, 1938. To quote myself: "But even if Goebbels was successful in increasing the level of bigotry among the Germans, the evidence of <u>Kristallnacht</u> suggests that he never developed it to the point where the public condoned violence against the Jews." This is what requires our further contemplation.

I would agree with Professor Burke that there is not always a direct causal relation between values and actions (fear, lethargy, distraction, and a host of other frailties can keep men from doing what they think they ought to do). Indeed, my essay shows that <u>Kristallnacht</u> was just such a case. Despite all the complaints there was hardly any action. But sometimes values do cause actions. Thus a major purpose of my essay was to question the simplistic assumption that a <u>sufficient</u> cause of the Holocaust was popular German antisemitism.

I also agree that "a focus on <u>Kristallnacht</u> [could] prove too narrow." However, it would have exceeded the scope of my assignment to deal with the entire Third Reich. One can still draw conclusions from this significant event. That is because <u>Kristallnacht</u> was, as I pointed out, the sole overt, visible, and nationwide act of violence against Germany's Jews and thus has very useful qualities as a test case for the issues I wanted to raised. If Professor Burke means that follow-up research is needed (my inference rather than his suggestion) I certainly concur wholeheartedly since stimulating that was a major goal of my challenge.

As to Professor Burke's other criticisms, I find them less worthy of serious response. In quibbling over my statement that Holocaust studies have hitherto assumed "that the pressure of popular

antisemitism in Germany made the Holocaust occur, or
at least facilitated it" he is simply ignoring the
Aristotelian distinction between "necessary" and
"sufficient" causes. I think it self-evident that
the Holocaust could not have happend <u>without</u> a
prior tradition of not just German but also European
and Christian antisemitism, but that does not mean
that we thereby explain <u>why</u> (let alone, when,
where, and how) the Holocaust happened. In any case,
the reader can quickly check my statement by reading
works as old as Raul Hilberg's <u>Destruction of the
European Jews</u> or as recent as Lucy Dawidowicz's <u>The
War Against the Jews</u>, and judge for themselves
whether my summary is accurate.

Concerning Professor Burke's objections to my
use of the concept of value hierarchies, I wish that
he had provided an alternative explanation for the
undisputed fact that in the wake of <u>Kristallnacht</u>
there was widespread and open criticism of it,
couched in the terms I have categorized. And as for
my failure to consider a host of other values, my
reason is obvious: they were not expressed on this
occasion and thus are pertinent only as abstract
possibilities rather than as concrete and
documentable factors. Historians must deal first and
foremost with whatever recorded reality they can
discover.

I confess to bafflement about the charge of
"circular reasoning" regarding my use of the German
popular response to <u>Kristallnacht</u> as an example of
value hierarchies and also using it to show how such
values conflicted with antisemitic violence. The
facts are that (1) people <u>did</u> reject
<u>Kristallnacht</u> and (2) in doing so they expressed
values that suggested rank orderings in which
antisemitism was subordinate to other values. An
interpretation emerges from the data which then helps
order and explain the data. That is called "the
scientific method," though in order to be complete
theories need further testing, refinement, and so
forth. Theories always arise from some factual or
observational basis, though criticisms do not
necessarily follow this rule.

Method aside, there remains the data and in his
critique of my conclusions Professor Burke has simply
ignored that data. For example, I concluded that "at
least with respect to <u>Kristallnacht</u>, German value
hierarchies won out over Nazi propaganda." No one
disputes that Nazi propaganda urged violence against
Jews. Yet when such violence happened, unprecedented
numbers of Germans complained and in their complaints
appealed to other values. It is conceivable that
some very convoluted process was going on here, but

applying "Occam's Razor" one should conclude that the other values overrode the ones the Nazis were tying to impose. And to say that such values were insufficient to prevent genocide is quite irrelevant because it shifts the basis of the issue while ignoring the new variables that such a shift requires. The evidence is also clear, for example, that the German people were overwhelmingly opposed to war in 1939,[3] yet they got war and there was little they could do to prevent it. Here the question was not about abstract values but was about their own lives. Who asks "How could Hitler get away with starting World War II in view of adverse public sentiment in Germany?" The answer is obvious to all who have studied the internal workings of the Nazi dictatorship. In short, Professor Burke has posed a question long since answered in the context of other issues.

He is similarly uninformed about the claims advanced by Nazi propagandists, from Hitler and Goebbels on. Admittedly these claims were exaggerated, wrongheaded, and vulgar, but they involved nothing less than the flat assertion that people could be made to believe anything that the propagandist wished them to believe. Unfortunately some historians, impressed by the vigor and sophistication with which Nazi propagandists tried to give substance to these claims, have concluded that the claims themselves must have been valid.[4] They were not. Propaganda, as has been shown in other instances, has very limited "mind bending" capabilities. Often its "success" is due to other factors: coercion, social pressure, terror, "obedience to authority," prior values being reinforced, group conformity, etc. Above all, the general evidence of its failure in Nazi Germany in crucial cases is abundant. I refer the reader back to my original examples.

Increasingly it seems to me that a chief function of Nazi antisemitic propaganda was not to redirect the public at large but to legitimize the extant intentions of the Nazi leadership. This is quite another causal factor for the Holocaust. In fact the element of self-justifying motivation through propaganda in a society technologically susceptible to centralized manipulation may well be the most pernicious element of the whole issue; the manipulators reinforce themselves.

One formulation I used, "that Hitler and his henchmen murdered the Jews of Germany and the rest of Europe against the will of the German people..." has been criticized by Professors Burke, Menze, and others. Upon reflection I agree that this phrase is susceptible to misinterpretation, though I thought my point was clear within its original context. But let me restate it in other terms. The German people publicly expressed their opposition to (and disapproval of) Nazi antisemitic violence on the occasion of <u>Kristallnacht</u>. They may have done so out of lamentable values, but still they objected. From this it follows that they did not sanction, desire, or promote violent action against the Jews, for a variety of reasons. Overall, they did not accept the totalistic causality chain that led Nazi leaders from "paranoid antisemitism"[5] to mass murder because somewhere along that causality chain they interposed idiosyncratic exceptions or culturally derived objections. Thus Hitler, when he decided to do unrestricted violence against the Jews, had to consider the unsupportive attitudes of the German people before risking the legitimacy of his "plebiscitary dictatorship." If he activated genocide through deception, circumlocution, obfuscation, etc., that was because he was afraid of the response of--and certainly not pressured by the wishes of--German public opinion. The "will of the German people," as recorded by reactions to <u>Kristallnacht</u>, was clearly not in favor of violence against the Jews. Again, it is possible that these opinions later changed, but I have seen no evidence of this. "Possible" should not be confused with "plausible." The burden of proof thus shifts.

Precisely for these reasons we need to confront the paradox of a people permitting what they are on record as opposing. In the course of analysing that problem we can perhaps also factor out the role, within a terroristic dictatorship, of public opinion, or also value hierarchies, in preventing future genocides. Here is where Professor Menze's critique shows the heuristic possibilities of revisionist interpretations.

His first question concerns the reliability of the data. Can the reports of the SPD underground be treated as reliable or were there political motivations, possibly even understandable "wish dreams," mixed in? I believe that the editor of the <u>Deutschland-Berichte</u> was not only aware of that problem but also determined to cope with it.[6] After all, the SPD was dependent on accurate reports in order to plan its anti-Nazi strategy. But a researcher can check this by comparing the raw reports with the edited conclusions (both available in the <u>Archiv der Sozialen Demokratie</u>, Bad Godesberg). Were the reports of Nazi surveillance agencies corroborative? The researcher can find them in the <u>Bundesarchiv</u>, Koblenz (<u>S.D.</u>, <u>Gestapo</u>,

<u>Propaganda Ministerium</u>, <u>Regierungs-Präsidenten</u>:
all filed monthly reports). As for the reports of
foreign journalists or diplomats, the sources are
obvious and, in most cases, published. But
ultimately it is the multiplicity of corroborative
evidence that validates: they all agree. In fact,
that is what raised the initial question.

Professor Menze accepts this interlocking
evidence and moves on to ask its significance. His
emphasis on Hitler's personal reaction strikes me as
consistent with the prevailing interpretations of
Hitler's behavior and, in view of the <u>Führer</u>'s
decisive position in Nazi Germany, terribly
important. And yet we know that Hitler was also a
responsive politician. He did modify policies in
response to external inhibitants, such as economic
limitations, though he was also ingenious in finding
ways to circumvent inhibiting factors in pursuit of
his insane goals.[7] At issue, then, is how he also
got around the problem of domestic non-approval of
his genocidal desires.

Professor Menze suggests that Hitler was attuned
to fundamental cultural facets of the Germanic
tradition plus certain psychological realities. The
former is speculative but the latter opens up many
research options. Traditional human defense
mechanisms in the fact of value conflicts have been
shown to include denial, displacement,
compartmentalization, identification with an
aggressor, and rationalization. These are
unconscious psychological responses; to them Menze
adds the conclusions from Milgram's disturbing
experiments on "Obedience to Authority." Can these
explain the German people's acquiescence in a
genocidal policy that had objected to in its origins?
Is the isolatable variable the degree of
consciousness, or perception? Or should we single
out a culturally determined factor, an acquired
association, such as the equation of external
orderliness with decent living, regularity =
controllability?

I do not know, but I do know that the analytical
framework has moved to a more sophisticated level,
thanks to the introduction of these considerations.
We have several new research topics to explore plus
some potential hypotheses within which to explore
them.

Professor Menze's citation of some isolated
underground reports from 1936, to the effect that
"Anti-Semitism, unquestionably, has taken root in
broad circles of the population," opens still other
research possibilities, though one should hasten to
add that there is an enormous difference between the

sort of low level prejudice noted and a general pressure for genocide. I would couple his citations with countless others than run through the Deutschland-Berichte as a recurrent theme, all concerning the progressive demoralization of the German people under the Nazi dictatorship. The single most frequently used descriptive term is "apathy" (Gleichgültigkeit), followed closely by "passivity" and "despair." A particular note of dismay enters the Social Democrats' reports when they noted the German workers' increasing drunkenness--after all those years in which the SPD had struggled, with growing success, against the proletariat's traditional retreat to the solace of alcohol.

Here comparative studies of populations forced to live under terroristic dictatorships should be instructive. Preliminary reports from Idi Amin's Uganda, though sketchy since serious and deep research has yet to be done, are particularly pertinent because the population had such radically different traditions from those of Germany. Yet according to a two-part report by the New York Times,[8] based on interviews, popular responses to Amin's mass murder were amazingly similar to the behavior of the German people. The reporter found that Ugandans "remained a-political and passive," though most were aware of "the horrors of the regime." They sought false refuge in a familiar myth: "If only the Presdient-for-Life knew..." The dictator used euphemisms in commanding murder ("Give him the V.I.P. treatment") while the people learned to talk in code about murder, too. The capriciousness of terror (a Kampala businessman's deepest impression: "There were no rules") caused Ugandans to withdraw into themselves: "The main problem and the main worry was that you knew something and you couldn't do anything about it, because your life was in jeopardy."). In sum: denial, rationalization, compartmentalization, and passivity were the consequences of living in a state of terror without predictable expectations. Déjà vu of Hitler's Reich.

What this suggests is that we need much more research on the general qualities of dictatorships like Nazi Germany's, on their internal dynamics, their effects upon their subjects, the ways they can be effectively influenced from within and without. The destruction (or at least questioning) of prior theories opens the way. And at least a focus on these realities will keep us from glib generalizations or simplistic moralisms.

But I return to my general impression, plus the apparent lessons of public reaction to <u>Kristallnacht</u>. Not much can be expected from popular responses once a terroristic dictatorship has established itself. The time for effective action is beforehand, in prevention.

NOTES

1. John Kenneth Galbraith: <u>The Affluent Society</u> (Boston: Houghton Mifflin, 1958), p. 9.

2. Another risk is inherent in all scholarship: the risk of being misquoted by those who wish to advance a tendentious and ideologically self-serving argument. In Holocaust studies this occurred when the very existence of this historical event was challenged by an American Professor of Engineering, Arthur Butz, in <u>The Hoax of the Twentieth Century</u>, (Torrance, Calif.: 1977?). This book, so contemptible that it never earned a single serious review, has now been followed by a pseudo-scholarly <u>Journal of Historical Review</u> (Vol. 1, No. 1, Spring 1980), published by a so-called "Institute for Historical Review" of Torrance, California, and claiming to contain the results of a "Revisionist Convention" held in Los Angeles. By my reading this is nothing more than neo-Nazi apologetics lurking behind historical revisionism. My professional opinion as a historian is that anyone who would believe Butz and his associates would also be likely to believe in the Easter Bunny. In any case, the distortion of serious research by political propagandists is something we will long have to endure and the only remedy is to expose its mendacity.

3. Virtually all the <u>Gestapo, S.D.</u>, underground reports concur, as do the foreign observers from newsmen to diplomats--see any memoir literature, <u>e.g.</u> Shirer's <u>Berlin Diary</u>. A synthesis is available in Marlis G. Steinert: <u>Hitlers Krieg und die Deutschen: Stimmung und Haltung der deutschen Bevölkerung im Zweiten Weltkrieg</u> (Düsseldorf, 1970); translated in abridged form as <u>Hitler's War and the Germans</u>.

4. Jay W. Baird: <u>The Mythical World of Nazi War Propaganda: 1939-1945</u> (Minneapolis: University of Minnesota Press, 1974). Also Robert Edwin Herzstein: <u>The War That Hitler Won: The Most Infamous Propaganda Campaign in History</u> (New York: Putnam, 1978).

5. Peter H. Merkl, <u>Political Violence Under the Swastika: 581 Early Nazis</u> (Princeton: Princeton University Press, 1975), pp. 498-501. The phrase is Sarah Gordon's (see note 3 in my main essay), who reworked Merkl's data.

6. See note 5 in my essay.

7. See Schleunes (note 2 in my main essay) but, in another context, Timothy W. Mason: <u>Sozialpolitik im Dritten Reich: Arbeiterklasse und Volksgemeinschaft</u> (Opladen: Westdeutscher Verlag, 1977), pp. 299ff.

8. John Darnton, "Idi Amin: A Savior Who Became the Creator of 8 Years of Horror," <u>New York Times</u>, April 30, 1979 and May 1, 1979.

4
Hannah Arendt in Jerusalem: The Controversy Revisited

Walter Laqueur

It is difficult to think of a book in living memory that stirred up as much controversy as Hannah Arendt's Eichmann in Jerusalem. Miss Arendt still has her angry detractors and fanatical supporters, but on the whole, I believe, it is easier now to understand what made the late Hannah Arendt write this book and why it provoked so much criticism. And it is also possible to comment on the impact of this controversy on the subsequent historiography of the Holocaust.

Hannah Arendt, thirty five years of age at the time, arrived in the United States in 1941, having escaped from France. Her main intellectual interests had been philosophy and modern literature. She had written a doctoral dissertation on the concept of love in the work of St. Augustine. Her first articles, published in Germany, were on Rilke's Duino Elegies and on Kierkegaaard. She belonged to a generation and a milieu that was basically unpolitical but which had developed a passionate interest in politics, in the widest sense, following Hitler's rise to power and the outbreak of World War II. Soon after her arrival in the United State she began to publish articles, first in the German language weekly Der Aufbau, later also in other periodicals. Her early journalistic work in the United States has been almost entirely neglected (or forgotten), yet it provides essential clues to the genesis of the book that created such a furor two decades later.[1] What emerged from these articles was that Hannah Arendt always had doubts about Zionism and that gradually she came to believe that Herzl had been a crackpot, that Zionism was a chauvinistic, fanatical, and hysterical phenomenon, and that it had never been a popular movement. It should be noted in passing however that she remained a Zionist until after 1943. Her open break came with the publication of an article in the Menorah Journal in Autumn

1945, "Zionism Reconsidered" in which she accused Zionism of cutting off Jewish history from European history and the rest of mankind, in which she affirmed that nationalism was dead in Europe and that the Soviet Union had shown an "entirely new and successful approach to nationality conflicts." This article also condemned Zionism for having been in constant contact with the Hitler government about the transfer business.

In 1942 Miss Arendt insisted on the establishment of a Jewish army to fight Nazism "for the glory and the honour of the Jewish people," and this was the theme of her very first article in the United States and of many that were to follow. Her demand was based on something like a Neo-Bundist ideology. An army is usually the function of a state, except perhaps in the case of Prussia, where according to an old saying, the state was a mere appendage of the army. But Hannah Arendt did not want a state for the Jews, and her demand for an army in these conditions was curious, to say the least. She was at this time very much preoccupied with the fate of the Jews in Europe and, above all, with Jewish resistance. Thus a report published in <u>Aufbau</u> about the <u>Musterghetto</u> Theresienstadt provided an occasion to develop a theory to explain Nazi policy towards the Jews: Jews are tolerated, and sometimes even protected, where their presence will create antisemitism among the local population; they will be deported from regions which are not antisemitic. Jews are deported from areas where their very presence could lead to resistance. ("If Mrs. Mueller in Germany sees that her neighbor, Mrs. Schmidt, behaves decently to Mrs. Cohn, she knows that she must not be afraid of Mrs. Schmidt--she may even talk openly to Mrs. Schmidt." [2] An ingenious theory no doubt, but quite wrong. On another occasion writing on the "part of the Jewish partisans in the European uprising" Hannah Arendt noted that the European Jews were not doomed: The Jews of Europe no longer faced a separate fate if they refused to accept it. [3] Or to put it into simpler language: the Jews did not have to die if they did not want to die. A small minority of Jewish millionaires and scoundrels had acted as traitors, but a very substantial part of the people had chosen the road of armed struggle: she wrote about a hundred thousand Jewish partisans in Poland, ten thousand in France... fighting the Nazis in the streets, fields and forests.

Even before the war ended Hannah Arendt gave her mind to the question of guilt, noting that the numbers of those responsible and guilty among the

Germans were relatively small; hence the conclusion that there was no political method of dealing with German mass crimes: "where all are guilty, nobody in the last analysis can be judged." Even in a murder camp, Miss Arendt noted, everyone, whether directly active or not, was forced to take part in one way or another in the workings of the machine: "that is the horrible thing."[4] This in brief outline was the origin of the concept of the 'banality of evil.' (I recently came across the phrase in Josef Conrad's preface to Under Western Eyes, written well before World War I, but it may have been used before.) Arendt was fearful of the great opportunities that would exist in Europe after the war for the reemergence of an international fascist organization. The arch evil of our time had been defeated but not completely eradicated, except in the areas under immediate Russian influence, where the "forces of yesterday" had been destroyed once and forever.[5]

I have concentrated on the issues that have a direct bearing on the controversy of the early sixties. A reading of Hannah Arendt's political journalism shows that she was far more often wrong than right both in her analysis and predictions. There was always an inclination on her part to exaggerate as well as to generalize (and theorize) on the basis of a slender factual basis. She had a great deal of intelligence but little common sense and apparently no political instinct; she was a philosophical not a political animal. The case of Theresienstadt is an extreme case in point: the obvious explanation provided in Aufbau, that of a Musterghetto, was quite right, which is more than can be said about the theories about 'selective deportation.' Again, the fears of a great revival of fascism after the war are psychologically understandable, but they were not at all borne out by subsequent events. But the fact that she had so often been wrong did not shake Miss Arendt's confidence in hew own judgment. In one of her very last essays Miss Arendt wrote that "Anti-Communism" was "at the root of all theories in Washington in sheer ignorance of all pertinent facts."[6] This from the woman who had been one of the most influential architects of the totalitarianism concept, who had explained in Burden of our Time that Nazi Germany and Soviet Russia were "two essentially identical systems."[7] True, Miss Arendt later retracted this: after the Hungarian revolt in 1956 (which profoundly influenced her), she wrote that the closed system of the Soviet Union was no longer totalitarian in the strict sense of the term; one of the reasons given was the food supplies sent to the Hungarians, another

the flowering of the arts in the Soviet Union.
Arendt had exaggerated in 1951, and again after 1956,
without, however, lasting damage to either her
self-confidence or her reputation.

There was a general tendency during the war and
indeed for quite a few years after to overrate the
importance (and the numerical strength) of Jewish
resistance in Europe. The same is true,
incidentally, with regard to wartime resistance in
general, excepting only Yugoslavia. I have dealt
with this topic in a recent study; all that need be
said in this context is that resistance was
physically possible only in a few countries to begin
with. The reports about tens and hundreds of
maquis, Jewish or non-Jewish, were of course sheer
fantasy. Thus, seen in retrospect, European Jews did
not live up to Miss Arendt's expectations as fighters
for the glory and honor of their people; as a result
they were punished. If they had fought they (or at
least many of them) would have survived; since most
of them did not fight, five or six million were
killed. Miss Arendt found mitigating circumstances
for non-Jews. Everyone in a murder camp was forced
to take part in the working of the machine. She did
not make such allowances for her fellow Jews.

Miss Arendt attended the Eichmann trial as a
journalist, and her account was published in five
installments in the New Yorker in late spring of
1963. It became a succès de scandal from the
first moment. Some critics were shocked by the
periodical chosen by Miss Arendt: witty,
entertaining, frivolous, intellectually pretentious,
and quite unserious. An investigation into mass
murder in between Mr. Arno's cartoons, the
advertisements for Cadillacs and Oldsmobiles, gin,
holidays in Bermuda, a little bit of holocaust, a
little bit of Tiffany and Saks Fifth Avenue; it was
quite a remarkable mixture. Others complained about
her style; the snide remarks, the flippancy and
superciliousness, and their concomitant, the
heartlessness. Yet others pointed to the unfortunate
tendency on the part of the author throughout her
book to use terms that were emotionally highly
charged and to apply a double yardstick. Thus, when
Gideon Hausner, the chief prosecutor, asked some of
the survivors of the death camps why they had not
offered armed resistance, Miss Arendt expressed
indignation about cruel and foolish questions of this
kind. But her own critique of the Jewish leadership
rests precisely on the same basis: those who did not
fight were guilty. [8] Again, any form of contract
between Jewish leaders and the Nazis even when the
aim was to make the emigration of Jews possible, or

to save lives, was 'collaboration' as far as Miss Arendt was concerned. But the term collaboration in the context of World War II has a certain connotation of which the author was no doubt quite aware. If she believed that Jews should not have talked to the Nazis under any circumstances, she should have said so. But she did not and for this reason the indiscriminate use of the term was irresponsible.

A German critic was taken aback by the fact that Miss Arendt had singled out two Germans who had resisted; one was the rightwing writer Reck-Malleczewen, the other the philosopher Karl Jaspers. [9] Reck-Malleczewen had died in a concentration camp, but there is no known evidence whatsoever that Professor Jaspers ever uttered a word of criticism between 1933 and 1945. Why then was he singled out? Becaue he was Miss Arendt's teacher to whom she remained devoted to the end of his life; he died in 1969. This little episode is revealing: while in no way central to Hannah Arendt's arguments, it was typical of her approach to history. But there is yet another aspect which, to the best of my knowledge, has not so far been noted, the curious resemblance between master and disciple: both were philosophers, both felt from time to time obliged to comment on politics, frequently in a high pitch, bordering on hysteria, from which their philosophical writings were quite free. Thus Jaspers, during the height of the cold war was one of the people advocating West Germany's nuclear rearmament. In the 1960s, on the other hand, he published a treatise in which he demonstrated that West Germany was well on the way towards abolishing parliamentary democracy and, to all intents and purpose, becoming fascist again. The book was published in the United States with a preface by Hannah Arendt in which she stated that "politically (this is) the most important book to appear after the second world war."[10] Had Arendt really believed this, she would certainly have published at least an article in the same vein. She did not, which shows that she had reservations. But filial piety nevertheless prevailed over intellectual integrity.

Among Hannah Arendt's critics, apart from those already noted, Gershom Sholem and Manes Sperber ought to be mentioned, as well as Norman Podhoretz's essay, the Bettelheim review in the <u>New Republic</u>, and the ensuing polemic with Judge Musmanno.[11] The most detailed and ambitious, but in many respects, least effective reply to Hannah Arendt was the late Jacob Robinson's <u>And the Crooked Shall be Made Straight</u>, a book of more than four hundred pages published by Macmillan in 1965. The late Dr. Robinson probably knew all there was to know about the factual background and with his training as a lawyer he was also an expert on the legal implications of war crime trials. His technique in the book was that of the lawyer who wishes to discredit a hostile witness by showing that he is not really master of the subject. And so he relentlessly subjected Arendt's every word to critical examination, pointing out that the correct spelling of a certain SS Obergruppenführer should be Hanns, not Hans as given by Miss Arendt, as if mistakes of this kind necessarily disqualified her from commenting on SS policy. Dr. Robinson's book was a case of overkill. He demonstrated that Miss Arendt had indeed committed many mistakes; partly owing to a cavalier attitude to facts, partly perhaps out of genuine ignorance. She knew, after all, neither Hebrew nor Yiddish, neither Polish nor Russian, and most of the relevant literature was at the time in these languages. She had to rely basically on Professor Hilberg's book (a book on the Nazis, not on the Jews) and on what she learned during the Eichmann trial. But Robinson's book, hastily written, also contained factual mistakes, it failed to tackle important issues, and it was inconsistent--claiming at one and the same time that much further study was needed on collaboration and that there had been no collaboration and treason at all among the Jews. Above all, Dr. Robinson, in the light of his background, training, and interests, was quite obviously the wrong person to 'refute' Hannah Arendt. Plodding, immersed in questions of detail, he could not possibly follow her to the rarified heights of abstractions where the moral philosopher could engage in a virtuoso performance, but where poor Dr. Robinson would be quite lost.

I should perhaps mention in passing my own involuntary involvement in the affair. I had reviewed Dr. Robinson's book at the time and had noted its shortcomings.[12] This produced an irate reply from Miss Arendt, far longer than the original review. It dealt largely with Dr. Robinson's book rather than my review, which mainly served as a peg for her rejoinder. My review had been more moderate than most and there has been no anger in it. But Miss Arendt, at the time already something of a cult figure among the New York intelligentsia, was far from satisfied. She did not mind being attacked, but she evidently disliked not being taken very seriously as a student of contemporary Jewish history. And so she imputed to the reviewer sinister motives: Mr. Laqueur, she implied, was dependent on Dr. Robinson, a vassal jumping to the aid of his seigneur. My relations with the late Dr. Robinson were neither close, nor, for a variety of reasons, friendly. Mrs. Arendt, who did not know me at all, could not possibly know about my relations, if any, with Dr. Robinson and yet she was quite ready to assume the worst, to insinuate, and to incriminate. Her reaction greatly intrigued me, even though I knew of course that statements made in the heat of a polemic should not be taken too seriously nor remembered for too long. Miss Arendt was certainly at the time in a state of near panic, as her writings show, firmly convinced that the Elders of Zion had conspired to 'get her.'

Hannah Arendt's main arguments are widely known and can be summarized therefore in briefest outline. Eichmann was guilty and deserved to be executed but he was an idealist in a perverted way, he had no criminal intent, he was basically a normal human being acting under the pressure of a totalitarian regime for which he was not personally responsible. Hence the conclusion that justice was not done in Jerusalem. It was the wrong court condemning him for the wrong reasons: he should have been hanged as <u>hostis generis humani</u> rather than as <u>hostis Judaeorum</u>. Miss Arendt attributed to this distinction enormous importance; I failed to see the crucial significance of this issue at the time and I have not become any wiser in the years between. Far more important are the charges she made against the Jewish leadership and its responsibility for the catastrophe. Without their active collaboration ("mere compliance would not have been enough") the destruction of so many millions of Jews would not have been possible; "there would have been either complete chaos or an impossible severe drain on German manpower."[13] The ghetto police, Miss Arendt reports, was an instrument in the hands of the murderers, the actual work of killing in the extermination centers was usually in the hands of Jewish commandos, who also dug the graves, extinguished the traces of mass murder, and had built the gas chambers in the first place. Thus Jewish cooperation put an end to the collapse among the victims. The leadership, almost without exception, cooperated in one way or another, for one reason or another, with the Nazis. If the Jewish people had been unorganized and leaderless, there would have been chaos and plenty of misery but the total number of victims would hardly have been between four and a half and six million people. Hence the conclusion that to a Jew this role of the Jewish leaders in the destruction of their own people is undoubtedly the darkest chapter of the whole dark story.

Some of these allegations are true, some are wrong, most are half true. There is no reason to assume that if the Jewish people had been leaderless, the Nazis would have found the killing more difficult or even impossible. It has frequently been pointed out that the extermination proceded quite smoothly even where there were no Jewish Councils, or where the Jewish Councils were not required to collaborate with the Nazis in the preparation for the final solution. Nor is it true that the division between murderers and victims was obliterated. But even if resistance would not have meant survival, this still leaves the painful issue of "Jewish appeasement." Arendt's condemnation of appeasement is basically correct as rule of political behavior when dealing with enemies of this kind. It is inexplicable how Dr. Robinson could possibly write in 1965 that "there is no evidence that the motivation in accepting and maintaining membership in the <u>Judenräte</u> was not generally honorable."[14] There was a great deal of such evidence. But there was no conspiracy of silence, no deliberate attempt to whitewash villains and make heroes out of doubtful characters, as Miss Arendt seems to have believed, seeing herself no doubt as a champion of truth which had been too long suppressed.

There was a certain reluctance to deal systematicaly with the most tragic subject of all, for the very same reason that there has been reluctance in every European country (including the neutral ones) to come to terms with the many manifestations of 'collaboration' in the Nazi era. The Jewish case was different, to be sure, because Frenchmen or Dutchmen, for instance, had freedom of choice: they did not <u>have</u> to collaborate. A recent French writer notes, "le collaborationisme n'était pas une fatalité. Un Louis Marin ou un Louis Vallon adhéraient en 1939 aux memes partis qu'un Philipple Henriot out un Marcel Déat."[15] The Jews did not have to collborate either, but the alternative was considerably more unpleasant.

There had been books and articles, countless autobiographies and memoirs on the Jewish Councils in Poland (by Philip Friedman and others), in Holland (by Abel Herzberg and others), in Theresienstadt (by H.G. Adler) and elsewhere. Professor Hilberg's book, which had many harsh things to say about the Jewish reaction, had already appeared, and it was Hannah Arendt's main source. The facts were known but they had not fully registered, even though, as in the Kastner trial, the basic issues had been discussed. If many of the facts referred to in Hannah Arendt's book had been known for a long time, what made so many people so angry about <u>Eichmann in Jerusalem</u>, and why did the book become a <u>cause celèbre</u>? Her series of articles, and the book that subsequently emerged, were of course far more widely read than the scholarly articles or mongraphs dealing with the same subject. The scholars, among whom there were and are quite a few no less extreme in the final analysis than Hannah Arendt in their condemnation of collaboration, were more cautious in stating their conclusions, not because they were afraid but because they were more aware of the complexity of the situation, the terrible pressures under which the Jewish Councils had been acting. Arendt's book, on the other hand, was impressionistic, subjective, and there was her usual tendency towards exaggeration and to be original at almost any price. She attacked without discrimination the entire Jewish leadership in Europe and made some exceedingly silly remarks which she probably later regretted (the reference to Leo Baeck as the "Jewish Führer" without quotation remarks). She attacked Zionism in view of its collaboration with the Nazis (meaning the organization of illegal immigration) and also because of certain ideological similarities, real or imaginary. Thus she antagonized all Zionists and pro-Zionists. But this again does not explain the vehement reactions triggered off by her book. The most telling criticism came from non-Zionists (such as Eva Reichmann) or anti-Zionists, or Zionists such as Ernst Simon, Buber, and Scholem who had belonged to the Magnes group (Ichud) that stood for Arab-Jewish collaboration and which had been actively supported by Hannah Arendt. Her attitude towards Zionism was by no means as consistent as commonly believed: while she supported Ichud, she also had sympathies for Mr. Begin's Irgun Zuai Leumi, which (in her words) attracted the most decent and idealist elements. This apparent paradox is not difficult to explain: Arendt hated 'conciliators' and 'appeasers' such as Weizmann, but she always had a weakness for those who fought and resisted. She belonged to those intellectuals about whom it has been said that <u>ils n'aiment que les trains qui partent</u>, the direction of the departure being a secondary consideration.

Hannah Arendt was bitterly attacked precisely because she was held in such high esteem by many of her contemporaries, <u>corruptio optimi pessima</u>. This, in a way, was quite unfair, for she had, after all, not made her name as a contemporary historian. She had moved very far from her national Jewish enthusiasm of 1942-43, but no one expected that she would want deliberately and unnecessarily to cause offence and pain. Hannah Arendt's attitude towards

116

her people (her personal 'Jewish problem') was complex, and there is little doubt that this had a bearing on the writing of this book. Sooner or later someone more familiar with this subject than the present writer will deal with this aspect of the affair.

Hannah Arendt was mainly attacked not for what she said, but for how she said it. She was a highly intelligent person and at the same time exceedingly insensitive. She would not, or could not, discriminate, see the nuances, and this in a context in which nuances were all-important. She certainly had the intellectual equipment to deal with the subject, but not the temperament. She was one of the cleverest writers of her generation, but the Holocaust is a subject in which cleverness can be a positive disadvantage. Her memory was selective: when she wrote about Eichmann, she had forgotten almost all she had written about the human condition in a totalitarian state. The Holocaust is a subject that has to be confronted in a spirit of humility; whatever Miss Arendt's many virtues, humility was not among them. "Judge not that ye not be judged" says the New Testament. But Hannah Arendt loved to judge, and was at her most effective in the role of magister humanitatis, invoking moral pathos. And thus she rushed in where wiser men and women feared to tread, writing about extreme situations which she in her life had never experienced, a writer by temperament always inclined to overstatement, most at ease when dealing with abstractions, at her weakest when analysing concrete situations and real people. The constellation was unfortunate, and the result predictable.

The Eichmann controversy did not do any lasting harm to Hannah Arendt's reputation. On the contrary, at the time of her death she was widely thought to be one of the most original and influential thinkers of our time. She was an erudite and brilliant woman, she wrote well, her ideas appealed to left and right alike, an almost unique case at the time. Even her confusion seemed attractive in the New York of the 1960s. The fact that her political comments and her historical obiter dicta were often wrong was quite immaterial. One can easily think of professional politicians being wrong most of the time; they seem not to be worse off as a result--in politics it is far more damaging to be right at the wrong time. Nor should it be forgotten that she had made her name as a political philosopher, not as a political journalist. True, Arendt's political philosophy has also baffled admirers and critics alike. One of them, a highly sympathetic commentator, admitted that

most of what she had written about totalitarianism
had been wrong, but still her book was a
"considerable work of art, vivid and enthralling,
intensely reflective. Even when it fails as history
it succeeds as reflection." It is certainly true
that when The Origins of Totalitarianism appeared
it was more enthusiastically welcomed by literary
figures than by students of history and politics.
The romantic streak in Hannah Arendt has been noted
by many. Perhaps Eichmann in Jerusalem too should
be treated as a work of art rather than historical
analysis? If so, it may well remain the only work of
art inspired by that trial. There still is a last
paradox, the relationship between the political
philosopher and the political journalist. Is a
political philosopher to be relied upon who can be
trusted only on the level of abstraction? I have
been assured that there is only a tenuous link
between these two activities, just as a great art
historian is not necessarily the best expert to
establish the provenance or genuineness of a picture.

It has been argued (by Leni Yahil among others)
that it was the merit of Hannah Arendt's book to
provide fresh impetus to the study of the Judenrat
phenomenon, and, speaking more generally, of the
issue of 'collaboration.' This is, I believe,
correct only in part, for even before Eichmann in
Jerusalem appeared there had been a great deal of
comment on the subject: Solomon Bloom had written a
memorable essay on Rumkovski and the Lodz Ghetto as
far back as 1949, Friedmann had written on Gens (of
the Vilna Ghetto) and Merin, Nahman Blumenthal on
Bialistok, and there were many more studies both for
the general public and of a more specialized
character. Two of the most important books on the
Jewish Councils appeared in 1965 and 1972
respectively; I refer to Presser's Ondergang and to
I. Trunk's Judenrat. But both had been many years
in the making: Presser owed nothing to the Arendt
controversy, and Trunk, I suppose, very little.
During the last fifteen years there have been more
specialized studies on the Jewish Councils in Holland
(Michman), in Hungary (Braham), in Theresienstadt (L.
Rothkirchen) and above all in Poland. Following the
publication of the Czerniakov diaries, there has been
much illuminating comment on the Judenrat
phenomenon. Some writers have recently tried to draw
an interim balance, comparing the findings of various
studies. Most of this work, I suppose, would have
been done in any case and thus the impact of the
'controversy' consists mainly in having compelled her
contemporaries to rethink the whole issue of Jewish
collaboration and resistance during World War II.

Whether anyone basically changed his views as a result, I doubt. There are some such as Dvorzhetzki and Eisenbach who see the Judenrat virtually without exception in a negative light. Nathan Blumenthal in his investigation of the Lublin Judenrat reaches the conclusion that not all were criminals and traitors, but that even those who were not objectively served as Nazi tools. Others, such as Z.A. Braun, Weiss, and Kaplinski, maintain that a wholesale condemnation of the Judenrat distorts history. They argue that there were enormous differences between conditions in one ghetto and in another, that in a few the Judenrat closely collaborated with the resistance, that in some (perhaps 20 percent according to Trunk) the German orders were carried out with excessive zeal and no attempt was made to circumvent and sabotage them, and that in most places the general strategy was to gain time. Yehuda Bauer has noted that if (I quote from memory) the Soviet army had reached Lodz a few months earlier Rumkovski, the 'King' of the local ghetto, would have entered the annals of Jewish history a hero, not a traitor. It is also true that one has to differentiate between the period before the deportations started, when the Judenrat engaged in the administration of the ghetto and the time thereafter when the Jewish leadership actively participated in the selection of the victims to be sent to the extermination camps.

Thus fifteen years after the controversy we are no nearer to a consensus than before and it is quite likely that there never will be agreement, partly because, as has been noted repeatedly, conditions varied so much from place to place, partly also because there are genuine differences of opinion with regard to what could have been expected from Jewish communities facing the Nazi terror machine. But if in many cases mitigating circumstances can be found, if some leaders in fact behaved heroically, the Judenrat phenomenon, as a whole, has acquired a negative connotation, and rightly so. From the moment at the very latest that the Jewish Councils were used by the Nazis to help in the 'final solution,' their action became indefensible. True, it can always be argued that they acted to prevent worse persecution, but this argument has been heard too often. Why was there so little resistance? The question deeply bothered Hannah Arendt and most contemporaries. The answer is in many ways obvious; given the isolation of the Jews, the demographic structure of the Jewish communities, the lack of psychological and organizational preparation, the hostility of the non-Jewish population in Eastern

Europe, the lack of arms, the unsuitability of the surrounding terrain, there could not have been much resistance, certainly not successful resistance. But there could have been more resistance than there was, and why did Jews let themselves be slaughtered like sheep? Hannah Arendt was doubly shocked, partly because during the war she had imagined that there had been a great deal of resistance, only to find out later that this had not been the case. But she was also by temperament one of the intellectuals who had great admiration for men or women of action (preferably intellectuals who were also doers, such as Rosa Luxemburg, even if the results were disastrous) and the meekness of the Jews seemed intolerable in retrospect. She look for a scapegoat and found it in the Jewish leadership.

Sixty years before Hannah Arendt published her book the greatest living Hebrew poet, after the Kishinev program, wrote his <u>Be'ir Ha'hariga</u> (In the City of Slaughter): "Great is the sorrow and great is the shame, and which of the two is greater, answer thou, O son of man... The grandsons of the Maccabeans--they ran like mice, they hid themselves like bedbugs and died the death of dogs wherever found." Bialik's indictment was far stronger than Hannah Arendt's but there were no irate reviews, no protests, no contradictions. His poem, unlike Hannah Arendt's book, influenced a whole generation. Was it because Arendt's book, pretending to be an objective historical account, contained much that was unfair or untrue? I do not think that this was the main reason, for her book also contained much that was true. His contemporaries felt that Bialik's attack was born out of agony. Hannah Arendt's reproaches were those of an outsider, lacking identification: they were almost inhumanly cold and they were, in part at least, rooted in an aesthetic approach. She would have hailed a great Jewish uprising, I suspect, for the same reason that Yeats welcomed the Easter Rising in 1916, for its "terrible beauty." But there could be no beauty and no glory in the Holocaust.

NOTES

1. The only exception known to me is a doctoral dissertation, R. Meyerson, Hannah Arendt, Romantic in a Totalitarian Age, 1928-63. Ann Arbor, 1972. There is a Hebrew dissertation by Yerahmiel Cohen (Jerusalem April 1973) on H. Arendt which does not however deal with her early writings.

2. "Musterghetto Theresienstadt," Aufbau,35, 1943; "Die wahren Gründe für Theresienstadt," 36, 1943.

3. "Die Gesetzmässigkeiten des jüdischen Sonderschicksals verloren immer ihre Gültigkeit wenn Juden sich weigerten, es als Schicksal zu akzeptieren," "Die jüdischen Partisanen im europäischen Aufstand," Aufbau, 36, 1944.

4. H. Arendt, "Organized Guilt and Universal Responsibility," Jewish Frontier, January 1945.

5. "The Seeds of a Fascist International," Jewish Frontier, June, 1945.

6. Crises of the Republic, New York: Harcourt Brace Jovanovich, 1972), p. 39.

7. (London: Secker and Warburg, 1951), p. 429.

8. H. Trevor Roper, New York Times, October 13, 1963; E. Simon: Nach dem Eichmann Prozess (Tel Aviv, 1963).

9. Golo Mann, Die Neue Rundschau, 4, 1963, and Die Zeit, January 24, 1964.

10. K. Jaspers: The Future of Germany (Chicago: University of Chicago Press, 1967).

11. Neue Zürcher Zeitung, October 19, 1963; Der Monat, May 1964; New Republic, June 15 and 29, 1963; Commentary, September, 1963.

12. New York Review of Books, November 11, 1965.

13. Eichmann in Jerusalem (New York: Viking Press, 1964), pp. 115, 117.

14. Robinson, p. 169.

15. Pascal Ory: Les collaborateurs, Paris 1976, p. 268.

16. Margaret Canovan: The Political Thought of Hannah Arendt (New York: Harcourt Brace Jovanovich, 1974), p. 47.

17. For instance, A. Weiss, articles in Gilead, Jerusalem 1976 and in Moreshet, November 1969 and November 1972.

18. For instance, A.A. Braun, Hahanhaga-darkeha ve'akhariuta, Jerusalem.

Comment: Insight Amidst Terror
William Sheridan Allen

To remove a side issue first, Hannah Arendt's _Eichmann in Jerusalem_ was certainly not viewed as insensitive by most American intellectuals because it first appeared in _The New Yorker_ (February and March, 1963) and because that journal is "frivolous. . .and quite unserious." Admittedly _The New Yorker_ is a remarkable mixture--its equally remarkable influence may stem from that--but it is also a forum for significant fiction and poetry, including translation, and for quite serious thinkers such as the late Edmund Wilson, George Steiner, Barry Commoner, etc. Indeed, it was about the time that _Eichmann in Jerusalem_ appeared there that the magazine's last bastion of determined superciliousness (the "Talk of the Town" section) began to print extremely thoughtful analysis of contemporary affairs rather than its earlier bemused flippancies. No one will forget the seriousness, even anguish, with which it confronted the Vietnam War. _The New Yorker_ was an entirely appropriate forum to reach a broad stratum of Americans concerned with significant questions--perhaps the best we had available.

This secondary issue aside, one must agree with Walter Laqueur that Arendt ought to be refuted (though not attacked) both for "what she said" and "how she said it" in _Eichmann in Jerusalem_. However, I would add that she can also be learned from, at key points. She was an erratic genius "far more often wrong than right in her analysis and predictions," but every now and then there would burst through her factual errors, wild generalizations, half-truths, misinterpretations, and general muddleheadedness, an insight of immense and often original brilliance.

Perhaps that was just the law of averages at work, but the bits of genius are what earned her some of the excessive reverence accorded her during her life. They are also ideas to be cherished and reaffirmed.

Laqueur is right in accusing Hannah Arendt of insensitivity, though inevitably his reasons as to why she was so have to be a bit speculative. And certainly he has marshalled enough evidence to show that one cannot rely on her judgment, which was at best idiosyncratic and, far more often than that, plain fuzzy. Both points are damning enough to suggest the entire _corpus_ of her work should be approached with a kilogram rather than a grain of salt. But some of his own critique is excessive.

For example, to summarize her attitude toward
Eichmann in Jerusalem by saying that she thought
its subject was "basically a normal human being" is
to distort the far subtler point she was making. The
court's medical examiners found him "normal" in the
sense that he was fit to stand trial. She noted that
his responses during the trial and before were petty,
cliché-ridden, and vapid. His concerns were more
often careerist than satanic. He had a "swiss cheese
superego." But precisely for these reasons she found
him a moral monstrosity. In practically the last
words of her book she would have had the judges say
to him: "no member of the human race can be expected
to want to share the earth with you." [1]
    Certainly she was not alone in her perception of
Eichmann as a rather commonplace figure. The head of
the Israeli intelligence team that captured Eichmann
in Argentina recorded these initial impressions:

> My first thought was, Well now, doesn't he look
> just like any other man!. . .I kept saying to
> myself, If I met him in the street I would see
> no difference between him and the thousands of
> other men passing by. And I kept asking myself,
> What makes such a creature, created in the
> likeness of man, into a monster? Is there no
> outward sign that distinguishes him from normal
> men? Or is that difference only in the corrupt
> soul? [2]

    That last question Hannah Arendt answered in the
affirmative, along the lines of what Reinhold Niebuhr
once said: "Not much evil is done by evil men. Most
of the evil is done by good people who do not know
they are not good." [3] This is an extremely important
point in multiple respects and one that she (rather
than Niebuhr, Conrad, or even Plato, who first
developed the idea) drilled into our consciousness by
her lengthy analysis of Eichmann's personality and by
subtitling her book "A Report on the Banality of
Evil." What is most valuable about this approach is
that it de-Luciferizes Hitler and the Nazis and thus
denies them even the awe sometimes accorded to
supposed giants of evil; in the end they were not
even that, but were dirty little murderers. In myth
the Devil breathes forth fire and brimstone; the
Hitler of reality had, as a major personal problem, a
tendency to fart under embarrassing circumstances.
    A second major contribution of Hannah Arendt's
book was her conclusion that evil corrupts almost
everyone it touches so that Hitler debauched the
morals of even his opponents; the Nazis made evil
banal in Europe. Again, her observation was hardly

original. Albert Camus raised much the same point in his "Letters to a German Friend," published in the French underground newspaper Combat during World War II.[4] But Arendt drove the point home with respect to Jewish complicity--even in this clear-cut case an attempt to combat evil may cause one to share in it.

Of course with respect to the particulars she got it all wrong. Jews did fight; they did flee or resist; they did not collaborate in the sense of a Laval or Quisling or Mussart. No Jew desired the success of Hitler's "New Order" though some did practice denial, did respond incorrectly, did facilitate the Holocaust through misconceived and inappropriate actions. Here again I would agree with Laqueur: she had no comprehension of, let alone sympathy for, the complexity of the situations facing the Judenräte and she distorted the issues by her reductionism and her censoriousness. Above all, she missed the essential point: that in the particular confrontation between Europe's Jews and the SS, there was no tactic that worked, including armed resistance (yet in a slightly different situation, Rumania, "traditional" strategies saved the lives of almost half the Jews under the control of that murderously antisemitic regime). To accomplish this, Rumania's Jews had to make some evil choices too, which reaffirms that evil begets evil, a point Americans are certainly in need of studying, and one that Arendt did try to get them to relearn on the eve of the Vietnam War.

Thirdly, I think Hannah Arendt was making a valuable point, the one that Laqueur seems to dismiss as irrelevant, when she distinguished between Hitler's "Final Solution" as a crime against humanity that was perpetrated upon the Jews (hostis generis humani), rather than simply a crime against the Jewish people (hostis Judaeorum). The latter is too easily subsumed under the heading "2,000 years of antisemitism" where its uniqueness can be lost. The former elevates the Holocaust into a universal moral problem, which is how it ought to be treated, not least out of respect for the victims.

I would also add one interpretive point to Walter Laqueur's analysis of why Hannah Arendt kept coming up with so many wrong-headed interpretations. She was an intellectual elitist with profoundly conservative attitudes. No one without such traits could have echoed Ortega y Gasset on the "masses" as faithfully as she did in Origins of Totalitarianism. That is also why she falsely elevated Reck-Malleczewen and Jaspers into the Resistance and never said anything about the hundreds of thousands of German socialists and communists who were thrown into Hitler's concentration camps because they really resisted the Third Reich rather than simply thinking heretical ideas and writing them into their secret diaries in elegant prose. In Arendt's value-hierarchy, conservative intellectuals were the only people who counted.

Perhaps this is a reason Hannah Arendt was lionized by one segment of American literati. But, pace Walter Laqueur, she was no cult figure to academic specialists. I know of no one working professionally on the rise, structure, and implications of Nazi Germany who took her Origins of Totalitarianism seriously. Instead she was (and still is) viewed as a popularizer who occasionally transcended that category. Because, in amongst all the rubbish, there were still those strangely disconcerting, often confused, amazingly brilliant flashes of insight.

NOTES

1. Hannah Arendt: Eichmann in Jerusalem: A Report on the Banality of Evil (New York: Viking, Rev. and Enl. Ed., 1964), p. 279.
2. Isser Harel: The House on Garibaldi Street (New York: Bantam Books, 1976), p. 218.
3. Quoted by Dr. Richard Hunt, "Entering the Future Looking Backwards," The Hastings Center Report, June 1978, p. 6.
4. Reprinted in an English translation in Albert Camus: Resistance, Rebellion, and Death (New York: Knopf, 1958).

Comment: The Importance of Arendt
David Schoenbaum

I have spent most of my professional life agreeing with Walter Laqueur, who has probably not even been aware of it, and I am not about to stop now.

I would nonetheless like to make a few supplementary points, or allow myself a mini-cadenza on several of his points. What I want to say falls into two general propositions.

The first is that while there were, and are, many reasons to object to Eichmann in Jerusalem, many of these were, and still are, bad. The second, notwithstanding the arrogance, errors, and excesses of Eichmann in Jerusalem, is that it is still, I think, an important and in many ways a good and interesting book.

One obviously bad reason for objection is the extraordinarily frequent resentment of the book's original appearance in The New Yorker. There may be circumstances where place of publication can be an issue--Harrison Salisbury in Penthouse, Jimmy Carter's famous interview in Playboy, for example. My personal rule in these things tends to be that those who have never been tempted find it easiest to reject temptation.

But none of these seems to me to have much relevance to Arendt and The New Yorker, which has been a vehicle for serious things as well as Charles Addams cartoons and Tiffany ads for as long as I can remember: a whole issue devoted to Hersey's Hiroshima on its appearance in 1946 comes to mind. The juxtaposition of Saks Fifth Avenue and the Eichmann trial is a bit of a frisson, I suppose. But one can also meet such things almost every week in the Sunday Magazine of the New York Times, where Walter Laqueur appears with some frequency, and I should imagine without measurable indignation from censorious readers.

Real conoisseurs of the frisson might, in fact, take notice of these very proceedings that bring us together. I am here to respond to Walter Laqueur, who is responding to Hannah Arendt, for reasons having to do with a genocide both of them only barely escaped, and that I escaped myself only because my grandfather had the good sense to emigrate to Sioux City. The immediate occasion for this meeting is the anniversary of a program that may well be part of the personal experience of people who are present. We are all comfortable and having a nice time. There is no way around the fact that we owe this pleasant and civilized occasion to Hitler. This

is obviously no reason not to meet. Life goes on.
It just confronts us with odd choices.

To return to Arendt, the point of my argument is
that she stepped on toes--quite a lot of them, I
suspect, and I assume with deliberate intention. But
I think much of the resulting controversy was also
inadvertent, having to do with both Arendt's blind
spots but also her readers'. If I, like Walter
Laqueur, may lapse briefly into the autobiographical,
I first became aware of the book when a cousin of
mine, a rabbi in Detroit, wrote me for my
professional opinion while I was sitting in a Cologne
apartment with acres of file cards, and writing what
became a kind of social history of Nazi Germany. I
answered him in ten single-spaced pages, as I
remember. I never got an answer. In part this may
be because I told him far more than he wanted to
know. But to a far larger extent, it was because I
told him something quite different from what he
wanted to hear, which was that she was wrong or
worse.

Much of the controversy the book aroused had to
do with just this lapse of mutual comprehension.
There were, as Laqueur points out, perfectly
legitimate grounds for exasperation. But at least
one of them was largely beyond the author's control,
and that is the intellectual baggage she inevitably
brought to the subject. This can be understood at
two levels. First, while Arendt was a remarkably
gifted representative of the species, she was
unmistakably a product of a milieu and tradition
hopelessly foreign to the vast majority of her
readers. They were not raised on Greek and the
German classical philosophy and all the rest of that
remarkable Central European inventory that people of
Arendt's generation and circumstances seem to have
absorbed like "Sesame Street." The tradition is
radical, polemical, a manifestation of people who
take ideas very seriously, sometimes for their
intrinsic value, sometimes for their utilitarian
value as tools or weapons, viz., Marx's famous
injunction that the philosopher's job is not merely
to describe the world, but it also has a tendency to
deduce things, a certain disposition to patronize
facts--to treat them as means to an end.

The second item in Arendt's intellectual baggage
was the peculiarity of her personal experience that
unquestionably colored her reaction to Eichmann in
Jerusalem and many other things as well. Laqueur
has referred to several of the elements in this
personal psychodrama. More can be found in a
remarkably revealing TV interview with Günter Gaus,

later published in the mid 60s. The interview confirms a good deal about her personality.

To stay in the Yeatsian mode Laqueur introduced, Arendt's was a personality in which the center didn't always hold, and the subject, to say the least, was full of passionate intensity. The interview also suggests some interesting things about Arendt's sense of Jewish identity, i.e., that for her, like countless thousands of her contemporary German Jews, there really wasn't very much of one, since there was neither religion, nor culture, nor national identity to fill the space. What there was instead was almost literally physical--"I knew as a child that I looked Jewish," she says in the interview--and was meant to be asserted almost like physical identity, that is, without pride or apology, but simply as a fact of life. When teachers at school said something antisemitic, she was to leave the class, come home, and tell her mother who then fired off a registered letter of complaint. When kids said something antisemitic, she was to deal with it herself. "You see, all Jewish children encountered antisemitism, and it poisoned the outlook of very many of them," Arendt told Gaus. "The difference with us was that my mother always took the position that you weren't supposed to duck, you were supposed to defend yourself."

My personal impression, which I concede is beyond any confirmation, is that Arendt--presumably for reasons of her own disposition and experience--expected more, not less, of Jews in this connection, and imaginably in other connections too. I suspect that the oft-cited double standard of Eichmann in Jerusalem, her tendency to argue in dubio contra reo as Ernst Simon has said where Jews are concerned but to let Eichmann off the hook, is actually the expression of a peculiar kind of Jewish chauvinism. I think she expected Jews to be better than other people--though of course without any very tangible indication of just what, save for assertive physical survival, Jews were supposed to be better about.

In any case, the combination of tone, premises, and unstated assumptions can only have been a burden for an American Jewish reader--like my cousin, to stay with one practical example. But when one adds the actual message, in both its positive and negative dimensions, one can hardly be surprised at the general outrage, quite irrespective of those errors of interpretations, taste, and historical fact of which Laqueur has reminded us. What the book said was that most of six million Jews were neither heroes nor martyrs, but victims; that most executors of the

Third Reich were not monsters, nor even necessarily interchangeable with Germans, but malignant bureaucratic twerps who might, under other circumstances, have sold used cars or insurance; and that there were certain affinities and identities of interest between the Third Reich and one or another manifestation of the Zionist cause. Quite irrespective of their objective merits, all three were propositions guaranteed to chill the livers of American Jewish readers for innumerable reasons. All three stomped purposefully and I think fearlessly on existing taboos.

The problem is, I think, that all three propositions are generally defensible, and that publishing them was a service to truth--or at least to "that continual and fearless sifting and winnowing by which alone the truth can be found," as the plaque at the University of Wisconsin says. The Jews of Europe were victims, trapped by circumstances and their hopes, no better and also no worse than any other population confronted with such fundamentally hopeless circumstances. The Nazi empire, for the most part, was run by normal and familiar people, not psychopaths, who accommodated themselves in a variety of ways to the temptations, the hazards, and the disorientations of their situation. Like other nationalisms before and since, the Zionist faith does include elements of populist, even biological, identity, of national exclusiveness, of missionary purpose, and ambivalence toward both minorities and assimilation. None of these is to say "tu quoque," nor do I believe this was Arendt's purpose. She was not really, I think, accusing the Jews of Europe of exterminating themselves, though I concede the obvious ambiguities in her argument. She was certainly not minimizing German guilt by suggesting that Eichmann was no monster. Rather the contrary, her point was that Nazi Germany was a place where even people as conventional as Eichmann found it painless to be complicit in mass murder. Her ambivalence about some of the paradoxes of Zionism, an apparent consequence of her personal history, is a problem both Israeli and non-Israeli Jews ignore at their peril, as I think we've seen since 1967, and still more since Mr. Begin's election as prime minister in 1977.

Do I agree with or approve of everything she says. No. Do I, as a professional historian, find Eichmann in Jerusalem good history? No. But I don't think these are the only appropriate standards. If there is such a thing as the banality of evil, which I think there is and which Arendt brought to our attention, I think there is also something we

could call the productiveness of error. It is no
coincidence, after all, that we are standing here
discussing neither Bill Allen nor me, nor even Walter
Laqueur, all of whom I think are generally right, but
Hannah Arendt. She might not have been right,
but--as good historians ordinarily do not--she made
people who don't ordinarily read history think hard
and unsentimentally about things that needed to be
thought about.

Rejoinder

(Professor Laqueur declined to add to his
initial presentation in response to the comments).

5
The Holocaust
and International Relations

Leo Mates

The unprecedented genocide which caused the destruction of the bulk of the Jewish populations of Germany and other Nazi-occupied countries has had a great impact on thinking and acting in our times. It has affected not only the attitude towards internal problems of the European and many other nations, but also international relations. Racial discrimination, persecution of minorities, and other forms of denial of human rights, were denounced and opposed by progressive individuals, groups, and parties, as well as prohibited by law in a growing number of countries, even before the criminal activities perpetrated by Nazis and their collaborators. Nevertheless, the experience of the genocide before and during World War II was an important turning point in history.

The prevailing theory and practice supporting the view of the relationship between a government and its citizens as a purely internal problem of each nation was seriously questioned, and even more, rejected by the victorious Allies after Wolrd War II. This was reflected in the Charter of the United Nations and in numerous other documents and international acts. From a special case, which was included in some treaties and conventions after World War I, the respect and observance of human rights, including especially the elimination of racial discrimination, became an accepted obligation of a general nature for all nations. The international community assumed a new role in the movement of humanity toward democracy and human rights.

This momentous impact of the Holocaust is a poor consolation to the survivors and was of no help to the victims. However, there is little doubt that the martyrdom of millions was not in vain. If it did not help those who suffered, it may have contributed to the prevention of similar massive crimes elsewhere and in the future. It certainly contributed to the

emergence of more enlightened views toward
populations of a different color of skin, culture, or
language. The conscience of European peoples was
awakened also in regard to colonialism and
responsibility towards the underdeveloped countries
of the formerly colonized parts of the world.

It must, though, be added that the evils of
racial arrogance and the ill treatment of minorities
and underprivileged communities still persist and
should not be underestimated. But even the beginning
of a public recognition on a global scale of the
indivisibility of human rights and the link between
them and peace in the world are important landmarks.
In this paper the various aspects of the impact of
the persecution of the Jews will not be examined
exhaustively. We shall turn our attention mainly to
the problem of human rights in the framework of
international relations.

The Impact of the Holocaust

The ruthless and criminal persecution and
massive slaughter of European Jews before and during
World War II was not the first or only act of cruel
oppression and destruction suffered by Jewish
populations. It was not even something quite new to
the Jews of Europe. On the other hand, acts of
massive persecution and destruction have been
suffered by other communities also--in Europe during
the Holocaust and earlier. Populations of other
continents too had their share in suffering acts of
extermination. But, still, the genocide of Jews by
Nazis and their collaborators remains an event of
extraordinary significance in history.

It is not easy to identify with certainty those
events that had the greatest impact. In different
circles and social environments different elements of
the whole may have had particular meanings, and some
could have caused more revulsion than others.
Historically it is important to point out the
circumstance that on most occasions of genocide in
the past, it occurred during or after the clash of
imcompatible communities. This, of course cannot be
accepted as an excuse, but it is a historical fact.
The Jews in Germany, however, were a well integrated
and constructive element of society and of the German
nation.

Hence, the extraordinary shock caused by this
unexpected and cruel onslaught, which was perceived
in other nations as some kind of a massive
fratricide. Among the various cases of genocide in
history, the most frequent were cases of conquest and

colonization of other continents by European nations and cases of genocide practiced in war. Perhaps one of the best known examples from ancient history is the extermination of the population of Melos by the Athenians during the Peloponnesian War, indicative of the long history of genocide in war. Instances of exterminations of native populations were of course not uncommon in the period of colonial conquest.

The case of the destruction of Jews by Nazism was exceptional in the sad train of events connected with World War II, since it was the initial case of discrimination and denial of human rights within a community. Other cases followed and were modeled after it. This applies to the persecution and destruction of Gypsies and Slavic populations in countries conquered by the Nazis, as well as the similar acts by quislings, e.g. the Ustashi in Yugoslavia, who slaughtered Jews, Serbs, and Gypsies on a massive scale. This was genocide in the purest sense, since there was no conflict between the Jewish community and the rest of the population preceding the acts of persecution and destruction. There can be detected no distinct motivation for the persecution based on political activities of any individual or of the Jewish community as a whole. The only reason and explanation was the prejudice, rather hate, stirred up against the whole Jewish community as a community and toward every single member of it.

This circumstance was received with additional horror because of the centuries of association between Jews and Germans and the imposing contribution of members of the Jewish community to German arts, culture, science, and economic development. Finally, the shock was amplified by the magnitude, cold-blooded thoroughness, and brutality of the persecution and destruction in specially designed establishments. There was no element of irrational behavior or spontaneity; it was rather a clear case of unprecedented, massive, and systematic cruelty planned in advance and carried out methodically.

The genocide was also the prologue to equally planned and systematic efforts to conquer other countries and subject them to a similar rule of terror and cruelty. Genocide at home and then extended to other countries, the provoking of the most devastating was in human history, carried on with the same callousness and cruelty, including genocide in conquered lands and massive killing of hostages--these were the shocking events which aroused mankind and which made a strong impact on the conduct of international relations after World War II.

The end of the war was, therefore, not experienced in the world as the end of a mere conflict between two sides, as a victory over an aggressor, but more as the end of a mightmare, of an attack on the very foundations of humanity. This explains also the first and immediate effects of the war on international relations, in particular with regard to the treatment of the leaders and instigators of the Holocaust and the other crimes derived from it, especially the extension of the practice of genocide to other countries. Among the first acts of the victorious Allies was the establishment of the International Military Tribunal, following an Agreement signed on August 8, 1945, by the governments of the United States, France, the United Kingdom, and the Soviet Union. The Charter of the Tribunal, annexed to the Agreement, extended its jurisdiction also to individuals responsible for crimes against peace, war crimes, and crimes against humanity, even if they did not thereby violate the law of their country and irrespective of orders given them from any established authority of their country.[1]

International law was applied to individuals and a new definition of the applicability of it was given in the judgment delivered in Nuremberg on September 30, 1946: "It was submitted that international law is concerned with the action of sovereign States, and provides no punishment for individuals; and further, that where the act in question is an act of State, those who carry it out are not personally responsible, but are protected by the doctrine of the sovereignty of the State. In the opinion of the Tribunal, both these submissions must be rejected....Crimes against international law are committed by men, not by abstract entities, and only by punishing individuals who commit such crimes can the provision of international law be enforced."[2]

The only earlier attempt to introduce criminal proceedings against an individual for crimes under international law occurred after World War I with the indictment of the German emperor by the victorious allies, but the Netherlands refused to extradite him and the matter was dropped. In connection with this precedent it should be underlined that World War I in its time also inflicted an enormous shock on the conscience of mankind, and Germany was viewed as the power responsible for it. Nevertheless, even the many millions of human beings killed and crippled, and untold sufferings of even more millions, were not a sufficient impulse for the changing of established usages in jurisprudence and the interpretation of international law. It was only after the horrors preceding and during World War II, and among them in the first place the Holocaust, that the decisive step was taken of setting up an International Military Tribunal.

There was another significant innovation in the interpretation of international law connected with the Nuremberg Tribunal. It was assumed that certain standards of behavior and certain obligations are understood with sufficient clarity and have a binding force governing international relations so that criminal prosecution is in order in the case of war crimes even without explicit prior legislation. This position was also stated in the Charter of the Tribunal and in the Judgment of September 30, 1946. But this concept was also formally stated in a number of resolutions of the General Assembly of the United Nations in the early stages of the activities of that organization. [3]

All these innovations are visible testimony to the strong impact of the cruelties which began with the Nuremberg Laws and Nazism, introducing the persecution and eventual genocide of the Jewish community in Germany, later extended to other communities and carried out in other countries conquered by German armies. The outstanding role of the horror created by the persecution and extermination of Jews is beyond doubt. In fact the stirring up of base instincts in the masses and the translation of violence and terror into normal legal practice, practiced on German people by the Nazis in the process of escalating the persecution of the German Jews, led directly to introduction of terrorism and violence in occupied countries and territories. The Holocaust made the decisive impact and was the basis for the drastic reaction of mankind to genocide in general and to all war crimes perpetrated by the Nazis and their allies during World War II.

International Concern for Human Rights

Quite naturally, one of the first concerns of the international community was to punish the major war criminals. Major trials were held in Nuremberg and in Tokyo, but also in all other allied countries. Simultaneously, however, the impact of the Holocaust gave rise to another important innovation in that human rights were defined as a concern of mankind as a whole. At the same time, the United Nations was constituted as a universal organization. The Charter was proclaimed as universal law, not merely as a

multilateral treaty binding only the contracting
powers. Under the Charter action is made possible to
uphold its principles in all parts of the world
irrespective of UN membership status.[4]

The universal character of the United Nations,
notwithstanding the limitation of the original
membership, served also as a basis for formulating
general principles concerning the conduct of states
in international affairs, and also in some domestic
matters regarded as universally important. This
applies to all the Principles and Purposes enumerated
in Arts. 1 and 2, but also to other provisions of the
Charter, and in particular to those connected with
international peace and security. Explicit reference
to non-member states is made in Arts. 2.6, 11.2, 32,
50, and 93 of the Charter. But the phrasing,
content, and scope of all operative provisions
indubitably reflect the idea of universality.

One of the early interpretations of the Charter,
by Leland Goodrich and Edvard Hambro, is quite
positive in this respect. "It is clear that the
Organization thereby actually assumes authority not
based on the consent of states affected." This is
written in connection with the interpretation of Art.
2.6 and is followed by the remark that this is not in
accord with established views and that ".... the
authority of the United Nations under this paragraph
is based exclusively upon the will and power of the
contracting parties." [5]

Since the first publication of this
interpretation in 1946 events have tended to prove
that the innovation was not merely a tour de force,
but reflected in reality a new consciousness of
mankind. Not only was there no challenge to this
amplified competence of the United Nations, but the
organization became practically universal by the
extension of its membership in the 1970s. The United
Nations did not live up to these principles and did
not perform as expected, also the world has not
become the scene of international brotherhood and
tranquility, but the idea of indivisibility and
interdependence has nevertheless spread and is
universally accepted.

We are here not so much interested in the
results achieved by the United Nations, but in the
emergence and acceptance of new ideas and concepts
developed after World War II and inaugurated shortly
after the end of the war. We are also interested in
the further development of these innovations in the
intervening decades, and in particular in the field
of human rights.

It was therefore necessary to review briefly the
new framework in which the international institutions

performed and developed, for this affords the proper perspective for the examination of the problem of human rights and in particular the growing internatinal concern for the observance of human rights in all countries. The insistence on human rights in the Charter is thereby projected on the widest field of international relations and world affairs. The acceptance of the universal character and role of the United Nations, although its resolutions are not always and immediately carried out, contributed to the strengthening of the idea that human rights are a matter of general concern.

It is interesting to note that the emphasis on human rights in the Charter did not exist in the original proposal formulated by the Dumbarton Oaks Conference of the United States, the USSR, Britain, and China of 21 August - 7 October, 1944. The only mention of human rights in the Proposal is among the purposes listed in Chapter IX, "Arrangements for International Economic and Social Cooperation." Furthermore, the mention is rather perfunctory:

"With a view to the creation of conditions of stability and well-being which are necessary for peaceful and friendly relations among nations, the Organization should facilitate solutions of international economic, social and humanitarian problems and promote respect for human rights and fundamental freedoms."

Specification regarding the application to "all without distinction as to race, sex, language, or religion" was inserted in San Francisco; the word "observance" was also added to the word "respect" with regard to human rights. This change can be found in Art. 55 which is the definitive version of the quoted Article of the proposal. More important is the inclusion of human rights in the Preamble and in Article 1, on General Purposes. Clearly, the participants in the San Francisco Conference, acting under the pressure of public opinion and representing a wide range of political opinion in the world, were much more responsive to the reaction of mankind to the horrors of racial discrimination, persecution, and genocide than were the top officials of the Four Powers assembled in the privacy of the Dumbarton Oaks Library in Washington. Hence the wording of Arts. 55:

"With a view to the creation of conditions of stability and well-being which are necessary for peaceful and friendly relations among nations based on respect for the principle of equal rights and self-determination of peoples, the United Nations shall promote:...universal respect for and observance of human rights and fundamental freedoms for all without distinction as to race, sex, language, or religion." And Art. 56 adds:

"All Members pledge themselves to take joint and separate action in cooperation with the Organization for the achievement of the purposes set forth in Article 55."

Without elaboration of these provisions and those contained in other Articles, there can be little doubt that the Charter took a decisive step forward from the earlier views and legal interpretations of domestic jurisdiction in the field of human rights.

In the first years of the Organization, a debate ensued regarding the true interpretation of these provisions. The occasion was the consideration of the treatment of Indians in South Africa, later expanded to cover other colored communites. The debate centered around the questions of what constitutes interference and of how far promotion of universal respect for and observance of human rights can be carried without becoming interference in domestic affairs. With the passing years and the growth of the anti-colonial movement, the attitude in the United Nations changed. It would be stretching the argument if one were to say that the anti-colonial movement was inspired by the increase in the sensitivity to human rights observance, but attitudes in the metropolitan powers were undoubtedly thus affected. The number of those opposed to the imposition of colonial rule on unwilling populations increased under the impact of memories of the horrors of occupation and genocide experienced during World War II. Thus, the resistance to maintaining colonial rule by force became an important factor in precipitating the withdrawal of European powers from their colonial empires.

This movement was slow, and in some cases stubborn resistance to the inevitable end of colonialism led to the use of force and to resort to brutality and terrorism by colonial powers, as well as to retaliatory acts of violence by the anti-colonial forces. However, colonial wars had happened in the past also, and they abounded with violence and massive repression. Only after the shock of the wartime genocide, which brought this kind of experience directly into the heart of Europe, did public opinion in Europe become sensitive to this problem.

As a result of this development, the initially timid attitude and mild opposition to racial practices in the southern part of Africa developed into a wide and practically universal condemnation. The first debates on South Africa ended in a half-hearted resolution that did not even openly condemn racial discrimination and still clung desperately to the concept of domestic jurisdiction. This position was quite obviously untenable. Once the issue was admitted for genuine discussion, and in light of the sensitivity to the racial persecutions of Nazism, it was impossible to condone racial persecutions anywhere in the world. The last attempt to maintain a double standard, distinguishing between the treatment of Europeans and "natives" in Africa, could not be sustained. Thus racial discrimination was exposed to growing criticism by the revulsion implanted in public opinion by the wartime experiences.

Thereafter, the practice of the United Nations changed rapidly. After the condemnation and severe censure concerning discrimination and oppression in South Africa and in other colonial possessions, international measures were introduced. In the context of this examination it is of little consequence that these measures, such as trade embargo and boycott, were not efficacious. The important development—despite a dwindling opposition to these measures from some Western powers with strategic and economic vested interest in the region—was the decisive change of attitude.

In the last few years all Western powers, including the United States and Britain, have gone so far as to exercise pressure on the regime in Salisbury and in the South African Republic. The denial of human rights there and in other places has, thus, been unanimously and unequivocally accepted as the concern of the United Nations, i.e. of the international community. These developments related to specific situations and to the acts of some governments hve been accompanied also by general efforts in the United Nations to codify the concept of human rights.

First came the Universal Declaration on Human Rights, adopted unanimously in the General Assembly of the United Nations.[6] The Declaration had, of course, no binding character, but it would be wrong to underestimate its actual role all over the world. After all, it was the formal codification of human rights as a concern of mankind. It was the belated fulfilment of the idea of some participants of the San Francisco Conference. It may be considered the definitive and precisely defined doument confirming the international nature of the problem. It started from the concise language of the Charter but encompassed in its ramifications the whole problem in all its details.

An important effect of the Declaration was the beginning of serious efforts to draft a binding Covenant on Human Rights. This led to the adoption of two covenants in 1966 by the General Assembly, one covering human rights in the economic, social, and cultural fields, and the other dealing with political rights. [7] Here again, the reluctance of governments to submit to international jurisdiction has made it difficult to enforce human rights everywhere. Many governments did not accept the jurisdiction of the special committee established under the covenants, and by no means all governments accepted the covenants themselves. [8] Nevertheless, there have been important advances.

The furthest step towards international enforcement has been made in Western Europe. There, already in 1950, the Convention for the Protection of Human Rights and Fundamental Freedoms, was concluded among the member states of the Council of Europe. [9] Here also there are good reasons for dissatisfaction concerning the observance of human rights in specific situations and in individual states. But, let us repeat, this is less important for the purposes of this paper, than the fact that human rights, at least in the regional framework of a certain number of countries, have definitively left the domain of purely domestic jurisdiction and become a legitimate concern of international bodies.

It is significant, on the other hand, that the widening of the scope of the Charter in the field of human rights caused also a restrictive addition to the Dumbarton Oaks Proposal. Article 2.7 was introduced with the aim of protecting states from undue interference in domestic affairs. [10] This restriction remains valid in all cases and overrides any other international agreement, as provided for in the Charter. [11] Hence an ambiguity developed. On the one hand the respect for, and the observance of, human rights has become an international concern, but at the same time the rule is upheld that there should be no interference in domestic affairs.

This ambiguity is a very important feature of the Charter and it means practically that international concern in regard to human rights must not exceed certain limits, which again must be agreed internationally and which are also variable over time. This means in other words that the reality of international relations will, and in fact does already, gradually widen the area of international

concern in reaction against the earlier very rigid
concept of domestic jurisdiction. This sense of flux
and change is reflected in the choice of words in the
Charter, where there is mention only of "matters
which are essentially within the domestic
jurisdiction of any state."[12] The emphasis here is
on the word <u>essentially</u>. It indicates that it is
no longer possible to draw a clear and rigid line
between domestic and international jurisdiction.
After all, the decision to bring war criminals to
trial in an international tribunal was already
prepared in the minds of the leading statesmen of the
United Nations. Public concern for human rights
anywhere in the world was too strong to be ignored;
the shock of the horrors of Nazism could not be wiped
out by referring to old concepts of domestic
jurisdiction as they were known in the past centuries
of the development of international law.

The Final Act of Helsinki and Human Rights

The Final Act, unanimously accepted by all
participating states, and signed at the end of the
Conference on Security and Cooperation in Europe on
August 1, 1975, led to acrimonious exchanges at the
follow-up Conference in Belgrade in 1977-1978. The
main subjects of the controversy were the provisions
and the interpretation, as well as implementation,
pertaining to human rights. The main protagonists
were the representatives of the United States and of
the Soviet Union, supported by other representatives
of the Soviet bloc, but other Western representatives
and the representatives of the neutral and nonaligned
countries of Europe also took part in this debate.
The Final Act is a lengthy document that has no
binding force comparable to a Covenant, yet it is
rather explicit in the field of human rights. In
this area, as well as in all other parts of the
document, intentions rather than obligations of the
signatories are expressed. Nevertheless, this opened
up the possibility of examining in the follow-up
conference how and to what extent the participating
states had made efforts to carry out the various
postulates of the Final Act.
In the Final Act human rights are expressly
enumerated in a section with the heading <u>Declaration
on Principles Guiding Relations between Participating
States</u>. Thus the problem of human rights is from
the beginning brought into direct connection with
international relations. The issue of human rights
is contained in Principle VII. The crucial passages
of the text are:

"The participating states will respect human
rights and fundamental freedoms, including the
freedom of thought, conscience, religion or
belief, for all without distinction as to race,
sex, langue or religion.

"They will promote and encourage the effective
exercise of civil, political, economic, social,
cultural and other rights and freedoms all of
which derive from the inherent dignity of the
human person and are essential for his free and
full development.

"The participating states recognize the
universal significance of human rights and
fundamental freedoms, respect of which is an
essential factor for the peace, justice and
well-being necessary to ensure the development
of friendly relations and cooperation among
themselves as among all states."

The very direct link established between the
respect for human rights and international relations
called, naturally, for the equally explicit statement
of the principle of noninterference in internal
affairs.   This matter is covered under Principle VI
of the Final Act.   In the text of this Principle we
find the usual provision expressed in a general way,
but then follows the specification of its meaning.
The most interesting passage is:

"They will likewise refrain in all circumstances
from any other act of military, or political,
economic or other coercion designed to
subordinate to their own interest the exercise
by another participating state of its rights
inherent in its sovereignty and thus to secure
advantages of any kind."

It appears to follow unequivocally from the
quoted text that the human rights situation in any of
the participating states can be freely discussed, and
in particular for the purpose of finding the degree
of compliance with undertakings accepted in the Final
Act.   This should of course be done without using
pressure of any nature and without seeking to obtain
advantages of any kind.   However, the debates in
Belgrade showed that there was no unanimity in this
matter.   Three positions developed during the general
debate at the opening of the meeting and were again
reflected in the concluding debate.

Before presenting the three positions, it may be interesting to point out that the issue of human rights among the participating states is not related to colonial problems or racial discrimination in Africa. It has been inserted into the Final Act as a problem existing and pertaining to conditions in Europe and, more generally, the area covered by the participating states. This would include the North American continent in view of the participation of the United States and Canada in the Conference and in the Belgrade Meeting. Hence, the issue can be more directly linked with the events of the last war and the genocide and persecution of peoples in occupied territories. This was clearly brought out in the private discussions where concrete cases were mentioned. Most of them concerned the denial of rights to Jews in some countries of Eastern Europe and, in particular, in the Soviet Union. If there could be any doubt of the direct linkage between the Holocaust and the current debate on human rights, these doubts were dispelled in the discussions at Belgrade.

Already in the opening statement the representative of the United States expressed the view that there was "encouraging evidence of progress," but he later qualified his statement. Referring to the countries of Eastern Europe he singled out in particular the failure to implement the provision on human rights. Although he stated that it was not his intention to approach this issue in a polemical way, the discussions, especially in the relative privacy of committee rooms, became highly polemical. The statement in the general debate, taken alone, did not differ much from statements made before or after the U.S. representative spoke.

In fact the first speaker in the opening debate was the Yugoslav Foreign Secretary Miloš Minić who opened the meeting on behalf of the Yugoslav Government, and made a straightforward statement on human rights as a subject of the meeting:

"We also believe that the realization of human rights should be constantly promoted through all-round, equal cooperation. Yugoslavia feels that the question of the realization of human rights should be approached in a comprehensive manner and considered with a full measure of responsibility and realism, all this with a view to ensuring the constant implementation and further improvement of the provisions of the Final Act in this field."[13]

The head of the Yugoslav delegation, Milorad Pešić, amplified this statement, warning against pressure and real interference in this or any other fields, but concluding, "national sovereignty should not be an obstacle to the enjoyment of human rights or be invoked in an attempt to justify their violations." [14]

Other participants from the group of neutral and nonaligned countries made similar statements. It may be of interest to quote only the statement of the Swedish representative, Ambassador Leifland, in the opening debate:

"The Swedish government will not refrain from drawing attention to violations of human rights. We cannot possibly regard this as interference in the affairs of other nations. The Final Act gives us good ground for holding this view.

"But, a government must also carefully consider what best benefits the cause it wants to promote. This is a difficult but not impossible balance to strike." [15]

Representatives of Western countries expressed similar views and there can be found little difference in the positions taken at the opening of the debate in Belgrade between all representatives, except for those from the Warsaw Pact countries. They did not enter into the debate directly, but tried to ignore the issue at first. In this respect, the opening statement of the Soviet representative, Ambassador Vorontsov, is typical:

"Those who oppose detente--and such circles exist in the West--by the same token hinder the implementation of the provisions of the Final Act." [16]

He reacted to the whole debate on human rights only in his concluding statement:

"Turning aside from serious consideration of the burning problems of European security, and above all those of limiting the arms race and of detente, those delegations attempted to switch attention to another subject, to challenge the socialist countries in the field of human rights, cooperation in the humanitarian fields. But these attempts, as we know, have failed fully." [17]

Without quoting further from the opening or the concluding statements of Western representatives or those of other countries, it appears that there were two fundamental positions represented at the meeting, the one advocating and the other rejecting the right of an international meeting to discuss human rights conditions in any country. But there were differences among those holding the first view. Western European representatives to a large extent, and those from neutral and nonaligned countries more forcefully, expressed the view that the issue should be treated with realism. This was an implicit, sometimes also explicit, criticism of the rather direct and sharp tone of the American representative. The difference was most visible in the private meetings and then again publicly in the presentation of drafts for the concluding document of the meeting. Other Western delegations to some extent, and the neutrals and nonaligned more explicitly, disagreed with the exclusive position of the United States vetoing any issue of substance if strong censure of the Eastern position on human rights were omitted. This led, as is well known, to the elimination of practically all substance from the Concluding Document of Belgrade. Thus, no statement on human rights remained on the record at the conclusion of the meeting.

The outcome of the meeting was received with misgivings by many delegations. The British representative Lord Goronwy Roberts expressed disappointment in his speech at the end of the meeting, in which he summarized the frustrating efforts to draft a meaningful concluding document: "As a result, the concluding document, the end product of all our long debates, is short and thin. It is a severe disappointment."[18]

This, however, is probably not the end of the discussion of all the questions on the agenda, and certainly not of the debate about human rights. This was forcefully brought out by another Swedish representative, Ambassador Arvidsson. He expressed regret about the "great number of proposals [which] have been forwarded" and promised that "they still exist in our minds and we are convinced... this will give new impetus..."[19] The Danish representative Melbin, who presented the short version of the Concluding Document, expressed his misgivings over its lack of content, but he also saw the reason for accepting it in the circumstances:

"We were, however, convinced that common responsibility required a concentrated effort to establish overall agreement on a concluding document which, although short, would at least briefly reflect the proceedings at the Belgrade Meeting, state if only a few essential conclusions thereof, and above all include such decisions on follow-up, that the continuation of the multilateral process initiated by the CSCE was ensured." 20

It is therefore justified to conclude that the momentous, although necessarily heated and antagonistic, debate on human rights will continue in the European framework. The first occasion will be in Madrid. The breakthrough based on the impact of the Holocaust, and resumed in the drafting of the Charter of the United Nations and further activities of the Organization, has come up again for a thorough discussion in Europe and North America. It did not get very far in Hilsinki, and it remained without concrete results in Belgrade, but the debate continues. It does not seem likely that national sovereignty could be successfully invoked in an attempt to justify the violation of human rights.

It may well be that, in retrospect, the whole period covering the most inhumane and abhorrent acts of genocide, the expression of revulsion and determination to eliminate such acts, and the current efforts to discuss human rights globally will be regarded as an important turning point in the evolution of human values. If the gains were dearly bought by untold sufferings and loss of life, it was so with most other achievements in history. What counts is the lesson learned and the benefit created for future generations, who will mourn the victims and remember those who drew the correct conclusions from the Holocuast.

NOTES

1. United Nations Treaty Series 279.
2. American Journal of International Law, 41, 1 9 4 7 , p . 2 2 0 , quoted in L. Oppenheimer: International Law, Vol. 1, p. 210. See also Marx Sorenson (ed.): Manual of Public International Law (London: Macmillan, 1968), p, 516.
3. Res. 95.I, of 11 December 1946, confirming principles sustained by the Tribunal, Res. 96.I, of December 1946, defining the crime of Genocide and introducing proceedings for the drafting of a Convention of Genocide, Res. 117.II, of 21 November 1947, instructing the International Law commission to

draft a Code of Offences against the peace and
security of mankind. This work was further carried
on in other resolutions based on these initial steps.
The outcome was a convention on Genocide, which came
into force in 1954, and further work on the
codification of international law.

   4. Article 2.6 is the most explicit statement
of this principle: "The Organization shall ensure
that states which are not Members of the United
Nations act in accordnce with these Principles so far
as may be necessary for the maintenance of
international peace and security."

   5. Leland Goodrich and Edvard Hambro: <u>Charter</u>
<u>of the United Nations; Commentary and Documents</u>
(London: Stevens & Sons, 1947), pp. 108f.

   6. General Assembly Resolution 217, III. of 10
December 1948.

   7. General Assembly Resolution 2200, XXI. of 16
December 1966.

   8. The two Covenants entered into force on 23
March 1976 three months after the ratification by
Czechoslovakia as the twenty-fifth country accepting
them.

   9. United Nations Treaty Series 221.

   10. Nevertheless, Article 2.7 does not restrict
the application of enforcement measures under Chapter
VII of the Charter.

   11. Article 103 of the Charter.

   12. Article 2.7.

   13. Verbatim Record of the Belgrade Meeting
CSCE.BM. VR.1, 4 October 1977.

   14. CSCE.BM. VR.3, 5 October 1977.

   15. <u>Ibid</u>.

   16. CSCE.BM. VR.6, 6 October 1977.

   17. Provisional Records of the Belgrade meeting,
CSCE.BM. PV 2 of 9 March 1978.

   18. CCSE.BM. PV 2, 9 March 1978.

   19. CSCE.BM. PV 1, 8 March 1978.

   20. CSCE.BM. PV 2, 9 March 1978.

Comment: Human Rights and the Memory of the
Holocaust—Is There a Connection?
Henry R. Huttenbach

True to the spirit of this conference, Leo Mates
has reviewed post-World War II involvement with the
preservation of human rights as a partial by-product
of an international conscience profoundly stirred by
its confrontation with the genocidal slaughter of
European Jewry. In so doing, he has adopted the
unstated assumption inherent in the theme that
embraces this gathering: "Western Society after the
Holocaust" tacitly presumes that there is indeed an
intimate relationship between post-1945 humanistic
concerns in the international arena and recollections
of the death camps. Is there, however, a
demonstrable link between the moral and ethical and,
therefore, legal history of human rights since the
conclusion of World War II and the termination of the
Final Solution? Does the dark cloud of human ashes
that rose out of the crematoria cast a shadow over
subsequent deliberations on the human condition? Or
is this attempt to bring human rights history and
Holocaust history in tandem an exercise in wishful
thinking? Has Mates made a successful case for human
rights history as experiencing a new stage as a
result of its encounter with Auschwitz?

At the heart of this conference, and hence, by
logical extension at the core of Mates' subject, lies
the central question of the historical character of
the Holocaust: was the genocide of the Jews of
Europe an actual turning point or merely one so
perceived by subsequent generations? Is the
Holocaust a real watershed in history whose impact on
the European mind (and, therefore, on subsequent
decision-making) was immediate; or has the
realization of the mass murder of Jews come more
slowly, if at all? [1] How systematically has Mates
raised the possibility that the history of human
rights declarations may not be written and
interpreted without direct reference to the Holocaust
as an integral stimulus, motivator, or modifier?
What must be answered, with unflinching honesty, is
the following question: did the genocide of Jews
heighten the moral sensitivity of those participating
in the dialogues on human rights?

It is Mates' contention that as Europe struggled
to reconstruct itself after having witnessed the
crimes of the Nazis, the architects of a new
international order and its human rights component
operated with the memory of the Holocaust deeply
etched in their collective consciousness. "The
momentous impact of the Holocaust...," Mates begins,

"certainly contributed to the emergence of more enlightened views toward populations of a different color of skin, culture, or language." And, in concluding, Mates states that the human rights debate on an international scale gained its "breakthrough based on the impact of the Holocaust." Clearly, both the assumption as premise and as conclusion must be rigorously tested before human rights history is linked to Holocaust history. To do so, it might be well to begin with the relationship of the war aims embraced by Hitler's foes to the fatal plight of the Jewish masses trapped in Nazi Europe.

At what point in its six years duration did World War II also become a war to liberate the Jewish people? At no time, to be sure, did the intensification of antisemitic legislation and policy between 1933 and 1939 ever approach the status of a casus belli. On the contrary, international awareness of the persecution of Germany Jewry never once distracted the diplomacy of appeasement: neither the Munich Agreement nor the Nazi-Soviet Pact was derailed by any overt or covert concern for Jews.[2] Once war had broken out and news of the extermination of Jews reached London, Moscow, and Washington,[3] the general strategy and specific tactics of the military effort remained unaffected: repeated requests to bomb the death camps and the rail lines leading to them were steadfastly refused on grounds that they were not military targets. None of the pronunciamentos emanating from the sundry summits made reference to Hitler's war on the Jews: Tehran, Yalta, and Potsdam are eloquent testimony to the low priority enjoyed by the Jewish tragedy. Though Hitler identified the Jews as his primary enemy, generously allocating war resources towards the total elimination of that foe, the alliance marshalled against him never once saw fit to make common cause with that doomed minority.

Even in its declarations against Nazism, the alliance buried the crime against the Jews in generalities: Hitler and his subordinates would be held accountable for "atrocities" and "crimes against humanity." The camouflaging of the Holocaust that would begin soon after the war had its roots in the ambivalent stance taken by the governments fighting Nazi Germany, an inauspicious beginning to what Mates would have one believe to be otherwise. "The experience of genocide before and during World II was an important turning point in history"... "The unprecedented genocide which caused the destruction of the bulk of the Jewish populations of Germany and other Nazi-occupied countries had a great impact on thinking and acting in our times." Unfortunately, this metamorphosis of attitudes cannot be found in the war policies of those seeking to erase the evils of Nazism, at least in as much as it concerned the Jews. In the thought and actions of the allies, the crime committed against Jews did not rank sufficiently high to warrant special comment or to embark on a separate campaign.

Only after the war, when Germnay lay in ruins, when the time for retribution and revenge called for a legitimization of the war trials, was the extermination of the Jews resurrected and retroactively elevated as the crime of crimes, an immorality with which the victors would be painfully associated by reason of their inexcusable inaction, a policy whose roots grew out of the prewar Evian Conference and which was symbolized by the pathetic St. Louis affair. This inconsistency marred the proceedings of the Nuremberg Trials in which Nazi war criminals stood accused of genocide by those who had stood idly by and were themselves guilty of various shades of collaboration.[4] As the trials ran their course, focus on the genocide of the Jews shifted determinedly away to the millions of non-Jewish victims of Nazism until this crime was equated with the other inhumane policies of the Third Reich.

More important as a barometer of local and international sensitivity towards Jews was the immediate postwar treatment of the survivors who faced an uncertain future in a Europe struggling to rebuild in the context of rival superpower occupation and domination. Even as the Nuremberg Trials opened, murderous violence greeted Jews who sought to return to homes in Poland, pogrom-like outbursts that received no public condemnation.[5] As for the tens of thousands trapped in the limbo of the displaced persons camps, they became pawns in a political cat-and-mouse game reminiscent of the evasive prewar tactics in which each nation sought to place the responsibility for Jewish refugees upon the other. While England kept the doors to Palestine hermetically sealed, the United States operated from behind inflexible quota restrictions. As before World War II, the world simply did not want to extend a haven to Jews. Despite the knowledge of the Holocaust--the films of Bergen-Belsen had been seen by tens of millions and reports of the trials filled the daily newspapers--the revolution of sensitivity, the moral mutation claimed by Mates, just did not exist as far as the Jews were concerned. Which leads one to the second point of disputation that arises out of Mates' paper and with which the conference must grapple, if only for the sake of clarification.

If the approach so far has been historical in order to initiate accuracy for purposes of challenging Mates' optimistic claims of the dawn of a new era of sensitivity for human rights as a direct result from the encounter with the Jewish tragedy, this response now shifts to a definition of terminology, namely, to the meaning of the term Holocaust. On hearing Mates, it soon becomes evident that while Holocaust includes the Jewish experience, it is by no means restricted or limited to it. Throughout his essay, Mates always speaks of the Holocaust in conjunction with all the war crimes, those against Jews and non-Jews. "[T]he drastic reaction of mankind to genocide in general and to all war crimes perpetrated by the Nazis" came not, as he insists, from the knowledge of the slaughter of the Jews but from a revulsion to crimes perpetrated against other peoples. For the world, as for him, Holocaust means the sum-total of the Nazi horror. When it came time to commemorate the memory of the victims and to condemn the crimes of Nazism, the Jews were an invisible entity, only a part of the "greater" Holocaust: in the French left-inspired film, "Night and Fog," the deportees are simply identified as "les victimes," no mention of Jews;[6] the monument outside Kiev had inscribed on it "Soviet citizens," again no mention of Jews,[7] and the original information posters guiding visitors to Auschwitz referred to "Peoples from many nations." The anonymity of the Jews was testimony not only to the desire to steer attention away from their experience, but proof that the contemporary World War II conscience was quickened not by the fate of the Jews but by the deaths of one's own fellow countrymen whose ranks were conveniently inflated by the inclusion of millions of Jews. It was a Holocaust not because the storm had struck the Jews but precisely because it had struck at others.

As the term Holocaust became common currency, originally to give expression to the Jewish experience, it was rapidly adopted to convey a broader meaning, most recently, by the Jewish philosopher Arthur Cohen. For him, the Hell conveyed by Holocaust, was a flaming fury of violence that not only consumed Jews, but was the surfacing of an Evil that showed its face before and after World War II.[8] The Jews were only part witnesses: prior to 1939, according to Cohen, there were the countless millions who disappeared in Stalin's Gulag, and after 1945 he points to the masses who died in Vietnam. For Cohen, as for Mates, these are but "modalities" of the same crime of man against man.[9] In expanding the contextual meaning of Holocaust to become synonymous with all categories of mass killing, Cohen can conveniently focus on the limitless human capacity for cruelty, of which the genocide of the Jews is but one example, and Mates can construct the logic for his evolution of sensitivity towards suppressed minorities which underlies the human rights dialogues and which, he reasons, stemmed directly from the revelations of Auschwitz and whose most poignant message was that of the Jewish dead. Unfortunately, this is a misuse of the term, an abuse if it is meant to lump the genocide of Jews alongside other atrocities categorically separate.

In Mates' case, his argument rests upon this "expanded" Holocaust which did, indeed, serve as a catalyst for world opinion and which did, in fact, stimulate sensitivities in favor of the security of individuals and minorities. But, in this sense, as has already been shown, it was not the plight of the Jews that quickened the moral consciences of governments but the desire to protect their own citizens from the fate that had overrun them during World War II. As such, the statistical evidence of the genocide of the Jews served the purpose of further emphasizing the enormity of the other crimes but not to demonstrate it per se. That was already a foregone conclusion. Not only does the historical record of postwar behavior towards Jews contradict Mates' claim of a moral reawakening, but it also robs him of his logic. The sequence of awareness of the depth of Nazi criminality within the context of a broader understanding of Holocaust (of which the Jews become but a quantitatively significant part) did not originate with the evidence of the six million dead but with the knowledge of the murder of the other millions. Unless he can demonstrate, despite the available evidence to the contrary, that there had emerged a genuine sense of humanity for Jews qua Jews in the immediate aftermath of their genocidal slaughter, the entire history of human rights since 1945 rests less on a moral premise based on a respect for Jews than on the principle of self-preservation. That, of course, does not require any profound conversion or exposure to the Jewish Holocaust, which, because of its uniqueness, insists on a moral response, for it challenges the family of nations to respond not to a threat to themselves but a threat to others—to Jews.

Seen in this perspective, post-World War II history assumes a far less promising interpretation. What has been the international response to the continued plight of Jewish minorities now that the crimes of Nazism have been exposed and disseminated? The forced expulsions of Jewish minorities from Arab countries did not cause a ripple of discomfort let alone a strong condemnation from appropriate organizations associated with the United Nations.[10] Jewish communities remaining in Islamic countries live a precarious existence, with violence never far away. Jews living under rightist regimes such as that of Argentina experience constant intimidation and live in perpetual fear. The antisemitic policies of the Soviet Union need no further amplification except to remind one that neither the Holocaust, which reached deep into Stalin's Russia, nor Khrushchev's condemnation of the excesses of Stalinism tempered the viciousness of Soviet-sponsored antisemitism. Its ideological twin, anti-Zionism, has reached global[11] proportions leading to two symptomatic events: 1) the equation of Zionism with racism, and 2) challenges to the legitimacy of the Jewish state, Israel. These traditional and new forms of rejection of Jewish minorities and of a Jewish country point against a world which Mates insists has learned a lesson from the Holocaust.

As I show elsewhere,[12] the legacy of the Nuremberg Trials in the international arena is spotty, to state the case mildly. It was and remains an _ad_ _hoc_ phenomenon. The Genocide Convention of the United Nations remains, at best, an exercise in pietism. The world has not become safer from genocide since 1945. There exists neither a choate body of anti-genocide international law nor a viable organizational machinery to offer a minimal sense of security to threatened minorities, human rights declarations notwithstanding. Close scrutiny of the published materials associated with the human right dialogues divulges no reference to the Holocaust. In particular, of those landmarks referred to by Mates--the Charter of the United Nations, the Universal Declaration on Human Rights, the Convention for the Protection of Human Rights and Fundamental Freedoms, and the Helsinkin Declaration--none speaks openly of the genocide of Jews as a rallying thought. The evidence Mates needs to link human rights history to Holocaust history is dramatically absent. There is unfortunately little proof that the Holocaust ushered in an era of moral enlightenment, that concern for the destiny of Jews served as a first premise to reason towards universal principles, such proof unfortunately is lacking.

Mates is quite correct in linking anticolonial sentiment to the memories of World War II. Fewer and fewer Frenchmen wished to be associated with an unpopular and increasingly tyrannical policy in Algeria which, according to effective propaganda, equated them with Nazi Germany. However, never once was the killing of thousands of Moslems equated with the killing of Jews by the Nazis,13 despite the hundreds of thousands of pamphlets and editorials condemning the brutality of the French colonial army. Nor can the emerging international isolation of South Africa be attributed directly or indirectly to a memory of the Holocaust. In the United States, certainly, the public's revulsion against Apartheid can be traced directly and almost exclusively to memories of segregation and discrimination, a conscience pricked by the civil rights movement. Besides, far more cynical analysis may explain the shift in policy against the government in South Africa: given the retreat of the Portuguese, the balance of power is shifting inexorably in favor of Black-dominated regimes. Therefore, given the dependence of industrial powers upon even scarcer raw materials, it is only wise diplomacy to back the probable winner. Again there is no need to make the Holocaust an artificial _leitmotif_ to account for the sympathy expressed for individual martyrs like Biko or for the sufferings of those in the slums of Soweto. The sentiments for Blacks in Africa, whether popular or official, are _sui generis_, and, in a historical context, need no Holocaust to serve as a point of departure. While morally the Holocaust may be central to any human rights discussion, in terms of African history it is essentially peripheral with the exception of the Ibos, who, during the Biafran secession attempt, consciously spoke of genocide and made specific reference to the experience of the Jews as evidence that genocide is a real possibility in the contemporary world.

In closing, upon examination of Mates' evidence and argumentation, it is difficult to find an historic link between the universal expressions of concern for human rights and the Holocaust. Ironically, he himself supplies the strongest proof favoring the separation of the two histories. Even as the original Declaration of the United Nations drafted in January, 1942, was modified at Dumbarton Oaks in the autumn of 1944, to all intents and purposes the issue of human rights, that is the drafting of an _effective_ declaration in their favor, received a significant setback. While the range of human rights increased, Article 2.7 unambiguously placed national sovereignty above the protection of citizens deprived of their personal sovereignty. Between January, 1942, and October, 1944, the knowledge of the genocide of the Jews had become an indisputable fact. The salvation of the Jews depended upon the unambiguous principle of intervention if declarations on human rights were to possess any credibility. Yet, while the reality of the Holocaust generated the starkest of truths allowing for no ambiguity both in the realm of thought and action, Mates admits that at the very moment when the Final Solution took place, the international dialogue on human rights (which was supposed to have the Holocaust as its quintessential part) still permitted itself the luxury of what he dubs as "ambiguity." It is difficult to reconcile what Mates calls an international concern for human rights with the principle of non-interference in domestic affairs. That is squaring the circle, a hopeless contradiction whose coexistence he steadfastly seeks to maintain despite the glaring inconsistency of logic and of historic record. As long as the two are allowed to coexist, one is hard put to ascribe the international dialogue on human rights to an awareness of the Holocaust. The actual pursuit of human rights and the memory of the Holocaust are still far apart. The convergence of the two does not lie in the past, in 1945, but still in some unspecified point of time in the remote future. There is as yet no concrete connection, however much one might will it.

Turning once again to the theme of the conference, "Western Society after the Holocaust," one must end on a note of caution, avoiding both pessimism, as insinuated by this response, and guarded optimism as expressed by Mates. Nevertheless, if "a new consciousness" is to emerge, it will not come via a miracle or some mysterious process of osmosis but due to a determined effort to integrate the Holocaust experience into the ethical consciousness of those social elements most responsible for generating sensitivity towards Jews and hence, by extension, towards all. So far there are few signs that the training grounds of those professions who participated in genocide have taken radical steps to examine themselves in depth. Where is there a Medical School which asks its graduates to swear the Hippocratic Oath in the light of the Mengele Syndrome? Where is there a Law School mentioning the dangers of legalism as a path to genocide? What Schools of Busines include in their curriculum a case study of I.G. Farben and its pursuit of profit all the way to Auschwitz? [14] Is there a seminary that asks about the final implications of the silence of the Christian Churches during the martyrdom of the Jewish people? Do Schools of International Law and Diplomacy teach the merits of drafting anti-genocide law and policy? Not until a Holocaust-conscious elite permeates western society will it be possible to speak of an historic encounter with the Holocaust. A long as one can demonstrate an abyss between the human rights movement and a universal regard for the Jew, no one is secure.

NOTES

1. When assessing the influence of a particular event, one must first establish the chronology of its impact. On the simplest level, there are three categories into which historical events can be put according to this criterion: a) instant, b) cumulative, and c) delayed. Mates, in tracing the history of human rights, assumes the Holocaust to exert a combination of (a) and (b), a contention which I challenge. Historians, including myself, generally agree that the United Nations vote favoring the establishment of Israel may not have been favorable had the Holocaust not taken place. This, however, does not permit an automatic assumption of a similar influence in another area, a methodological flaw that mars Mates' argument throughout, for it tacitly rests on this false analogy.

2. Despite attempts to internationalize the plight of German Jews by various organizations and agencies, the problem never attained sufficient urgency to appear on the agendas of governments negotiating with Germany.

3. By the autumn of 1942, all three capitals had received a variety of scattered and unconfirmed reports. By November, 1942, these had all been corroborated by several independent sources and finally presented with incontestable documentary evidence leaving absolutely no room for doubt as to the genocidal character of Nazi policy towards the Jews of Europe. See a report in Jewish Frontier (September 1942), pp. 28-29. The journal devoted its entire issue to the problem in November; this formed the basis of Rabbi Stephen Wise's twenty-four page report presented on December 8 to the White House, entitled Blueprint for Extermination. See Arthur D. Morse; While Six Million Died (New York: Random House, 1968), p. 28. It should be emphasized that the State Department had already received all this information by that time.

4. Over the Russians hovered the cloud cast by the Katyn Forest Massacre, which, despite the controversy surrounding the evidence, nevertheless pointed a damning finger at one of the major accusers of the Germans of atrocities. Wladyslaw Anders: The Crime of Katyn (London: Polish Cultural Foundation, 1965).

5. Nora Levin: The Holocaust: The Destruction of European Jewry, 1933-1945 (New York: Crowell, 1973), p. 711.

6. In a conversation in March, 1974, with Olga-Migot (author of Le Systeme Concentrationnaire Nazi) who participated in the making of this film, in response to the question of the "invisibility" of the Jews, she replied that emphasis upon them would distract from "the greater moral issues." The same attitude and rationalization for a "higher" morality of "universal" values characterized the arguments of the producers of the stage version of Anna Frank's Diary, who, in the name of "broader appeal," literally dejudaized the script by purging from it all of Frank's specific references to Jews and Judaism.

7. It was only due to Yevtushenko's extraordinary intervention and the resulting publicity that grudging changes were made, which, coincidentally, took place at the same time as virulent antisemitism sponsored by the government once again swept through Soviet society, a new wave of hate-literature originating with Trofim Kichko's Judaism and Zionism.

8. Arthur A. Cohen: Thinking the Tremendum (New York: Leo Baeck Institute, 1974).

9. Ibid., p. 20.

10. See Maurice M. Roumani: The Case of the Jew from Arab Countries: A Neglected Issue (Jerusalem, 1975).

11. The linking of Judaism and Zionism for anti-Israel propaganda has its roots in the Soviet Union. The tract by Kichko (see note 7) was but a popularized recapitulation of a long-standing ideological position. More recently, this formula was given theological support at the Fourth Conference of the Academy of Islamic Research held in Cairo in 1970. The proceedings of this international gathering of Moslem religious scholars were published the same year in Arabic (2 volumes) and English (1 volume). See D.F. Green (ed.): Arab Theologians on

Jews and Israel (Geneva 1971). Its conclusions form part of the attitudes of the Palestine Liberation Organization and, most recently, were formally and publicly reexpressed by Ayatollah Khomeini in his writings before assuming power and in his speeches after the fall of the Shah.

12. "The Limits of International Law and Diplomacy: Case Studies of suspected genocide since the Holocaust," a paper to be presented later at this conference.

13. See Alistair Horne: A Savage War of Peace: Algeria 1954-1962 (New York: Viking Press, 1978).

14. Joseph Borkin's The Crime and Punishment of I.G. Farben (New York: Free Press, 1978) ought to be required reading for all aspiring young executives.

Comment: A More Realistic View of Human Rights
Daniel S. Lev

Leo Mates has two cases to make: one that the Holocaust is a root cause of present-day commitments to human rights, the other that the commitment to human rights around the world is serious and growing. On the first I suspect he is largely wrong. On the second, he may be right but too optimistic.

Out of respect for those who died, one naturally wishes that the Holocaust had in fact produced something of undoubted, universal significance. In our time nothing less grand than human rights, whatever we mean by the term, seems adequate to justify the horror that Nazi Germany caused the Jews of Europe. But Dr. Mates' attempt to make the link seems tenuously grounded. The evidence that European and North American leaders were shocked by what happened into creating safeguards for the future is rather weak, and the counter-evidence that, except for Jews, most have taken the Holocaust in historical stride is depressingly convincing.

If it could be shown that the struggle for human rights was fundamentally a post-war phenomenon, the argument for the Holocaust as cause would be much stronger. But, after all, the Congress of Vienna also concerned itself with human rights, with about as much success as the universal declaration, and human rights in war and peace were the subject of international conferences and treaties during the late nineteneeth and early twentieth centuries. It is not at all clear that, despite the Holocaust, a great deal more has been accomplished diplomatically since 1945. Slavery, for example, was dealt with more successfully in those earlier efforts than anything accomplished in our era. As Mates points out, when the hard issues of national sovereignty have arisen during the last thiry years of negotiations, human rights have been relegated, at best, to second place. State interests assume priority, even more perhaps than in the nineteenth century; and there is legitimate suspicion that human rights issues have now been used a bit cynically as a political weapon, another card in the game of international contention. From a perspective less generous than Mates', the human rights memorial to the Holocaust is rather shoddy. In this brutal but realistic perspective, the Holocaust, innovative only in its passionlessness, merely added to a few centuries worth of evidence that terrifying savagery can be committed on behalf of the modern state. As a genocidal masacre it was neither the first nor the last, and its influence, even indirectly (and questionably) through the universal declaration, the covenants, and Helsinki, on the behavior of state leaders has yet to be demonstrated.

Yet, on different grounds than Mates considers, human rights issues have indeed become global in recent decades, not because of the Holocaust, but because the modern state, and, with it, some consciousness of the inhumanity made possible in its name, have spread over the globe. In those countries with the most serious political and socio-economic human rights problems, the Holocaust has no obvious meaning at all; that was Europe's heritage, while Asia and Africa have their own. Nearly everywhere, however, there have been courageous efforts to protect people from their own governments. Consistent leadership of this struggle has not, pace Carter, been exercised by governments anywhere, but by non-governmental organizations. State leadership is normally preoccupied with state interests, which are seldom defined to include the fundamental well-being of non-citizens and too often not even of citizens. It is conceivable that the Holocaust had some influence, at least in Europe and the United States, upon the ideological development of a few non-governmental organizations. Resistance to state oppression, however, has a history about as long as the history of the state itself. It is in the continuing abuse of political authority and the social degradation of the human condition that the essential causes of the human rights movement are to be found.

Mates ends, typically, on an upbeat note, and I wish I could follow suit. But it is not self-evident that current human rights efforts represent a turning point, let alone that the Holocaust has its redeeming benefits. If anything, what has happened since World War II indicates that the struggle for human rights really is a perpetual struggle, all uphill and against powerful odds.

Rejoinder
Leo Mates

I am grateful to the commentators, Professors Lev and Huttenbach, for their responses to my paper, but in most cases I cannot accept their criticism.

The major fault of both commentaries is that they read into my text what is not in it and thus fail to reflect my meaning correctly. One misreading is that I tried to establish a strict causal link between the Holocaust and the increased concern for human rights in the world. This is then followed by another, namely, that I assumed that all this happened with the intent to help the Jews, for their sake. I stated, however, only that the persecution of the Jews in Europe gave an impulse to the quest of human rights in the world in general, that it was a contributing factor in a historical process.

I share their view that the effort to advance the cause of human rights is an everlasting uphill struggle, and this is also reflected in my paper. What is more, I believe that it is not an altruistic effort of some communities to help others, but, as I said in my paper, that it is a quest for universal rights, for the benefit of all. Hence, it is an enlightened self-interest, and not a good deed. Therefore, I did not try to show any benefit to the Jews through the advancement of human rights. As a matter of fact, I did not speak of the praxis of human rights, but only of the increase in concern, as reflected in official declarations nad international conventions. The sole exception was my mention of the Western European Human Rights Court.

Turning now more specifically to the comment of Huttenbach, I shall pursue the same point further. I do not believe that it is advisble, or admissible on scholarly grounds, to transfer from science the law of causality in its strict application. Phenomena in society are influenced by so many factors, including the frequently confused human will, that a clear cause-effect link cannot be established, cannot be proven, and does in most cases not exist in this simple form.

Anyhow, if one were to accept in a specific case a clear and straight causality, it could not be proven. The proof of causality in science is the experiment. Only its repetition, with gradual elimination of irrelevant factors, can establish causality. Hence I cannot accept methodologically the demand for proof, nor can I accept an interpretatin of my text alleging my acceptance of causality. In fact, Huttenbach's demand for proof follows his own correct introductory statement of my thesis:"...[the] involvement with the preservation of human rights as a partial by-product of an international conscience profoundly stirred by the confrontation with the genocidal slaughter of European Jewry."

It seems evident, that this is not a cause-effect linkage in the strict sense, but rather an instance when many factors influence a development, one of these being examined here for its relevance to the outcome. This would plainly indicate that the factor mentioned, the stirred conscience, did not alone cause involvement. The involvement was a product of many factors and actors, the stirred conscience being one of them. The same outcome might have occurred even within this one factor. This however can not be proved or disproved.

On the positive side, I believe that I adduced enough facts to corroborate the thesis that the outcome was at least to some extent influenced by the Holocaust, or, more precisely, by the reaction to the Holocaust. Huttenbach, having correctly stated my thesis proceeds to the sense of causality. This position is stated even more clearly in a further demand. Huttenbach asks the direct question whether I had established that "human rights history" was "experiencing a new stage as a result [my emphasis] of its encounter with Auschwitz?"

After this leap from circumstance to cause, Huttenbach makes a further departure from my argument. He devotes considerable effort to show how the change in attitude on human rights did not occur with the intent to help the persecuted Jews. He had no great problem in convincing the reader of this. I accept it also, but it is irrelevant to my thesis in the paper. In no way did I try to argue that any of the changes I speak of had been made for the benefit of Jews. Reacting to the tragedy of Jewry does not necessarily mean doing something to help them specifically. This is, regrettably, the most common pattern of behavior of humanity.

This does not mean that the Jews would be exempt from any beneficial changes. Here, however, we have come to another point of misunderstanding. I was not claiming that a sudden change had occurred in the praxis of human rights. Hence the effort to demonstrate that no such drastic change occurred does not affect my thesis or change the meaning of events which I have described.

This leaves open the question whether changes in attitudes are relevant for praxis. This is a question which has long since been answered, and I do not intend to expand on it. Let me only mention that I have witnessed several instances when states, having opposed certain recommendations in the United Nations, nevertheless felt obliged to follow them subsequently. There have been instances showing the impact of the internationalization of the right to emigrate. The strict and prohibitive rules on the emigration of Jews from the Soviet Union have been relaxed. International pressure, and in particular the actions of President Carter, have been explicitly based on the new concepts of human rights. This is a case in point, showing even some changes in praxis, although I do not consider this relevant to the thesis of my paper, which only expressed hope for changes in the praxis of the future, expressing hope very cautiously at that.

Huttenbach then proceeds to show the insensitivity of governments and government officials, as if I had claimed that they were stirred by the horrors of the slaughter of the Jews. In fact, I underlined that the stirring of consciences became visible only after the discussion came into the open in San Francisco, as distinct from the in camera sessions of government officials at Dumbarton Oaks in Washington D.C. Huttenbach tries to use this reference against my thesis, as if it were a contradiction. The salient fact is rather that delegates from Europe were closer to the crimes and were at that time under very strong pressure from public opinion after all the pictures and photographs had been shown publicly and the survivors had returned home.

This is what preceded and surrounded the public deliberations of the United Nations at the end of the war. The crimes, their extent and cruelty, as well as the lack of understandable cause, created a shock permeating the atmosphere of the conference halls and streaming, so to speak, from the galleries. The main outcome of the debates was the internationalization of human rights. They were taken out of the domain of purely domestic jurisdiction. This was also the moral basis for the Nuremberg Tribunal.

I shall now mention only briefly some of the minor points raised by Huttenbach. I did not use the term Holocaust so as to cover other genocides, and I consider it completely irrelevant to discuss the behavior of the official French Left or the USSR. They erred frequently in respect to human rights, but this has no connection with my argument. The lack of reaction to the Holocaust during the war is also irrelevant. It was caused by a great number of contributing factors, one being the concentration on the prosecution of the war in the free countries, another the lack of opportunity for public expression in occupied countries. Of the insensitivity of officials, I have already written. Finally, I never considered the Holocaust to be the "quintessential part of the human rights dialogue."

Lev made some of the points already answered above. In connection with causality he has his own way of expressing it, making me say that the Holocaust was "the root cause" of changes in the human rights problem. He also makes the point that I was too optimistic. However, I only presented a train of events and changes in attitude. This is in no sense a matter of optimism or pessimism. I came close to the dilemma only in the conclusion, speaking of the possible effect of changes in attitudes on future praxis regarding human rights. Here I expressed great, perhaps even undue, caution. However, it is not possible to argue about impressions. What is optimism to one may be pessimism to another.

6
Anticipations of the Holocaust in the Political Sociology of Max Weber

Richard L. Rubenstein

No thinker of the twentieth century has had so profound an influence on modern social thought as the German sociologist Max Weber. He has with justice been called "the towering figure of modern sociology." From his earliest writings on the problems of agriculture in East Prussia in the 1890s to his lectures on "Science as a Vocation" and "Politics as a Vocation," delivered to German university students in a strife-ridden, revolutionary period, Weber was a keen and dispassionate observer of his nation's economic, social, and political problems as well as a passionate participant in its political struggles. The period in which Weber flourished witnessed the astounding transformation of Germany into a modern industrial society, with all of its attendant social problems. It also witnessed Germany's military collapse at the end of World War I which laid the foundations for the subsequent triumph of National Socialism. Because of the universal scope of Weber's intellectual concerns, there is hardly a political or social problem of the period for which his writings lack relevance.

It is perhaps inevitable that men and women read the work of their intellectual predecessors in the light of their own history and experience. In the aftermath of World War II, it was to be expected that sooner or later the career and the writings of so preeminent a figure as Weber would be reexamined in the light of the experience of National Socialism. In Germany, the reexamination of Weber has been carried on largely in response of Wolfgang Mommsen's book, **Max Weber und die Deutsche Politik** (1959) and his recent work, translated into English as **The Age of Bureaucracy: Perspectives on the Political Sociology of Max Weber** (1974).1 Indeed, my own reconsideration of Weber in the light of the National

Socialist era has largely been the fruit of my reading of Mommsen.

In considering Weber's work, we must at all times be aware of the fact that his analysis of social phenomena was not meant to be prescriptive. What is important for our purposes is the extent to which Weber's analysis of some of the most important social institutions of the modern period anticipates potentialities in these institutions which were to become fully manifest in the period of National Socialism. Even before reading Wolfgang Mommsen, I was struck by the degree to which Weber's model of bureaucracy as a coldly rational impersonal instrument of domination could be taken as a blueprint for the role of the SS in the extermination of the European Jews.[2] There is, of course, nothing in Weber's writings to suggest that Weber envisaged state-sponsored mass murder as one of the capacities of bureaucracy. Nevertheless, when read in the light of the Holocaust, Weber's reflections on the organization, methods, and personnel of bureaucracy have a chilling aura of prophecy about them.

It is my conviction that, in addition to Weber's writings on bureaucracy, there are a number of other areas of significance in Weber's thought that take on profoundly altered significance in the light of the Holocaust. These include: his analysis of post-exilic Judaism as a pariah religion, his conception of the value-free nature of the scientific enterprise, and his insights into the problem of political leadership in modern society. I would, however, stress that this retrospective rereading of Weber in the light of subsequent events is <u>not</u> intended as an effort to discover <u>causal connections</u> between Weber's thought and those events. Let us keep in mind the title of this eassay. We are interested in "anticipations of the Holocaust," not causes.

Let us begin with a necessarily brief consideration of Weber's analysis of post-exilic Judaism. Weber held that since the exile, the Jews have been a "pariah people."[3] Weber used the term pariah in a completely non-pejorative sense, but he deemed it to be the most precise sociological characterization of the Jews as a people and Judaism as a religion.[4] He defined a pariah people as "a group which lacks an autonomous political association and which is confined to an hereditary separate community by limitations . . . on commensality and intermarriage on the one hand, and by political and social underprivilege, associated with radical separation in economic activity, on the other."[5] Weber saw many similarities between the Indian pariah

caste and the Jews. In both cases, Weber argued that
pariah religion tended to bind its adherents more
closely to each other and to their outcast status as
their objective status became more oppressive. In
both cases, "the lowest castes . . . clung most
tenaciously to their caste obligations" and saw
fulfillment of these obligations as the only means of
attaining salvation from pariah status.[6]

Weber was also aware of crucial differences
between the two systems. According to Weber, the
Hindu system is profoundly conservative. It does not
look forward to the eventual elimination of pariah
status, although it does offer the individual pariah
the hope that, if he fulfills scrupulously the
obligations of this status, he may be reincarnated as
a member of a higher caste in another life. The
practical effect of this doctrine is to root the
pariah all the more firmly in his place in a rigid
and unchanging social hierarchy.[7] In the case of the
Jews, Weber held that their messianism anticipates a
radical overturn of the present social hierarchy in
which today's pariahs or their descendents will
eventually become the dominant class. Weber's words
are worth quoting, if only for the hint of contempt
which is intermingled with the value-free analysis:

"The Jew, by contrast, hopes that his
descendents will have a share in the Messianic
kingdom, which will release the entire pariah
community from its inferior position and make
them instead lords of the world. For by the
promise that all peoples shall borrow from the
Jews, while he will borrow from no one, Yahweh
did not mean that he would make the Jews into
small-time pawnbrokers and money-lenders in the
ghetto: the meaning of the promise was that
they would become a powerful ancient city-state,
whose debtors and debt-slaves were the
inhabitants of the villages and small towns
which it had subjugated....For his people is one
chosen and called by God for his position of
highest prestige, not that of pariahs."[8]

Weber thus identified the doctrine of the chosen
people as both a compensatory reflection of the Jews'
pariah status and an expression, when combined with
messianism, of their hope for an ultimate overturn of
present social hierarchies. Following Nietzsche,
Weber regarded the Jewish refusal to accept current
hierarchies as an expression of ressentiment which,
Weber argued, refers "to a concommitant of the
religious ethos of the underprivileged, who . . .
trusted that the unequal distribution of chances in

life results from the sin and unrighteousness of the privileged, and therefore must sooner or later provoke God's vengeance." [9] In turn, this theodicy, according to Weber, serves as a means of justifying the "conscious or unconscious thirst for vengeance" of the underprivileged. [10]

As the religion which introduced the element of ressentiment, Judaism is depicted as motivated primarily by the pariah's thirst for revenge. This is true of the Psalms, which "express in the most blatant form the moralistic satisfaction and self-justification of a pariah people's need for revenge," as it is of Israel's monotheism.[11] According to Weber, "in all the religions of the world, there is no universal God who has Israel's unparalleled thirst for vengeance."[12] While Weber admits that it would be a "grotesque distortion" to identify the feeling of ressentiment as the source of Jewish religious thought, he nevertheless asserts that "ressentiment reveals one of the specific traits of Judaism and in no other religion of the underprivileged does it play such a conspicuous role." [13]

Weber's insights have been both challenged and defended by later sociologists. The task of evaluating the merits of his analysis lies outside of the scope of this paper. What is relevant for us is the question of what Weber's analysis may reveal about the situation of Germany's doomed community in the period of the Weimar Republic. Even if we grant, as this author most certainly does, that Weber was devoid of personal animus towards Jews and Judaism in his scientific work, it is legitimate to ask whether the picture he drew of (a) Judaism as an institutionalized expression of a pariah people's thirst for vengeance and of (b) that people's long-range aim to overturn existing social hierarchies might have reflected a perception concerning Judaism among educated, non-extremist Germans that, given the embittered political atmosphere of post-World War I Germany, could easily have been distorted by others into National Socialist accusations that all classes of Jews without exception were a principal agent in the political, cultural, and economic disasters that beset the Germans in World War I and its aftermath.

The idea that Jews and Judaism were destructive of existing social hierarchies was in any event strongly reinforced by the high visibility of Jews among the leaders of the Bolshevik revolution in Russia, the Spartacists, the revolutionary government of Kurt Eisner in Bavaria, and the subsequent short-lived Munich Räterepublik. Nor ought we to forget that Weber became Professor of Sociology at the University of Munich in 1919 and witnessed at first hand both the left-wing regimes and the right-wing reaction, although his writings on Jews and Judaism precede his Munich appointment. In the words of the German historian Karl Dietrich Bracher, the Räterepublik was depicted by the German Right as responsible for a "pogrom against the German people staged by the Jews, a phase in the Jewish conspiracy for world domination." [14] According to Marianne Weber, although Weber emphatically rejected antisemitism in the face of the events of the period, he was convinced that it was politically unwise for Jews to be as prominent as they were in Germany's left-wing parties.[15] Subsequent events were, of course, to prove him correct in his judgment. During the same period, large numbers of uprooted and embittered White Russians, who were convinced that the Jews were responsible for their misfortune, congregated in Munich and were responsible for initiating the widespread dissemination of The Protocols of the Elders of Zion, with its myth of a Jewish conspiracy for world domination, throughout Germnay and the West. Political myths do not take hold among large numbers of people, as did the Protocols, unless they have some degree of symmetry, however, distorted, with widely held social or political perceptions. One root of the myth of Jewish world conspiracy was obviously the role of the Jews in the revolutionary movements of the times. Another root may have been found in perceptions such as those expressed by Weber that Judaism is a pariah religion whose ultimate aim is to overturn existing social hierarchies and the values they engender. This perception had already been expressed by Nietzsche and, as such, had become embedded in the fabric of German culture.[16] It was, however, given enhanced credibility and scientific dignity when espoused by Weber.

Moreover, in assigning to Jews a social and ritual status resembling that of Hindu pariahs, Weber does not dwell on a decisive aspect of pariah existence that the National Socialists were to emphasize: the pariah pollutes and hence contact with him must be avoided whenever possible.[17] Nazi racial laws prohibiting sexual contact between Jews and non-Jews stressed this element of racial pollution and in so doing elicited from the German people some of the oldest and most deeply rooted feelings of primal revulsion toward people who were seen as polluting agents.[18] Weber's value-neutral identification of the Jews thus implied far more than it stated. While his sociological analysis can in no

way be held responsible for National Socialist racial
laws, his perceptions about Judaism are as important
for what they anticipate as for what they indicate.
When the National Socialists attempted to "defend"
the German people against Jewish "racial pollution,"
they were not creating something de novo, as
Weber's writings indicate. They were building on
feelings and perceptions which had already taken very
deep root even among respectable scholars who were
not antisemites. Weber's characterization of the
Jews as pariahs gave scientific expression to social
perceptions that were widespread among all classes of
Germans. Within a short time, the National
Socialists were to carry the practical consequences
of such perceptions to an extreme never before
experienced in the history of European civilization.

Finally, in view of the fact that Weber regarded
ressentiment and messianic revolutionary
aspirations as intrinsic to Judaism and hence not
subject to reforming amelioration, we must ask
whether his analysis could have been used, again
quite apart from his own intentions, to render
plausible the National Socialist program for the
radical elimination (Entfernung) of the Jews from
every sphere of German society and culture as the
only means of terminating their radically
destabilizing influence on German society.

It would seem that both the racial and religious
antisemites could have found much reinforcement from
a reading of Weber's writings on Judaism. Weber's
writings hardly constitute a defense of the thesis so
ardently maintained by the German-Jewish mainstream
since the emancipation that were was no fundamental
conflict between commitment to Jewish religious
belief and practice and civic loyalty as members of
the German state or its smaller predecessors. The
role assigned by Weber to the Jews is that which he
clearly states: they were a Gastvolk, a pariah
people, whose religion and ultimate aspirations were
at odds and perhaps incompatible with the
civilization of their hosts. As such, it would not
have been difficult for others to draw the conclusion
that their influence ought to be minimized or, in
times of stress, to conclude that Germany would be
better off without them.

At the very least, Weber's writings on Jews and
Judaism constitute a highly significant social fact.
His place within the German elite was assured. His
writings possessed great authority. As social fact,
it hardly matters whether his judgments about Jews
and Judaism were valid. By virtue of his preeminent
intellectual authority, Weber can be taken as a
representative figure who gave conceptual formulation

to the felt perceptions about Jews and Judaism of a large number of his educated, non-extremist contemporaries.

It must be remembered that there is nothing intrinsic about pariah status. It is a dominant group's social definition of a subordinate group. In her discussion of the caste status of Polish Jews before the catastrophe, Celia Heller quotes W.I. Thomas' theorem: "If people define things as real they are real in their consequences."[19] Thomas' theorem is as relevant to the status of pre-Holocaust German Jews as it is to Polish Jews.

In reality, Weber's evaluation is all the more significant because he was not an antisemite and because of the distance he placed between himself and extremist groups both during and after the war. If a scholar of Weber's moral and intellectual integrity could so regard Jews and Judaism, we must ask whether the position of German Jews would have been ultimately viable even if National Socialism had not triumphed. In the aftermath of a catastrophic national defeat, is it realistic to believe that any sector of the German people would have looked with favor on the continued presence in their midst of what Weber himself had characterized as an alien, guest community which was perceived as religiously motivated by the yearning to revenge itself for its historic degradation? In the aftermath of the war, Germany was itself a revisionist state. Weber had in fact commented that one of the consequences of defeat was to turn Germany into a pariah among the nations.[20] Rightly or wrongly, almost all Germans were bitterly resentful of the peace they had been compelled to accept and were resolved eventually to overturn the new postwar international order. There was little, if any, disagreement on the need for revision; there was only disagreement concerning when and how it would take place.

Moreover, as we know, Germany's military defeat was followed by years of aggravated economic crises, with all of their attendant mass social dislocations. In such an atmosphere, is it likely that a minority community that was regarded by Germany's best minds as alien to the religion, culture, and society of their community could have long continued their sojourn on German soil? Incidentally, a fruitful area for further research might be a sociological, anthropological, and psychological investigation into the roots of the radical asymmetry between Jewish self-perceptions in pre-Hitler Germany and the definition of their status by the dominant group. Unfortunately, this and other issues tend to be obscured when the negative responses of the dominant

group are categorized without further qualification
as antisemitism. In any event, looking back from the
perspective of November 1978, forty years after
Kristallnacht, if Weber's analysis of Judaism is
representative, it would appear that German Jews
belonged to a doomed community, although under other
circumstances their departure from Germany might have
been less laden with mortal travail.

Let us now turn to Weber's conception of the
value-free nature of the scientific enterprise and
his insights into the problem of political leadership
in modern society. As early as his Inaugural Lecture
at Freiburg in 1895, Weber argued that science can
neither establish nor prove the valdity of ultimate
values. Weber's reflections on science, fact, and
value were further elaborated in his essay on
"'Objectivity' in Social Science and Social Policy"
(1904). In that essay, Weber distinguished between
"knowledge of what 'is'" or "existential
knowledge"--what we would call factual knowledge--and
"knowledge of 'what should be'" or "normative
knowledge." [21] He asserted that "it can never be the
task of an empirical science to provide binding norms
and ideals from which directives for immediate
practical activity can be derived." [22] Nevertheless,
Weber argued that value-judgments "rest on certain
ideals" and are "subjective" in origin. [23]

Weber's rejection of the idea that the empirical
sciences could establish values was based in part on
his view of the nature of culture, which he regarded
as a humanly constructed order devoid of any
intrinsic meaning or value. Moreover, in arguing
that values are inherently subjective, Weber
emphatically denied that the social sciences can
adjudicate between values in conflict. [24]

This conviction is again expressed in Weber's
1918 Munich lecture, "Science as a Vocation," in
which he utilized the example of medical science to
illustrate his view concerning the relationship among
science, fact, and value. Weber asserted that
medical science is based on the presupposition that
it has "the task of maintaining life . . . and
diminishing suffering." [25] The presupposition is,
however, pretheoretical and largely unexamined, for
"whether life is worth living and when" is a question
that medical scientists cannot ask in their role as
scientists. [26] If we grant that the preservation of
life is an end worth pursuing, medicine can become
the appropriate means for its attainment.
Nevertheless, no science can enable us to decide when
and even whether we ought to preserve life. Thus,
Weber insists upon (a) a rigidly instrumental,
value-neutral status for both the practical and the

theoretical sciences and (b) a thoroughly subjectivist view of values. Values define goals; science provides the means for their attainment.

As one reads Weber's reflections on science, fact, and value from the perspective of 1978, one gets the feeling that Weber could not possibly have realized the full implications of the strictly instrumental, value-neutral status he had accorded to science and technology. This is especially apparent in the discussion of medicine we have just cited. Within less than two decades it would no longer be self-evident to the German medical profession, as it apparently had been to Weber, that the maintenance of life and the diminution of suffering constitute the presuppositions of medical science. As we know, during World War II a number of Germany's leading medical scientists lent their skills in good conscience to their government's programs for the deliberate mutilation and destruction of the lives of whole categories of non-combatants, both German and non-German.[27] In his 1918 essay on science, Weber had assumed that "the presuppositions of medicine and the penal code prevent the physician from relinquishing his therapeutic efforts" even in the case of mentally ill patients who no longer desire to go on living.[28] Had Weber survived to World War II, he would have been compelled to correct that assumption. He also would have been compelled to recognize that no horror perpetrated by the German medical profession or German technocrats was inconsistent with the view that values are inherently subjective and that science is intrinsically instrumental and value-free.

In spite of the fact that Weber believed that science is incapable of adjudicating between competing values, he recognized that some values do play a dominant role in the realm of practical affairs while others tend to become subordinate or disappear altogether. Weber's interpretation of how this takes place has a strong affinity to Social Darwinism, as does much of his thinking, as well as to Nietzsche. Weber believed that all social life involves "the struggle of man against man" and that the struggle has become more intense since the advent of capitalism.[29] He held that "power is the essence of politics" and that in the final analysis conflict is resolved by power, which he defined as "the probability that one actor in a social situation will be able to carry out his own will despite resistance...."[30]

The ultimacy of power in the resolution of conflict is implicit in Weber's concept of domination (Herrschaft) which he defined as "the probability that a command with a given specific content will be obeyed by a given group of persons."[31] One of the most problematic aspects of Weber's theory of domination is that it does not appear to offer any criterion for distinguishing between legitimate and illegitimte domination. Weber discussed the problem of political leadership and authority in his theory of "the three types of legitimate domination," namely, legal or bureaucratic, traditional, and charismatic domination. Since Weber's interpretation of the phenomenon of political authority is wholly functionalist, Mommsen argues that Weber offers no basis for distinguishing between legitimate and illegitimate authority, good and bad charismatic leaders, or free and oppressive regimes.[32] This writer finds Mommsen's argument entirely persuasive. If this view is correct, there is only one kind of political domination for Weber, the kind that succeeds. Thus, the ultimate criterion of legitimate domination turns out to be the successful exercise of power. We now have an additional reason why Weber did not believe that science could either establish values or adjudicate between them: Weber believed that values are more likely to be established by power than by argument.

It should, however, be noted that nowhere does Weber necessarily equate power with physical coercion, although he regarded monopolistic control of the instruments of coercion as the fundamental attribute of the state. Weber was impressed by the extent to which non-material ideals had changed the course of world history. His celebrated thesis that Calvinism played a decisive role in the origins of modern capitalism is an expression of his conviction that non-material ideals can decisively affect history and culture. Values may be created and established through power, but the power to which Weber turned with restrained hope to alter the dehumanizing consequences of modern instrumental rationality was not regarded by Weber as necessarily rooted in physical coercion.

As with all Germans, the problem of political leadership came to a head for Weber with the collapse of the Empire and the departure of the Kaiser. Weber became convinced that the most likely way in which the negative social effects of bureaucracy and capitalism could be at least partly overcome was through charismatic political leadership.[33] Weber ruled out traditional patriarchal or patrimonial leadership as a source of new values in the modern period. His whole analysis of the period rested on the conviction that instrumentally-rational modes of domination and economic enterprise such as bureaucracy and capitalism have effectively dethroned traditional modes. Only the charismatic leader who is (a) a creator of values and (b) morally accountable to no one but himself seemed to Weber to offer modern society hope of overcoming the stultifying consequences of bureaucracy and capitalism. Weber offered a value-neutral definition of charisma: it is that quality of a person which creates a willingness on the part of his followers to subject themselves unquestioningly to his leadership.[34] Weber held that the followers' attachment was non-rational and charged with emotion.[35] As Mommsen and others hve observed, Weber's charismatic leader strongly resembles Nietzsche's superman who attempts to lead humanity to ever greater heights by setting new values for himself and his followers.[36] Paradoxically, Weber's espousal of charismatic leadership was not in conflict with a certain advocacy of democracy on his part. Weber called leaders chosen by popular election in mass society "dictators of the battlefield of elections." [37] He favored plebiscitary democracy, but he did so because he was convinced that it was the most effective means of choosing a charismatic leader under conditions of mass society.[38] Once elected, Weber believed that such a leader ought to be in full and unquestioning control of the entire apparatus of government, although he did believe that parliaments might play a useful role as a check on the leader. [39]

Since the charismatic leader is the creator of values, he himself is utterly beyond good and evil. He is a law unto himself. Law flows from him; he is not constrained by legal or customary limits. Moreover, since the leader controls the state's instruments of coercion, there is normally no countervailing force that could impose ethical restraints upon him. Let us remember that Weber offers us no way to distinguish between a tyrant and a leader who abides by constitutional, customary, or ethical norms. For Weber, one becomes a charismatic leader by acquiring a faithful and unquestioning following. Nor can the leader trouble himself about his followers' motives. Weber readily admits that these may be "predominantly base" when viewed from a traditional ethical perspective.[40] According to Weber, as long as followers accept his leadership, for whatever reason, there is no deed, however, rightful, that the leader cannot rightfully cause to be done. Clearly, in the case of the charismatic leader, values are altogether capable of creating social and political facts. The leader's omnicompetence as a creator of values leads to a sense of omnipotence in the creation of facts. In

The Origins of Totalitarianism, Hannah Arendt observed that followers of totalitarian movements often have the feeling that within their system all things are possible.[41] She did not, however, fully spell out why this is so. A reading of Weber on the value-creating function of the charismatic leader helps us to understand the reason for this phenomenon: the omnicompetence of the leader in the sphere of values, especially when combined with absolute, unquestioning obedience on the part of those reponsible for their implementation, creates a political situation which is potentially, if not actually, totalitarian. By creating new values under conditions of absolute power, there is no domain of human activity in which the leader's values cannot be translated into new social and political facts. This situation is exemplified by the recent excesses in Cambodia, where the values derived from a ruling elite rather than a single leader. Moreover, as Weber understood, <u>it is precisely the value-free nature of science operating in a desacralized, non-traditional world that makes possible the omnicompetence of the leader in the domain of values.</u>

Weber insisted that the political leader must be in a position to utilize the state bureaucracy without restraint for his own purposes. He had no utopian or romantic illusions that bureaucracy could be done away with in modern, mass society. For Weber the crucial issue was the quality of person who would control the state apparatus. Since bureaucracy is a value-neutral instrument and parliaments are weak or impotent, Weber believed the direction of modern politics would be decided by the person who gained control of and knew how to make use of the state apparatus.

Weber further emphasized the importance of the problem of leadership by distinguishing between <u>führerlose Demokratie</u>, leaderless democracy, defined as "the rule of professional politicians without a calling, without the inner charismatic qualities that make a leader" and <u>Führerdemokratie</u>, leadership democracy, a distinctive form of charismatic domination in which the leader is elected by the public but in which the real bond between leader and followers is emotional[42] Weber made it clear that for the second type of rule to work, "the following of such a leader must obey him blindly." [43]

For Weber, <u>Führerdemokratie</u> offers the greatest hope of effective government under modern conditions and this would require a union of charismatic and bureaucratic domination.[44] Only when the creative force of charisma is implemented by the efficiency of the bureaucratic machine can the leader hope to give enduring and effective expression to his values. Thus, bureaucratic rationalization and charismatic irrationalism need not be irreconcilable. Not only can they be compatible, but together they can form a system of domination sufficiently elastic to meet whatever contingencies confront any attempt to organize modern society.

According to Wolfgang Mommsen, in his emphasis on charismatic leadership, "Weber . . . came close to the Führerprinzip, the Fascist leadership principle."[45] It seems difficult to avoid the conclusion that Mommsen has understated the case and that Weber's political philosophy overtly and explicitly accepts the Führerprinzip, although it does not necessarily follow that Weber advocated an openly Fascist ideology since his ideal-typical analysis of the relation of leader and followers avoids any description of the actual values the leader ought to espouse. This, however, was partly because Weber regarded democratically elected leaders as caesarist in fact if not in theory.[46] His reluctance to spell out what the leader's values ought to be was also consistent with his view that only the charismatic leader could define values. For Weber to have attempted to do so would have been inconsistent with his own view of the limits of his vocation as a scientist.

Still, if one compares Weber's ideal-typical model of the compatibility of charismatic leadership and bureaucracy with the history of National Socialism, it becomes clear that Weber's conception of Führerdemokratie could easily have served as an anticipatory blueprint for National Socialism in power. There is a chilling correspondence between Weber's views and the actual relations between Hitler, the state, the various bureaucracies, and the German people. This does not mean that Weber was an anticipatory advocate of what was to become National Socialism or that he would have followed the movement had he lived until the regime came to power. Unlike the Nazis, in his own interventions in politics Weber tended to counsel moderation and a respect for limits.[47] Nevertheless, as we see, Weber does not regard the charismatic leader as bound by normal limits, and there is no intrinsic reason in the light of Weber's political sociology why so radical a political development as National Socialism could not have been brought into being by a value-creating charismatic leader.

Furthermore, Weber's definition of charisma corresponds to the actual relationship between Hitler and the German people, as his ideal-typical model of bureaucracy corresponded to a very large extent to the SS.[48] Weber did not entertain the possibility that a value-free instrument such as a police bureaucracy could be put in the service of genocide, but, again, given Weber's thought, there is no intrinsic reason why such a development should not have taken place. It is almost as if Hitler arrived intuitively at a view of politics not very different from that which Weber came to conceptually. Certainly, Hitler could not have found a better blueprint for either his **Führerprinzip** or the organization and the utilization of bureaucracy than Weber's ideal-typical models.

A very significant element in Hitler's eventual success, in the aftermath of the unsuccessful 1923 **Putsch**, was his decision to bring about his revolution by legal means. This involved a decision to reject the violent seizure of power and to seek, as would Weber's plebiscitary charismatic leader, to legitimate his rule by a popular mandate. Once he received the mandate, Hitler arrogated to himself the same role of absolute creator of values for the German people that Weber described as the role of the charismatic leader.[49] Moreover, when Hitler took command of the state bureaucracy, almost all of its personnel saw their fundamental responsibility as that of implementing without question the National Socialist program.[50] The behavior of the members of the state bureaucracy was anticipated by Weber in the description of the vocation of the civil servant in his 1919 essay, "Politics as a Vocation," in which the role of the bureaucratic civil servant of "official" was contrasted with that of the charismatic political leader:

> According to his proper vocation . . . the genuine official will not engage in politics. Rather he should engage in impartial administration. . .To take a stand, to be passionate is the politician's element, and above all the element of the political <u>leader</u> . . . The honor of the civil servant is vested in his ability to execute conscientiously the order of superior authorities, exactly as if the order agreed with his own conviction. <u>This holds even if the order seems wrong to him</u> and if, despite the civil servant's remonstrances, the authority insists on the order. <u>Without this moral discipline and self-denial, in the highest sense, the whole apparatus</u> would fall to pieces. The honor of the political leader, of the leading statesman, however lies precisely

in an exclusive <u>personal</u> responsibility for what he does, a responsibility he cannot and must not reject or transfer. (italics added)[51]

In the light of the history of National Socialism, these words have an infinitely more ominous ring than they could have had to his original audience in revolution-beset Munich in 1918. Weber accounted it part of the "moral discipline" and self-denial" of the administrator that he carry out the leader's directives "even if the order seems wrong." So too did Adolf Eichmann, Rudolf Höss and a host of others in National Socialist Germany. Furthermore, since, as we have noted, Weber assigned no limit to the value-creating function of the leader, there was no reason whatsoever why an official's "moral discipline" in the face of orders that "seemed wrong" should have faltered even when genocide, industrial slavery, human medical experiments, and involuntary euthanasia were involved. The question faced by the German civil service, German corporate executives in firms such as I.G. Farben, the army, and the police including the SS was not whether the leader's values were moral or immoral; such judgments were entirely beyond their competence. In a system led by a charismatic leader, followers have only the choice of blindly obeying or getting rid of the leader, the latter a step the vast majority of Germans were unwillng to countenance until the bitter end.

When the war was over, there was widespread popular distaste in Germany for war crimes trials. Apparently, the defendants' claim that they were not responsible for the policies they had faithfully implemented struck a responsive chord among large segments of the German public.[52] Perhaps one reason for this may have been that Weber, in articulating his conception of "the honor of a civil servant," spoke for the vast majority of his fellow countrymen.

What may be most disturbing about Weber's theory of the value-neutral character of science and his assertion that a charismatic leader who controls the state apparatus has the absolute right to create an entire society's values is that it may not be possible to refute him. It would indeed be comforting were we able to demonstrate that values are in fact grounded upon some objective basis in the nature of things. That, of course, is what theories of natural law and most theological systems claim. Such claims obviously did not impress Weber, as a social scientist, and, whether or not his views ultimately prove to be correct, they do tend to confirm the proposition that there is nothing self-evident about either the objectivity or the immutability of values in modern society. Furthermore, as we have repeatedly noted, Weber's advocacy of charismatic, autonomously value-creating leadership was motivated by a desire to find a way out of what he regarded as the dehumanizing effects of bureaucracy and capitalism. The negative effects of unrestrained legal domination caused him to turn to unrestrained charismatic domination. Unfortunately, recent history has amply demonstrated that Weber's proposed therapy can be infinitely more destructive than the disorder it was supposed to cure.

In effect, Weber tells us that, if God is no longer available as the ultimate source of values, some person must play God. Indeed Weber's charismatic leader has the power to create values and to demand blind obedience which in the past had been reserved to God alone. Weber translated into the terminology of political sociology the insight of his mentor Nietzsche that, if God no longer exists, at least the great man must become a god. Those of us who have even a cursory knowledge of the history of the twentieth century know how replete with the most extreme terror and devasation the rule of such a man-god can be.

NOTES

1. Wolfgang Mommsen: Max Weber und die Deutsche Politik, 1890-1920 (Tübingen: Mohr, 1959) and Mommsen: The Age of Bureaucracy: Perspectives on the Political Sociology of Max Weber (Oxford: Blackwell, 1974).
2. Richard L. Rubenstein: The Cunning of History: Mass Death and The American Future (New York: Harper & Row, 1975), pp. 22ff.
3. Max Weber: Economy and Society, ed. by Guenther Roth and Claus Wittich (New York: Bedminster Press, 1968), Vol. II, p. 493.
On Weber's conception of Judaism as a "pariah religion" see the contributions of Jakob Taubes, Joseph Maier, Benjamin Nelson, Christian Sigrist, and Wilhelm E. Muhlmann in Otto Stammer (ed.): Max Weber and Sociology Today, trans. Kathleen Morris (New York: Harper & Row, 1971). Stammer's volume is the abbreviated proceedings of the Fifteenth German Sociological Conference held in Heidelberg to commemorate the centenary of Weber's birth. On Weber's interpretation of ancient Judaism, see Freddy Raphael, "Max Weber et le judaisme antique,"

Archives of European Sociology, Vol. XI, (1970), pp. 297-336. For a rejoinder to Weber on the notion of Judaism as a "pariah religion," see Salo Baron: A *Social and Religious History of the Jews* (New York: Columbia University Press, 1937), Vol. I, p. 5.

4. Weber: *Economy and Society*, Vol. II, p. 493.

5. Weber: *Economy and Society*, Vol. II, p. 493.

6. Weber: *Economy and Society*, Vol. II, p. 493.

7. Weber: *Economy and Society*, Vol. II, pp. 493f.

8. Weber: *Economy and Society*, Vol. II, p. 494.

9. Weber: *Economy and Society*, Vol. II, p. 494.

10. Weber: *Economy and Society*, Vol. II, p. 495.

11. Weber: *Economy and Society*, Vol. II, p. 495.

12. Weber: *Economy and Society*, Vol. II, p. 495.

13. Weber: *Economy and Society*, Vol. II, pp. 495f.

14. Karl Dietrich Bracher: *The German Dictatorship: The Origins, Structure, and Effects of National Socialism*, trans. Jean Steinberg (New York: Praeger, 1970), p. 82. On the revolutionary situation in Munich immediately after World War I, see Allan Mitchell: *Revolution in Bavaria 1918-1919: The Eisner Regime and the Soviet Republic* (Princeton: Princeton University Press, 1965).

15. Marianne Weber: *Max Weber: A Biography*, trans. Harry Zohn (New York: Wiley, 1975), pp. 648f.

16. Friedrich Nietzsche: *The Genealogy of Morals*, trans. Walter Kaufmann and R.J. Hollindale (New York, 1969), pp. 33ff.

17. On the subject of pollution and its social consequences, see Mary Douglas: *Purity and Danger: An Analysis of Concepts of Pollution and Taboo* (New York: Praeger, 1966).

18. The "Nuremberg Law" forbidding marriage or other sexual liaisons between Jews and Germans is entitled "Law for the Protection of German Blood and Honor" and its purpose is to preserve "the purity of German blood." The text of the law is given in Joachim Remak: *The Nazi Years: A Documentary History* (Englewood Cliffs, N.J.: Prentice-Hall, 1969), pp. 149f.

19. Celia S. Heller: *On the Edge of Destruction: Jews of Poland Between the Two World*

182

<u>Wars</u> (New York: Columbia University Press, 1977), p. 62.

20. Marianne Weber: <u>Max Weber: A Biography</u>, p. 662.

21. Max Weber, "'Objectivity' in Social Science and Social Policy" in Weber: <u>The Methodology of the Social Sciences</u>, trans. and ed. by Edward A. Shils and Henry A. Finch (Glencoe, Ill.: Free Press, 1949), p. 51. Hereafter cited as "Shils".

22. Shils, p. 52.

23. Shils, p. 52.

24. Shils, p. 82.

25. Max Weber, "Science as a Vocation" in <u>From Max Weber: Essays in Sociology</u>, trans. and ed. H.H. Gerth and C. Wright Mills (New York: Oxford University Press, 1946), p. 144. Hereafter cited as "Gerth and Mills".

26. Gerth and Mills, p. 133.

27. See Alexander Mitscherlich and Fred Mielke: <u>Doctors of Infamy: The Story of the Nazi Medical Crimes</u> (New York: H. Schuman, 1949), pp. 131-145; Raul Hilberg: <u>The Destruction of the European Jews</u> (Chicago: Quadrangle, 1967), pp. 586, 609; Rubenstein: <u>The Cunning of History</u>, pp. 36-37.

28. Gerth and Mills, p. 144.

29. Weber: <u>Gesammelte Politische Schriften</u> (München: Drei Masken Verlag, 1921), p. 12. This was Weber's Inaugural Lecture at Freiburg, 1895.

30. Weber: <u>Economy and Society</u>, Vol. I, p. 53.

31. Weber: <u>Economy and Society</u>, Vol. I, p. 53.

32. Mommsen: <u>The Age of Bureaucracy</u>, pp. 83f. Weber does, however, offer the medieval city-state as an example of "illegitimate domination," but nowhere does he offer any example of illegitimate charismatic, patrimonial, or bureaucratic domination. On "illegitimate domination" in Weber, see <u>Economy and Society</u>, Vol. III, pp. 1212ff.

33. This reading of Weber follows Wolfgang Mommsen's interpretation of Weber's political sociology. See Mommsen, "Max Weber's Political Sociology and his Philosophy of World History" in <u>International Social Science Journal</u>, XVII, no. 1 (1965), reprinted in part in Dennis Wrong (ed.): <u>Max Weber</u> (Englewood Cliffs, N.J.: Prentice-Hall, 1970), pp. 183-194; Mommsen: <u>The Age of Bureaucracy</u>, pp. 73-94; Mommsen: <u>Max Weber und die deutsche Politik</u>, pp. 287ff.; for a contrary opinion, see Guenther Roth, "Political Critiques of Max Weber," <u>American Sociological Review</u>, XXX (April, 1965), pp. 213-223. For a discussion of the related issue of power politics in Weber's thought, see Raymond Aron, "Max Weber and Power Politics" in Otto Stammer: <u>Max Weber and Sociology Today</u>, pp. 83-100, as well

as the responses by Carl J. Friedrich, Hans Paul
Bahrndt, Wolfgang J. Mommsen, Karl W. Deutsch, Eduard
Baumgarten, and Adolf Arnt. See also J.P. Mayer:
Max Weber and German Politics: A Study in Political
Sociology, 2nd ed., (London: Faber and Faber, 1956),
pp. 72-109.

34. Weber: Economy and Society, Vol. I, p.
241.

35. Weber: Economy and Society, Vol. I, p.
243.

36. Mommsen: The Age of Bureaucracy, pp. 79
and 105ff.

37. Weber, "Politics as a Vocation" in Gerth and
Mills, p. 106.

38. Gerth and Mills, p. 107.

39. Gerth and Mills, p. 113.

40. Gerth and Mills, pp. 121 and 125.

41. Hannah Arendt: The Origins of
Totalitarianism (New York: Harcourt Brace, 1951),
pp.436f.

42. Gerth and Mills, p. 113.

43. Gerth and Mills, p. 113.

44. See Wolfgang J. Mommsen, "Zum Begriff der
Plebiszitären Führerdemokratie bei Max Weber,"
Kölner Zeitschrift für Soziologie und
Sozialpsychologie, Vol. 15, 1965, pp. 295ff.

45. Mommsen: The Age of Bureaucracy, p. 93.

46. Weber, "Politics as a Vocation" in Gerth and
Mills, pp. 112f.

47. This is especially evident in his wartime
political opinions. See Marianne Weber; Max Weber:
A Biography, pp. 151ff.

48. See Rubenstein: The Cunning of History,
pp. 22ff.

49. Bracher, The German Dictatorship, pp.
340-350.

50. Bracher, The German Dictatorship, pp.
229ff.

51. Weber, "Politics as a Vocation" in Gerth and
Mills, p. 95.

52. See Hilberg: The Destruction of the
European Jews, pp. 684ff.

Comment: The Problem of Anticipations
Gordon Zahn

I am pleased to note that the final edited version of Professor Rubenstein's paper omits several points which had caused me greatest difficulty when it was first presented. It is particularly gratifying, for example, that he has dropped the inserted remarks which had found some symbolic meaning in the fact that the first non-Italian pope for centuries had served for a time, years after the end of World War II, as bishop of the diocese within whose boundaries had been located the infamous Auschwitz death camp. I mention this only because it illustrates the major problem I still have with this paper. Rubenstein does not make at all clear precisely what he means by "anticipations" or what, if any, conclusions he would want us to draw from the anticipations he describes.

It would seem that the concept has at least three major meanings. There is, first of all, one which refers to nothing more than order of appearance in a time sequence. Rome, in this sense, would be "anticipation" of Berlin by many centuries in that it appeared first as a cosmopolitan capital and may have served in some undefined way as a "model" for the other. Then there is the "anticipation" in which there is more of a direct foreshadowing of what is to come, although it does not yet involve or even imply sufficient causality: the proverbial bent twig can later be seen in the finished form of a full-grown tree. Finally, there is the type of "anticipation" in which a more distinct causal link--though not necessarily intention--can be traced. Thus the tragedy of the American "dust bowl" has been explained as the natural result of imprudent and excessive land use and the removal of forest cover which previously had retained water for the area affected.

Rubenstein's disclaimers seem to exclude this third usage in that he insists he does not charge Weber with any blame for the anticipations of the Holocaust attributed to his writings (though, I must add, it is my impression that the tone of some of Rubenstein's observations belies these careful disclaimers). To the extent that the second would apply, it could be held that any social theorist, to the extent that he accurately discovers and describes significant aspects of his time and society, will inevitably become a factor in their future development and, therefore, an anticipation of what will come to be.

In both instances, however, we have a right to ask for more exposition and analysis of the links between Weber's work and the particular aberrations he is accused of anticipating. This is lacking here. Except for laudatory affirmations of the high standing Weber enjoyed in scholarly and academic circles and the influence his works are purported to have--neither affirmations, be it noted, supported by evidence to suggest that the Nazis were familiar with, or favorably disposed toward, the man or his works--no attempt is made to establish the anticipations as holding any significance beyond the first category and, as such, would be interesting but not particularly meaningful historical accidents.

Surely we are all aware that bureaucracy was well established in Germany and elsewhere before Weber produced his excellent and seminal theoretical analysis which spelled out in careful detail the nature of bureaucratic enterprises as such and their operations. That his analysis can be applied so well to the SS and other agencies of the Third Reich testifies to the accuracy of his generalization and nothing more. In the same fashion Henry Ford and Taylorism could be seen as "anticipations" of the efficiently organized "disposition of unwanted elements" of the German population once so defined by the Nazis. So, too, with Weber's treatment of Jewry as an "alien" and "pariah" people. This is again an accurate presentation of the "definition of the situation" prevailing throughout Europe, a definition that had been in force long before he ever appeared on the academic scene. Even Jewish writers pictured their own people as in "diaspora," "alien" to, and "set apart" from the populations and cultures in which they were living. Zionist literature, while not necessarily accepting the invidious connotations of the term "pariah," recognized the reality of that status and drew heavily upon it to support its appeal to the yearnings for a "homeland." Weber's only contribution (crime?) was to translate what was already established in "common sense" knowledge and practice into objective sociological usage.

The same is true of his leadership typology which, in my judgment, stands as one of Weber's more significant contributions. What he termed "charismatic" leadership had been known, through writings of great political philosophers and actual historical experience of real charismatic leaders, through the ages. Why, then, single this writer out as an "anticipation" of what, except for the specific term, had ben "anticipated" as long ago as Plato and Aristotle? True, all the ingredients for classifying Hitler as such can be drawn from Weber's

description--but they were also present, and more
directly influential, in Prussian tradition, in the
Mussolini pattern, in a variety of heroic myths and
belief systems (not excluding the Bible!), in Wagner
and Nietzche (as Rubenstein himself notes). Why
focus on Weber as "anticipation" when many, or most,
of these antedated him?

One point on which I am inclined to agree with
Rubenstein concerns our reaction to Weber's
insistence upon sociology as a "value-free" endeavor.
But here, too, one finds a far stronger source in
the image of science itself (or, as I would prefer,
with the scientism which had infected the social
sciences even before Weber). The demand that the
social analyst must rigorously suspend or exclude
value judgments from his work is one which I reject,
although I would insist that they not be permitted to
bias one's research and findings. Strangely enough,
however, it is here that Weber's "anticipation" is
most in doubt. As George Mosse has shown in Nazi
Culture, many of the leading figures in the German
academic community became ardent supporters of
Hitler's New Order and outdid themselves in finding
validation for his favored theories of racial
selection, world history, political ideology, etc.
Hitler thrived not on value indifference or denial on
the part of the scholarly community, but, rather, on
a scandalous display of value commitment.

In summary, Rubenstein succeeds to some extent
in suggesting anticipations of the first order in
Weber's works; but he never goes on to show why these
anticipations merit being singled out in so
portentous a manner as some kind of discovery. Once
we define any given event as pivotal for human
history--as Rubenstein clearly believes the Holocuast
to have been--everything that has gone before
becomes an "anticipation" in one sense or another.
To focus upon any single event or scholar or
contribution for special notice and treatment
imposes an obligation to show why and in what special
ways that selection is justified. Rubenstein makes
no attempt to do that here. Instead we are left with
an academic game almost anyone can play. Why Weber
for his "pariah" concept and not Eugene Sue for his
novel which, we may be sure, had much more of an
effect upon many more readers? Why Weber and not
Spencer or Darwin whose theories of society as
organism and an unending process of natural selection
clearly anticipated the Blut-und-Boden appeal and
the creation of a superrace and a Thousand Year
Reich? Why Weber and not Machiavelli for political
amorality? or the French School of sociology with
its anticipation of Goebbels and his manipulative

propaganda? Why not Frederick the Great, Hitler's own acknowledged source of inspiraton.

Without a more adequate justification for singling our Weber as source of anticipations, I cnanot but feel that, even making full allowance for the eloquence and style of its presentation, Rubenstein has given us little more than an impressive, but ultimately empty, non sequitur.

Comment: Against the Misapprehension of Weber
Guenther Roth

My disagreement with Professor Rubenstein is total. There is just about no sentence in his presentation that I can accept on empirical or analytical grounds, whether it involves Weber's scholarly work, political commitments, or historical influence. As a political man Weber was a liberal committed to constitutional government, to the rule of law. He affirmed the political enfranchisement of all citizens, including the working class, which suffered political discrimination in Imperial Germany. He strongly opposed the academic discrimination against Jews. It is striking that Rubenstein nowhere mentions Weber's advocacy of the ethic of responsibility, Weber's main idea in "Politics as a Vocation." It is equally striking that he nowhere mentions the purpose of Weber's comparative study of the world religions and does not even cite Ancient Judaism. Weber wanted to explain the distinctiveness of the ethical rationalism of the Judaeo-Christian tradition and found the beginnings of Western rationalism in the ethical prophecy of ancient Judaism. Rubenstein also ignores or fails to understand the purpose of Weber's sociology of dominaton--an empirical social theory of political formations, especially of the rise of the modern state; it cannot be a prescriptive political theory.

Time and again Professor Rubenstein confuses the empirical and the normative. His favorite device is the hypothetical statement. He does not want to assert a straight causal relationship--a direct guilt on Weber's part for Nazism--but by misconstruing Weber's meaning and especially by innuendo he makes him, so to speak, guilty by hypothesis, a novel form of "guilt by association." Item: "Weber's conception of Führerdemokratie could easily have served as an anticipatory blueprint for National Socialism in power"--but the fact is, it didn't. (All emphases mine.) "Hitler could not have found a better blueprint"--but he didn't read Weber, and

insofar as the Nazis took notice of him at all, they
condemned him as a decadent liberal in alliance with
Jews. "Weber did not entertain the possibility that
a <u>value-free</u> instrument such as a police
bureaucracy could be put in the service of
genocide"--he didn't, if only because he would never
have dreamed of viewing the police as a "value-free"
instrument. Bureaucracy exists, of course, for the
purpose of administering the modern state.
Throughout history, patrimonial staffs, civilian and
military, had been used for murderous purposes.
Modern bureaucracy too is not immune to misuse,
especially if the framework of the liberal
constitutioanl state is abandoned--but Weber always
affirmed the state. He never said that "the
political leader must be in a position to utilize the
state bureaucracy <u>without restraint</u> for his own
purposes." His examples for "leadership democracy"
are Lincoln, Theodore Roosevelt, Gladstone, and
Joseph Chamberlain--all charismatic leaders in the
heartland of western democracy. For many years Weber
fought for strengthening the powers of the German
federal parliament; it was no contradiction when he
advocated the direct election, in imitation of the
U.S. constitution, of the President in the Weimar
Republic because the monarchical head of state had
disappeared in 1918.

Professor Rubenstein totally misconstrues
Weber's worldview--his acute perception of the
multivalent nature of Western rationalism.
Bureaucracy was not just "a coldy rational,
impersonal instrument of domination," but a major
achievement in the struggle against age-old personal
dependency. Democracy, constitutional government,
and civil rights are inconceivable without
bureaucracy, but the complex relationship between
formal and substantive rationality also involves
irresolvable tension. Moreover, the so-called
Weberian ideal type of bureaucracy is the empirical
counterpart of the normative theory of public
administration. Every American or English civil
servant is supposed to adhere to the ethos of
bureaucracy--quoted at length and disapprovingly by
Rubenstein--but in another hypothetical twist he
makes it appear that "Weber's model of bureaucracy...
<u>could</u> be taken as a blueprint for the role of the
SS in the extermination of the European Jews"--when
in fact it could not and was not. For Weber modern
bureaucracy presupposes the rule of the law. The SS
was, in Weber's terms, not a bureaucracy but a
charismatic organization sworn to absolute, blind,
and personal obedience. The first requirement was to
conquer <u>"den inneren Schweinehund"</u>--that basically

untranslatable pejorative term for the Judaeo-Christian conscience.

Rubenstein does not hesitate to call Nietzsche Weber's "mentor," when in fact almost every mention of Nietzsche on Weber's part is critical. Neitzsche's superman was for Weber a typical product of the mind of a German philistine. Weber's charismatic leader never had "omnipotence as a creator of values." Weber's whole emphasis is not on'superhuman' capacities but on the social dialectic between leaders and followers. The leader makes demands, but his power depends on the willingness of the followers to support him. Again, Rubenstein uses here the phrase "according to Weber" as if the latter had given us a prescription instead of a typological description of charismatic leadership. Weber never asserted "that a charismatic leader who controls the state apparatus has the <u>absolute right</u> to create an an entire society's values"--a leader can only claim it.

Another major misinterpretation is Professor Rubenstein's assertion that Weber "has a strong affinity to Social Darwinism," when much of the analytical framework of his greatest work, <u>Economy and Society</u>, is directed against the Social Darwinism of the time. Weber wrote hundreds of pages on the normative role of religion, law, and the rules of formally peaceful market exchange to demonstrate, among other things, that "the survival of the fittest" depended very much on the normative regulations of a society and was therefore not a matter of "natural" factors such as "race."

Finally, Rubenstein misrepresents Weber's portrayal of Judaism, the finished parts of which deal mainly with ancient Judaism in a world historical typology of salvation religions. The passages to which Rebenstein refers have almost nothing to do with the position of German Jewry in Weber's time. The fact that Weber used sociological categories such as "pariah people" (a coinage by a 19th century Jewish writer) and ethical "resentment" (which account for part of the dynamic and innovative potential of the West) is warrant enough for Rubenstein to argue that, if "Germany's best mind" could think in such categories, "it would appear that German Jews belonged to a doomed community." With Rubenstein, we know from hindsight that millions of Jews and millions of others were indeed doomed to die in a new world conflagration, but we can understand this adequately only if we abandon the easy strategy of creating intellectual chains of guilt.

Ultimately, writers cannot protect themselves against the misuse of their ideas. It is true that

190

Professor Rubenstein does not allege a use or misuse
of Weber's ideas by the Nazis, but his political
denunciation is not mitigated by his disclaimer that
he does not hold Weber personally responsible. His
attack is more radical: by reading into Weber's
work, one of the great achievements of modern
scholarship, an "anticipation of the Holocaust," he
also undercuts the moral justification for "science
as a vocation."

Rejoinder
Richard L. Rubenstein

I am grateful to Professor Gordon Zahn for his
response to my paper; I am also grateful to him for
the courtesy and good will with which he expressed
his critique both at the conference and in writing.
I fully appreciate his discomfort about my
concentration on Weber in seeking out "anticipations"
of the Holocaust. I must, however, remind Zahn that
I cautioned my readers that Weber's analysis of the
social phenomena under consideration "was not meant
to be prescriptive." Moreover, I clearly stated what
it was in Weber's writings that interested me:
namely, "what is important for our purposes is the
extent to which Weber's analysis of some of the most
important social institutions of the modern period
anticipates potentialities in these institutions
which were to become fully manifest in the period of
National Socialism." I also stated that my
"retrospective rereading of Weber in the
light of subsequent events is not intended as
an effort to discover causal connections between
Weber's thought and those events." In general, Zahn
takes me at my word--something Professor Roth
apparently has difficulty in doing--when I insist
that I am in no sense attempting to lay any blame for
the Holocuast on Weber. Nevertheless, Zahn concludes
by asking, in effect, why I concentrate on Weber
rather than Darwin or Spencer in searching out
"anticipations" of the Holocaust. Part of the answer
is that I have already considered the connections
between Darwin, Malthus, and Spencer on the one hand
and state-sponsored programs of mass population
elimination on the other in a previously published
article entitled "The Elect and the Preterite" which
is to be the first chapter of a forthcoming book by
that name. [1]
I also had other reasons for concentrating on
Weber. In my book The Cunning of History I argue
that the Holocaust was "the expression of some of the

most significant political, moral, religious and demographic tendencies of Western civilization in the twentieth century."[2] I have consistently taken issue with the notion that the Nazi movement and the Holocaust represented an aberrational revolt against Western civilization and its values. On the contrary, I would argue that the Holocaust was an important, albeit unintended, consequence of both the dominant trends and the most significant values of Judaeo-Christian civilization in the modern period, especially since the Industrial Revolution. This is the principal thesis of The Cunning of History. It is further elaborated in my forthcoming book The Age of Triage. I agree with Weber that the ethical rationalism of the Judaeo-Christian tradition led to the value-neutral functional rationality of modern capitalism. Building on Weber's insights, I argued in The Cunning of History that the triumph of functional rationality in the West produced monumental surplus populations and both the bureaucrratic institutions and the value-neutral attitudes that made possible their elimination. Put differently, I have reluctantly come to the conclusion that modern civilization, whether capitalist or socialist, has a very strong tendency to resort, in times of great stress, to programs of large-scale population elimination, such as mass expulsion, war, and genocide.

Having come to the conclusion that programs of systematic mass population removal, such as the Holocaust, were an expression of normal trends within Western Civilization in our times, I have devoted much of my research to demonstrating the validity of that conclusion. At the International Scholars Symposium I elected to explore the ways in which the thought of Max Weber anticipates the Holocaust because I know of no other classical social theorist whose analysis of modern Western Civilization is as authoritative or as enlightening. In a chapter in The Cunning of History entitled "Bureaucratic Dominaton," I attempted to show how Weber's ideal-typical analysis of bureaucracy anticipates the SS.[3] As I stated in that chapter, I did not in any sense blame Weber for the SS. I was, however, struck by the fact that the SS was an empirical exemplification of a form and an ethos of domination that Weber had described so brilliantly. In the current paper I turn to other social phenomena that were investigated by Weber, such as the charismatic leader, the value-neutral character of science, the ethic of obedience of the public functionary, and his interpretation of Judaism. In each case Weber's analysis anticipated developments that became fully manifest in National Socialism.

For example, while I make it perfectly clear that I understand that Weber never expected a leader to arise who would conduct himself as did Hitler, Hitler was the leader who came closest to embodying the charismatic leader unconstrained by any traditional political or ethical limitation of whom Weber writes. Apart from the willingness of the leader's followers to obey, there is in Weber's analysis no limitation on what the charismatic leader can and cannot do. To say this is not to hold Weber responsible for Hitler, as my other respondent suggests I do, but to understand how useful a conceptual tool Weber's ideal-typical contruction can be for the understanding of both National Socialism and the Holocaust. I find it striking that Hitler, acting on his own intuitive grasp of the political situation, behaved in a way that is fully consistent with Weber's analysis. I have also found exceedingly helpful Wolfgang Mommsen's observation that charismatic domination and bureaucratic domination, as described by Weber, are not necessarily contradictory, that the modern charismatic leader can utilize bureaucracy as his organizational instrument, and that bureaucracy may require the decision-making initiatives of the charismatic leader to function well.[4] I see this reciprocal relationship most completely embodied in the relationship between Hitler and the various branches of the German bureaucracy, although obviously there were pockets of dissidence and resistance to various aspects of National Socialism within the state bureaucracies. I admire Weber's prescience and his magisterial grasp of the demonic potentialities of modern society and politics. It is for that reason that Weber remains, as Erich Fromm has said, a "living presence" among us in contrast to lesser figures. [5]

I repeat that my purpose, here as elsewhere, is to demonstrate the continuities between the Holocaust and European civilization in modern times. As perhaps the last truly universal, Renaissance scholar Europe produced, Weber's political and social theories constitute an important body of data for that purpose.

As far as Professor Roth is concerned, it is a most serious matter when a man of his preeminent authority as a Weber scholar writes that "there is just about no sentence in his (i.e., Rubenstein's) presentation that I can accept." I would be more disturbed were the positions he refutes positions that I actually hold in the paper, but to a very great extent they are not. For example, he quotes me

for the purpose of refutation as having stated that
Weber's charismatic leader had "omnipotence as a
creator of values" (italics added) but that is not
what I wrote. In attempting to relate Weber's ideal
typical construction of the charismatic leader to
Hannah Arendt's analysis of totalitarian movements, I
wrote, "The leader's omnicompetence as a creator of
values leads to a sense of omnipotence in the
creation of facts" (italics added). That is a very
different observation than the one ascribed to me and
then refuted by the respondent.

Roth accuses me of confusing the "empirical with
the normative," whereas I stated quite explicitly
that I write about Weber's analyses. Moreover, as I
have already indicated, I caution the reader that his
analyses are in no sense meant to be prescriptive. I
do not know how I could have made myself clearer, but
to no avail as far as Roth is concerned. I was also
surprised to learn from Roth that I try to make Weber
"guilty by hypothesis, a novel form of guilt by
association." Roth then proceeds to defend Weber
against a series of accusations that I never made.
For example, Roth denies that Hitler had read Weber
on bureaucracy, thereby imputing to Weber some
respnsibility for Hitler, as if I had suggested that
he had. The basis of my interest in Weber on
bureaucracy is that his ideal-typical construction
anticpates developments that reveal the full gruesome
potentialities of an institution which, in Weber's
words, "develops the more perfectly the more
bureaucracy is 'dehumanized'." The SS was a
nigh-perfect embodiment of this development. Far
from holding Weber reponsible, I admire his insight.

Nor am I unaware of Weber's perception of "the
multivalent character of Western rationalism," as
Roth would suggest. I am cognizant of Weber's
evaluation of both the positive contributions and the
problematics of bureaucracy in the development of
modern economic, social, and political institutions,
but I submit that Roth glosses over Weber's pessimism
about the future of a civilization based upon legal
domination, as well as the reasons why Weber saw
charismatic leadership as a possible way out of "the
iron cage." Actually, Roth's quarrel is not with me
but with Professor Mommsen. In my paper, I fully
acknowledge my debt to him for my reading of Weber.
Having listened to Roth and having read his rsponse I
still find Mommsen persuasive.

On the subject of the charismatic leader, I do
state that Weber's concept of Führerdemokratie
could easily have served as "an anticipatory
blueprint for National Socialism in power." However,
that statement is immediately qualified by the

observations that (a) Weber cannot be seen as an "anticipatory advocate of what was to bcome National Socialism" and (b) "...in his own interventions in politics Weber tended to counsel moderation and a respect for limits." This does not prevent Roth from simply denying that the Nazis used Weber as a blueprint, as if I had stated or implied that they had.

Roth also takes issue with my statements that there are Nietzschean and Social Darwinist components in Weber's thought. Roth may very well be correct, but, given his knowledge of the literature, he is certainly aware of the fact that both these issues remain matters of debate among scholars. I find evidence for Weber's Social Darwinism in what Raymond Aron and Mommsen have called his nationalist power-politics,[7] the strongest evidence for which is his oft-quoted <u>Antrittsrede</u>, his Inaugural Lecture at Freiburg in 1895, in which he declares:

> It is not peace and human happiness that we have to hand on to our descendants, but the eternal struggle for the maintenance and cultivation of our national characteristics..."[8]

I may be in error on this issue, but, if so, I am in very good company. Similarly, on the subject of Nietzschean elements in Weber, there is no consensus among the scholars. I find the case for Nietzschean elements, especially in Weber's analysis of the role of <u>ressentiment</u> in creating both the values and the eschatology of Judaism, to be persuasive.[9] Similarly, Weber's discussion of the disenchantment of the world and the subsequent development of organizational and economic rationalization in capitalism is largely anticipated by Nietzsche's observations on the Christian origins of the bourgeois-capitalist world.

When Roth turns to my discussion of Weber's analysis of Judaism as a "pariah religion," he once again accuses me of indulging in "the easy strategy of creating intellectual chains of guilt." whereas I state that I regard Weber's writings on Jews and Judaism as "a highly significant social fact," important for what they "may reveal about the situation of German's doomed Jewish community during the Weimar Republic." Moreover, there is nothing in Weber's treatment to suggest that his interpretation of Judaism as a pariah religion was limited to ancient times, as Roth maintains. It is my opinion that Weber was essentially correct in regarding the Jews as a "pariah" community in the specifically non-perjorative sense in which he used that term. I do not take Weber's analysis as evidence of Weber's guilt, as Roth alleges, but of the precarious situation of Germany's Jews. Moreover, I regard the radical asymmetry between the way German Jews regarded themselves and the way even so unbiased an observer as Weber saw them as a further indication of their endangered situation. In this regard, it is interesting to note how few serious German Jewish scholars or intellectuals have attempted to deal with Weber's interpretation of Judaism. [10]

Roth and I do not disagree on our estimation that Weber's work is one of the truly great achievements of modern scholarship. Where ultimately we differ is perhaps in our assessment of modern civilization itself. I have no yearning to return to any other time. Modern civilization is our destiny, but I believe that I write in a spirit consistent with what I have learned from Weber when I see that civilization and its major institutions, including dispassionate scientific investigation, as having profoundly genocidal potentialities. There is nothing exceptional in my seeing "anticipations of the Holocaust" in Weber's work. I see them in almost evey great achievement of the modern world, including its art, literature, and music.

I would like to conclude this reponse to my critics with a few lines from the conclusion of The Cunning History. Perhaps they will help to clarify some of my reasons for seeing genocidal potentialities in our civilization:

> "....the world of the death camps and the society it engenders reveals the progressively intensifying night side of Judeo-Christian civilization. Civilization means slavery, wars, exploitation, and death camps. It also means medical hygiene, elevated religious ideals, beautiful art, and exquisite music. It is an error to imagine that civilization and savage cruelty are antitheses. On the contrary, in every organic process, the antitheses always reflect a unified totality, and civilization is an organic process... In our times the cruelities, like most other aspects of our world, have become far more effectively administered than ever before. They have not and will not cease to exist. Both creation and destruction are inseparable aspects of what we call civilization. [11]

NOTES

1. Richard L. Rubenstein, "The Elected and the Preterite", Soundings, Winter, 1976.

2. Richard L. Rubenstein: The Cunning of History (New York: Harper & Row, 1975), p. 6.

3. Ibid., pp. 22-35.

4. Wolfgang Mommsen: The Age of Bureaucracy: Perspectives on the Political Sociology of Max Weber (Oxford: Blackwell, 1974), pp. 75ff.

5. Erich Fromm, Foreword to T.B. Bottomore (ed.): Karl Marx: Early Writings (New York: McGraw-Hill, 1964), p. i.

6. Max Weber: Economy and Society: An Outline of Interpretive Sociology, edited by Guenther Roth and Claus Wittich (New York: Bedminster Press 1968), Vol. III, p. 975.

7. See Raymond Aron, "Max Weber and Power-Politics" in Otto Stammer (ed.): Max Weber and Sociology Today (New York: Harper & Row, 1971), pp. 83. See also responses to Aron's paper by Carl Friedrich, Hans Paul Bahrdt, Wolfgang J. Mommsen, Karl W. Duetsch, Eduard Baumgarten, and Adolf Arndt.

8. Max Weber: Gesammelte politische Schriften (Tübingen, 1958), p. 14.

9. See the discussion by Jakob Taubes in Stammer: Max Weber and Sociology Today, pp. 187ff. and the responses by Joseph Maier, Benjamin Nelson, and Talcott Parsons.

10. Weber's characterization of Judaism as a "pariah" religion is rejected by Salo W. Baron: A Social and Religious History of the Jews, (New York: Columbia University Press, 1952), Vol. I, p. 7. It is also contested by Julius Carlebach: Karl Marx and the Radical Critique of Judaism (London: Routledge and Kegan Paul, 1978), pp. 214ff. For other critical responses by Jews, see Ignaz Schipper, "Max Weber on the Sociological Basis of Judaism" in Jewish Journal of Sociology, 1, 1959, pp. 250-261; Toni Oelsner, "The Place of the Jews in Economic History as Viewed by German Scholars," in Leo Baeck Institute Yearbook, 7, 1962, pp. 183-212. A more sympathetic interpretation is offered by Hans Liebeschutz, "Max Weber's Historical Interpretation of Judaism," Leo Baeck Institute Yearbook, 9, 1964, pp. 41-68. Jakob Taubes' views are cited above in note 9.

11. Rubenstein: The Cunning of History, p. 92.

Contributors

- William Sheridan Allen, Department of History, State University of New York at Buffalo.
- Yehuda Bauer, Institute of Contemporary Jewry, Hebrew University, Jerusalem.
- Eric H. Boehm, International Academy, Santa Barbara, California.
- John P. Burke, Department of Philosophy, University of Puget Sound, Tacoma.
- Henry Huttenbach, Department of History, City College of New York.
- Leszek Kolakowski, All Souls College, Oxford.
- Gavin I. Langmuir, Department of History, Stanford University.
- Walter Laqueur, Institute of Strategic and International Studies, Georgetown University.
- Lyman H. Legters, School of International Studies, University of Washington.
- Daniel Lev, Department of Political Science, University of Washington.
- Franklin H. Littell, Department of Religion, Temple University.
- Leo Mates, Belgrade, Yugoslavia.
- Ernest Menze, Department of History, Iona College.
- Guenther Roth, Department of Sociology, University of Washington.
- John K. Roth, Department of Philosophy and Religion, Claremont McKenna College.
- Richard Rubenstein, Department of Religion, Florida State University.
- David Schoenbaum, Department of History, University of Iowa.
- Marie Syrkin, Santa Monica, California.
- Gordon Zahn, Department of Sociology, University of Massachusetts.